D0709403

PORN GENERATION

PORN GENERATION

How Social Liberalism Is Corrupting Our Future

BEN SHAPIRO

Since 1947
REGNERY
PUBLISHING, INC.
An Eagle Publishing Company • Washington, DC

Copyright © 2005 by Ben Shapiro

All rights reserved. No part of this publication may be reproduced or transmitted in any form or by any means electronic or mechanical, including photocopy, recording, or any information storage and retrieval system now known or to be invented, without permission in writing from the publisher, except by a reviewer who wishes to quote brief passages in connection with a review written for inclusion in a magazine, newspaper, or broadcast.

Library of Congress Cataloging-in-Publication Data
Shapiro, Ben.
  Porn generation / Ben Shapiro.
     p. cm.
  Includes index.
  ISBN 0-89526-016-6
  1. Sexual ethics—United States. 2. Promiscuity—United States. 3. Sex in popular culture—United States. 4. Popular culture—Moral and ethical aspects—United States. 5. Social values—United States. 6. United States—Moral conditions. I. Title.
  HN90.M6S52 2005
  363.4'7—dc22

                                    2005011544

Published in the United States by
Regnery Publishing, Inc.
One Massachusetts Avenue, NW
Washington, DC 20001
www.regnery.com

Distributed to the trade by
National Book Network
Lanham, MD 20706
Manufactured in the United States of America

10 9 8 7 6 5 4 3 2 1

Books are available in quantity for promotional or premium use. Write to Director of Special Sales, Regnery Publishing, Inc., One Massachusetts Avenue NW, Washington, DC 20001, for information on discounts and terms or call (202) 216-0600.

To all members of my generation striving to maintain their dignity, honor, virtue, and innocence in a chaotic culture—and to their parents.

Contents

CHAPTER ONE

A GENERATION LOST

"Virtue is harder to be got than knowledge of the world; and, if lost in a young man, is seldom recovered."

JOHN LOCKE

I am a member of a lost generation. We have lost our values. We have lost our faith. And we have lost ourselves.

As societal standards and traditional values have declined, and the crassest elements of sexual deviancy and pornography have taken over the public square, it is the youngest Americans who have paid the price. Never in our country's history has a generation been so empowered, so wealthy, so privileged—and yet so empty.

This book is not written from the perspective of a parent, a sociologist, or a teacher—but of a peer. This is my generation: the porn generation. And for good or ill, we are America's future.

Over the latter half of the twentieth century, the forces of moral relativism, radical feminism, and generational nihilism have gradually destroyed the foundation of our own greatness. Instead of adopting stronger moral standards, our society has embraced the lure of personal fulfillment.

In a world where all values are equal, where everything is simply a matter of choice, narcissism rules the day. Our culture has bred hollow young men, obsessed with self-gratification. Young women are told to act like sex objects—and enjoy it. The revisionist historians have effectively labeled obscenity as a right that the Founding Fathers sought to protect. Society told the porn generation that final moral authority rests inside each of us—and in our vanity, we listened.

The mainstream acceptance of pornography has become a social fact. Order a movie. Walk past your local news shop. Log on to the Internet. It's everywhere—in your Blockbuster, your newspaper, your inbox. We've replaced faith and family with a warped image of sex and self-satisfaction that ridicules the concept of purity and mangles the most sacred ideals of matrimony.

Traditional authority figures—parents, community leaders, even God—have been discarded. The new authority figures of the porn generation are many, and nearly all are members of a coarsened pop culture—one fed by the destructive malaise of the relativist world. Sex ed instructors, university professors, advertisers, Hollywood actors, MTV artists and assorted celebrities (A-, B-, and C-list) act as the new elders of a church of corrupt, shallow, and materialistic humanism.

The porn generation now inhabits a world where "empowerment" means sex with no strings attached. The old faith and traditional morality was too bourgeois, archaic, sexist, and close-minded for this brave new world. Our new god is Tolerance of all behavior, our new credo "live and let live."

The real Charlotte Simmons

As children, members of the porn generation are presented with morally subversive sexual education programs at increasingly younger ages. Nine-year-olds are lectured about condom use. Twelve-year-olds are pushed to make decisions about their sexual orientation. Fifteen-year-olds are expected to have said goodbye to virginity.

In college, drug use, alcohol use, and sexual experimentation are the norm. As one Harvard girl told me, "We're jaded, and it's fun." Fun to this girl meant trips to Amsterdam to smoke different types of mari-juana.[1] To others, fun means binge drinking or random sex.

According to a survey of college students conducted by *Details* mag-azine and Random House, 46 percent had had a one-night stand, 43 per-cent had cheated on a steady partner, 21 percent had tried to get someone drunk or high to get them in bed, and 32 percent had slept with some-one knowing they would never call again. On average, respondents had had 6.4 sex partners in their lives; 14 percent had 6–9 sex partners, 7 per-cent had 10–14, 4 percent had 15–19, and 3 percent had 25 or more. Thirty-six percent of respondents had had sex with someone they didn't like, and 28 percent had used pot during sex.[2]

The limitless sexual license of the porn generation is not without con-sequence. It leads to spiritual desensitization, emotional removal, and lack of commitment. The sad fact is that Tom Wolfe's literary character-ization of a young girl, Charlotte Simmons, carries enormous weight because it is so true.

Simmons starts her college experience as a leader, a fighter, a moral-ist at fictional Dupont University. Early on, she protests the "live and let live" morality that pervades the university:

> At Dupont...everybody thinks you're kind of—of—some kind
> of twisted...uptight...pathetic little goody-goody if you haven't
> had sex. Girls will come right out and ask you—girls you hardly
> even know. They'll come right out and ask you—in front of
> other girls—if you're a V.C., a member of the Virgin's Club, and
> if you're stupid enough to say yes, it's an *admission*, like you
> have some sort of terrible character defect.... There's something
> perverted about that.[3]

Simmons realizes that without the safety net of family morality, she is in serious moral danger:

> Right here was the point where she either cried out or she
> didn't cry out. Momma, only you can help me! Who else do I

have! Listen to me! Let me tell you the truth! Beverly doesn't just
return in the dead of the night and 'go to bed really late'! She
brings boys into bed—and they rut-rut-rut *do* it—barely four feet
from *my* bed! She leads a wanton sex life! The whole place does!
Girls *sexile* each other! Rich girls with 1500 SATs cry out "I need
some ass!" "I'm gonna go out and get laid!"...Momma—what
am I to do...[4]

But Charlotte doesn't cry out to her family for help, and she doesn't
extract herself from the moral mire that surrounds her. By the end of the
book, she has capitulated to peer pressure, lost her virginity, and given
in to the values of her surrounding environment. She has undergone deep
depression, and she has emerged a shallower person for her experiences.

There are thousands of Charlotte Simmonses in the porn generation.
When you're surrounded by encouragement leading you toward subjective morality, sexuality and hedonism, when you can't retreat to a safe
haven, it's simply easier to capitulate than to fight.

The lure of sexual privacy is so strong that it tends to overwhelm even
the most moral among us. Most of us carry the belief that no one else
should be privy to knowledge about our sexual practices—a belief primarily based on the most basic principles of monogamy. Something inside
us resonates to the words of Justice William O. Douglas in *Griswold* v.
Connecticut, the Supreme Court case first creating the nonexistent Constitutional "right to privacy": "Would we allow the police to search the
sacred precincts of marital bedrooms for telltale signs of the use of contraceptives?...We deal with a right of privacy older than the Bill of
Rights—older than our political parties, older than our school system."[5]

It is no accident that the social liberals chose sexuality as the starting point in their crusade against traditional morality. Purveyors of the
new morality have been hard at work, "defining deviancy down," as
Senator Daniel Patrick Moynihan explained in 1993. He posited that
"the amount of deviant behavior in American society has increased
beyond the levels the community can 'afford to recognize' and that,
accordingly, we have been re-defining deviancy so as to exempt much

conduct previously stigmatized, and also quietly raising the 'normal' level in categories where behavior is now abnormal by any earlier standard."[6] This has meant encouraging all forms of sexual expression, among other things.

Syndicated columnist Charles Krauthammer pointed out that alongside the movement to "define deviancy down," there is a concurrent movement to "define deviancy up": "As part of the vast social project of moral leveling, it is not enough for the deviant to be normalized," Krauthammer wrote. "The normal must be found to be deviant."[7]

Defining deviancy up has meant stigmatizing those who obey the dictates of traditional sexual morality as fools, ascetics, or latent homosexuals. It has also meant stigmatizing moralists as fascists and hypocrites—fascists, because we wish to impose our morality on others; hypocrites, because inevitably, some of us have not been completely pure.

We are not fascists—in fact, fascism's Nietzschean ideals are antithetical to traditional morality. We are Republicans and Democrats. We have the right to vote for general societal morality as expressed by our duly elected lawmakers. Social liberals seek to impose their amorality, albeit far less democratically; they push their viewpoint through pop culture, the education system, the judiciary, and the media. As for hypocrisy, that too is a weak argument—it is always better to do the wrong thing but say the right thing than to both say *and* do the wrong thing.

Yet it is impossible for all but the most extreme liberals in our society to ignore the truth: that tolerance of every social behavior is now the norm. In the absence of community-promoted traditional standards, subjectivism reigns. Nothing is expected of anyone; everyone may make his own rules about what is best.

The "live and let live" societal model is a recipe for societal disaster. The myopic question posed by advocates of the new, "Tolerant," morality is: "How does my immoral behavior hurt you?" But the overwhelming truth is that these are not individual acts, but inherently social acts with social consequences. And when society sanctions and encourages your immoral behavior, that *does* have an impact—it doesn't just hurt me, but it hurts my future children as well.

Truth and consequences

If millions of people accept the deviant as normal, that reshapes society in vastly destructive ways. Moral self-destruction may seem to have no consequences for an individual, but the destruction of societal standards always has consequences.

When the stigma left single motherhood, society felt the sting in rising rates of single motherhood and juvenile crime. When the stigma left sexual licentiousness, society felt the sting in rising rates of teen pregnancy, sexually transmitted disease, emotional emptiness, and nihilism. Your immoral personal behavior may not affect me, but exempting your immoral behavior from societal scrutiny certainly does. A society without standards is an unhappy, unhealthy society—a society with no future. And all of us have to live in that society.[8]

Nihilism, narcissism, and hedonism are natural results of the chaotic existential subjectivism popularized by the Left. If the hallmark of the baby boomers was rebellion, the hallmark of my generation is jadedness. Nothing really matters—we're cosmically alone. As Dr. Eddie Jessup puts it in Paddy Chayefsky's *Altered States*, "Ever since we dispensed with God, we've got nothing but ourselves to explain this meaningless horror of life."[9] Life *is* truly a horror when the only moral authority is ourselves, because escapism—hedonism—is the logical result.

No generation has ever had the benefits of convenience that my generation does, but instead of using our extra time to live, we seek to kill it. People eight to eighteen years old now spend an average of six hours and twenty-one minutes each day watching television, listening to the radio or to CDs, using the computer for non-school purposes, and playing video games. That's as opposed to just over two hours per day spent hanging out with parents, only an hour and a half doing physical activity, and under an hour doing homework.[10]

Drug use is another form of escapism. Forty percent of twelfth graders have tried illegal drugs.[11] While only 18 percent of parents believe that their children have tried marijuana, 39 percent actually have; 60 percent of teens say their friends have tried it.[12] Smoking pot is so commonplace that Democratic presidential candidates are now expected to discuss their experiences with weed on MTV. When I told one of my classmates that I wouldn't date girls who had tried drugs, he stated quite seriously, "Dude, that's just unrealistic."

Finally, there's sex. Existentialism and subjectivism are lonely because narcissism is lonely. If you build the world to your own specifications, and everyone else does as well, social contact becomes nearly impossible. Love—the attempt to reach out to another person, to bring that person into your world—requires a faith to which the jaded can never aspire. It is becoming rarer and rarer to find true romantics. In an age of jadedness, the only human contact becomes solely physical, an outward expression of the nihilism that consumes the soul. As society accepts solely physical relationships as an inevitable outgrowth of the destruction of traditional morality, solely physical sex becomes more common.

After they helped toss out traditional sexual mores in the name of "Tolerance," some in the media have recognized the disturbing social trends, and have given front-page coverage to the "shocking" rise of teen oral sex and promiscuity. And so we have Katie Couric stating that "Whether it's the cover of your favorite magazine, the music videos your kids are watching, or primetime TV, sex is everywhere,"[13] and noting that "No matter your child's age, S-E-X either has or will come up at some point. I recently spent a weekend with twenty teens from all across the country between the ages of thirteen and seventeen for a revealing and sometimes shocking conversation."[14]

But why should the mainstream media be shocked? After all, they've been promoting the breakdown of traditional morality for years. The social liberals in Hollywood, television, and the media are learning a difficult lesson: You can't chop away at the foundations of sexual morality for decades and still expect the structure to stand.

Today, one in five adolescents says that they had sex before age fifteen.[15] Two-thirds of suburban and urban twelfth-graders have had sex; 43 percent of suburban and 39 percent of urban twelfth-graders have had sex outside of a "romantic relationship."[16] Each day, eight thousand teenagers in the United States contract a sexually transmitted disease.[17]

Believe it or not, the number of young people who call themselves virgins is actually on the rise—but "virgin" often means that young people
are having oral sex, rather than vaginal intercourse. One study, by Peter
Bearman of Columbia University and Hanna Brockner of Yale, found
that 88 percent of teens who took virginity-until-marriage pledges broke
them.[18]

Meanwhile, the founders of the new society are desperately attempting to tell us that we are happy. We are supposed to measure happiness
in terms of sexual experience. In return for the abandonment of traditional morality, we have been given unrestrained sexual license. The
world is our harem. And so, from television to movies to music to
pornography, from public schools to college campuses, from the mainstream media to the Internet to the ad industry, American society pushes
sex. This is what the culture has been selling. And this is what we've
bought and paid for.

The social Left touts sex without consequences as the reward for our
abdication of societal morality. But sex—just like our abdication of societal morality—does have consequences.

These are not victimless acts. The high percentage of sexually active
young people is wreaking enormous damage to the emotional stability of
my generation. Both girls and boys who are sexually active before marriage are more likely to be depressed and attempt suicide. A full 25.3 percent of sexually active girls say they are depressed all, most, or a lot of
the time; only 7.7 percent of non-active girls feel that way. A shocking
14.3 percent of girls who are sexually active have attempted suicide; 5.1
percent of non–sexually active girls have. While 60.2 percent of sexually
inactive girls report that they are "rarely or never" depressed, only 36.8
percent of sexually active girls feel that way. Meanwhile, 8.3 percent of
sexually active boys are depressed all, most, or a lot of the time, as
opposed to 3.4 percent of teenage boys who are sexually inactive. And
while only 0.7 percent of boys who are sexually inactive report attempting suicide, 6.0 percent of sexually active boys report having done so.[19]

Young girls are the primary victims of the new society. For girls, sex
is unquestionably more precious than it is for boys; according to the

National Campaign to Prevent Teen Pregnancy, 77 percent of sexually experienced teenage girls wish they had waited to have sex.[20] Girls are now mutilating their own bodies, either through worries about their weight leading to anorexia and bulimia, or through actual self-mutilation, which entails using "knives, razor blades, or even safety pins to deliberately harm one's own body."[21]

But both boys and girls are damaged most by the desensitization they suffer as a result of an oversexed society. As 2001 Princeton University grad Laura Vanderkam stated in *USA Today*, "Hookups do satisfy biology, but the emotional detachment doesn't satisfy the soul. And that's the real problem—not the promiscuity, but the lack of meaning."[22] Dr. Marsha Levy-Warren sees the same problem with children buying into the sex culture: "Developmentally, they just aren't ready," she told the *New York Times*. "They're trying to figure out who they are, and unlike adults who obsess first and then act, kids do the opposite—they act and then obsess. They jump into this, and are left with intense feelings they're unable to sort out." Levy-Warren notes the rise of what she calls "body-part sex": "The kids don't even look at each other. It's mechanical, dehumanizing. The fallout is that later in life they have trouble forming relationships. They're jaded."[23]

Sexual licentiousness was the aphrodisiac that blinded us to the dangers of discarding traditional morality; now it is supposed to be our reward for discarding traditional morality. And yet we, as a society, are not happier. The liberal's favorite value—tolerance—excuses our cultural immorality and is our societal undoing. As columnist James Hitchcock writes:

> Tolerance fails as a virtue, first of all, because it is in some ways demeaning to people. It is much better to speak of "respect" or "empathy." But that is precisely the problem—common sense tells us that there are people who cannot and ought not to command our respect or empathy. We regard what they stand for as stupid, crazy, evil, or all three. To be respectful of them would be to abandon all moral sense, so that a completely tolerant person would be totally passive, without a moral center. Thus we fall

back on "tolerance," which merely means conceding to people
the right to be who they are, while withholding our respect. But
the determined advocates of tolerance are not content with that
and keep slipping back into making tolerance imply the neces-
sity of respect... Thus the obligation of tolerance leads inex-
orably to intolerance, turning the claim to be tolerant into a
tautology, a statement that merely repeats itself—"I am tolerant
except about those things of which I am intolerant."[24]

This book is meant to force us to reexamine the true consequences of tol-
erating immorality and the oversexed society in which we live. If we see
clearly the moral pit which we have dug for ourselves, maybe we can
stop digging—and maybe, just maybe, restore the standards that have
served American society well in the past.

It is also an attempt to reach out to my peers. Yes, sex is fun, and
good, and in the right context, healthy. But let's keep it in the right context. Let's think about *our* prospective children. Do we want our kids
growing up in the over-sexualized world that we do? Let's learn from history. Let's not repeat the mistakes of our parents' generation.

The baby boomers and liberals who make up the current leadership
in this country need to take a good, hard look at what they've done to
American society. If they don't feel that the children giving blowjobs at
age twelve are the products of a broken nation, they aren't looking hard
enough. It is the baby boomers and the grown-up flower children who
began the trend of oversexed culture. They produced the television
shows, made the movies, bought the albums, corrupted the school system, and ushered in a new era of "tolerance." They tore down the traditional moral system in the name of youthful rebellion.

It is not right that children be dunked headfirst into the vat of
garbage we call popular culture. Ten-year-old girls should not have
anorexia, and ten-year-old boys should not have to question their sexuality. It is the responsibility of parents to teach their children about sex,
not the schools'. It is the responsibility of parents to teach their children
values.

In the end, if prior generations aren't willing to condemn the consequences of their misguided passions, my generation must do it for them. If parents continue to ignore the truth or won't take the responsibility to act, we are required take this responsibility on ourselves. The baby boomers told their parents to take a hike back in the 1960s and 1970s—my generation can and must do the same. We must start the long journey back to an America that honors virtue and the foundational moral principles that make this country great.

CHAPTER TWO

FUN WITH BANANAS

"In public school systems across the country, they're indoctrinating kids to be 'sexual' under the guise of protecting them, when you know that's not true. I think it is indoctrination for left-wing agendas."

DR. LAURA SCHLESSINGER[1]

"I was nine years old in fourth grade," says Katie, a cute twenty-two-year-old suburban girl from the Northeast.[2] She's a brilliant Harvard Law student and a relatively happy person. At her upper-middle-class elementary school, she had her first brush with sex ed, porn generation style.

"One day, they told us they were going to teach us about 'Family Life.' They didn't separate us or anything. They said that people could engage in oral, anal, and regular sex, but didn't explain what the terms meant. I can't remember any moral judgments being made. They gave us booklets with line drawings of what happens as puberty progresses. They also told us that sex can get you pregnant, and that it can give you diseases. There was a lot of focus on HIV. They said that the only way to be 100 percent safe was abstinence. Then they sent all the girls to the nurse, who told us that if we bled we weren't dying, and handed out maxi pads and tampons."

Katie's parents were given the option to opt out of this explicit instruction for their nine-year-old, but they didn't. In fact, no one opted out in fourth grade, and only one person opted out in the following years of sex ed. According to Katie, she got sex ed nine times over, every year from fourth to twelfth grade: "The classes were co-ed all the way through. In seventh grade, they were showing condoms—we made balloons out of them. They had a goody box full of birth control implements: condoms, diaphragms.

"In seventh grade, someone said that their friend in eighth grade was already having sex, but that wasn't common. If I had to guess, I'd say that by the end of high school, about 15 percent of the kids in the class were having sex, and they were all the popular kids. But I was in the advanced class, where no one was really doing anything."

Katie believes that sex ed is a good thing for kids to hear. "The disease and pregnancy stuff was good because it scared people off—they realized there were consequences to sex. There should be education about it so that there are less half-truths and complete lies floating around and people can make an informed decision. Because *sooner or later they will do it*, and the more info they have, the better they are equipped to determine when they will do it." She also believes that parental inactivity makes taxpayer-funded sex education more vital, citing her own parents as an example: "My parents wouldn't have talked to me about this if I hadn't had sex ed in school. By now, at our house if they start something, it's like 'Chill, I'm not fifteen anymore.'"

Katie isn't a virgin, and she isn't ashamed of it. She became sexually active at age nineteen and has had three sexual partners. "There's nothing wrong with premarital sex," she tells me. "I got over that idea. I feel I can make rational decisions armed with what I learned in nine years of the same class repeating...Sex is appropriate when the person is mentally ready to have sex, and when it's not a result of pressure to fit in, and when she's mature enough not to have any regrets."

Still, Katie doesn't want her parents to know about her sexual history because "they still think it's wrong, and I don't want to open that can of worms."[3] For that reason, her name has been changed to protect her privacy.

Katie is an above-average girl, and would be considered in this day and age a sexually well-adjusted citizen. Her views on sex education and sex in general are shared by many of her peers. Premarital sex isn't seen as wrong, as long as you're ready for it, and sex education is supposed to prepare you for it.

With this kind of logic, it's not hard to see why kids are being sexualized at younger and younger ages. The younger the kids are when sex ed begins, the more they know at a younger age. The more they know, the more prepared they are. The more prepared they are, the more societal approval they will receive when they do have sex. And societal approval means societal encouragement.

The "have sex as soon as you're ready" logic also means that having sex becomes a mark of maturity. Those who are more mature and mentally prepared will have sex younger. Those who wait until marriage to have sex, conversely, must be immature social outcasts or for some reason unprepared.

The truth is that knowledge and information aren't cure-alls. In fact, they can do serious damage to children. What supporters of the full-frontal version of sex ed don't understand is that knowledge is power only when the person armed with the knowledge is capable of making a fully rational and informed decision. Children are not capable of such a rational decision, and treating them as adults does them no favors. Kay Hymowitz, author of *Ready or Not: What Happens When We Treat Children as Small Adults*, argues that the "anticulturalists"—people who believe that childhood sexuality, left on its own, free of social interference, will flourish and grow in healthy ways—have overestimated the choosing power of children.

> Drained of all feeling but physical pleasure, rationalized into
> Filofax personal organizer entries, the sex given to us by this
> ministry is little more than techno-fantasy." They do not see the

alternately insecure and grandiose, idealistic and crude, perpet-
ually glandular teenager most of us know. Their teenager, like
that of so many other experts, is rational, self-aware, and
autonomous. Information is all these kids need, they say. Information and some deprogramming to counteract society's continuing efforts to pervert their healthy sexual natures. So now we
have a nation of teenagers who are information rich but knowledge poor. They—and their ten-year-old brothers and sisters, for
that matter—may be adults when it comes to technical information; certainly their putative sophistication about sexual matters
is the subject of endless head shaking by parents and the media.
But as they approach graduation in the anticultural school of
self-sufficiency, they remain predictably illiterate when it comes
to real human connection.[4]

In the view of the social liberals, children are fully capable of making
informed decisions about sex. With that premise in mind, liberals are
constantly harping about the right-wing sex education agenda of "scaring kids." "Scaring kids" means abstinence-only education, telling them
that the only way to ensure prevention of STDs and pregnancy is abstinence. "These programs are completely out of control," rages William
Smith, director of public policy at the Sexuality Information and Education Council of the United States (SIECUS). "They're using millions of
taxpayer dollars to provide medical misinformation to use fear and
shame-based messages in an effort to convince young people to change
their behavior."[5] Dr. Drew Pinsky, host of "Loveline," agrees: "[A]s a
pure program, the sort of scare tactics that are used with abstinence-only
educations really don't seem to work."[6]

Yes, using scare tactics is wrong in most situations. But when the subject cannot comprehend the harmful consequences of an action not yet
taken, then fear is an appropriate motivator to inhibit such an action. It's
always comical to watch a parent engage a two-year-old child in a
Socratic dialogue about why the kid can't cross the street without an
adult present. A two-year-old child can't understand the concept of

death, just as a ten-year-old child can't understand the crucial emotional loss and desensitization suffered as a result of sex without rules. Fear of consequences, whether those consequences are spiritual or physical, is a critical component to teaching restraint.

Social liberals also argue, as Katie does, that kids will have sex "sooner or later," so it's better to prepare them for it while they're young. This kind of cynical resignation has less to do with realism than with promoting a certain political agenda.

In reality, social liberals abandon determinism whenever it conflicts with their moral outlook. They say that educating kids about cigarette use means telling them to say no under all circumstances, instead of teaching them that if they do decide to smoke, they should use filters to minimize the health risks. Apparently, kids won't smoke "sooner or later" if we tell them no. Social liberals want to prevent children from knowing anything about gun use, instead of training children to use firearms responsibly. Apparently, kids won't use guns "sooner or later" if we tell them no. For liberals, premarital sex is less morally repugnant than smoking or hunting.

Many social liberals would prefer that kids be sexualized younger, so that they can become more "tolerant" of deviant lifestyles and what everyone used to acknowledge as immoral choices. The liberal sexual agenda underlies the teaching of sex education. As David Campos, author of *Sex, Youth, and Sex Education: A Reference Handbook*, proclaims: "To achieve a sexually healthy lifestyle, youth must acquire a positive and comfortable attitude about sex. Frank and fact-based discussions about topics once considered taboo are essential. Abortions, condoms, masturbation, oral sex, and homosexuality are among the topics to be found in comprehensive sex education programs."[7]

Katie's statement that she "can't remember any moral judgments being made" sums up today's sex education. Debra W. Haffner, former president of SIECUS, writes that the goals of sex education should be: "to provide young people with accurate information about sexuality, to give them an opportunity to develop their values and increase self-esteem, to help them develop interpersonal skills and to help them exercise responsibility in their relationships."[8] Develop *their* values, increase *their* self-esteem. This is subjectivism, and it is forcing kids without capabilities into choices with serious consequences.

As April Cornell[9], a twenty-three-year-old black woman from Harvard Law, explained to me, "Being a teenager sucks. Teenagers have way more choice today than they had 50 years ago; I have way more choice than my parents did when they were 15 or 16. It never would have occurred to my mom not to decide not to have sex or decide not to use drugs. There are decisions that I had to make, as opposed to 'this is the way it is.' I think kids are being forced into choices they're not ready to handle."[10]

April's classmate, Michelle McCaughey[11], concurs: "I think there's a lot more pressure because so many things are accepted. There's already enough pressure on teenagers to be cool and social, and when you get rid of any moral constraints that would weigh upon them, it makes life a lot harder."[12]

Because social liberals would prefer that kids gain "tolerance" rather than maintaining their innocence, they scorn abstinence itself. This is a textbook example of defining deviancy up to include normal, healthy, even moral behavior. The NARAL (formerly the National Abortion Rights Action League, now just NARAL) Pro-Choice America website contains a Pennsylvania campaign mocking chastity. It urges viewers to send the following letter to President Bush: "I am writing today as a supporter of NARAL Pro-Choice America to order a chastity belt. You might wonder why I am asking you for a chastity belt. Well, in your latest budget proposal to Congress, you ask for more funding for abstinence-only until marriage programs but do not provide any more funding for the Federal Family Planning Program. . . . Until you give us real choices, please rush me the only thing that you seem to want to provide to protect my reproductive health: a chastity belt. My address appears below."[13]

The choice not to have sex is, apparently, not a "real choice." A real choice is whether to use a condom, or whether to get an abortion after having unprotected sex.

Sex in the classroom

It's easy enough to find anecdotal evidence regarding the dangers of comprehensive sex ed: young teens being taught about the benefits of oral sex, masturbation, and homosexual activity, all without parental notification;[14] the Massachusetts Department of Public Health creating a video in 1989 explaining what to do before, during, and after sex;[15] "Focus on Kids," an organization promoted by the Centers for Disease Control and Prevention, telling kids to embark on "condom hunt[s]" at local stores;[16] the "Be Proud! Be Responsible!" program encouraging bisexuality and homosexuality;[17] the Sex Information and Education Council of the United States' (SIECUS) and the Centers for Disease Control's "Guidelines for Comprehensive Sex Education" telling children "homosexual love relationships can be as satisfying as heterosexual relationships."[18]

But anecdotes don't tell the full story. Today's sex education is systemically different than it was when it first began, in the early twentieth century. Sex education first arose for public health reasons; "sex hygiene" was the phrase of the day. Such teaching of "sex hygiene" was largely—and correctly—couched in moral terms. "The only way to cure the sexual evils thoroughly, the only way to dig them up by the roots, [according to sex hygiene pioneer Prince Morrow] was to prescribe the same standard of morality for man as for woman...Men must be as chaste as women."[19]

The fact that this message had to be taught in schools, though, already signified the beginning of the end for traditional morality. If parents were abdicating their responsibilities to such an extent that the schools had to step in, it was only a matter of time before taxpayer-funded sex ed became the dominant experience it is today.

It didn't take long. With growing sexual licentiousness and the beginnings of moral decline in the 1920s, sex education became more and more prevalent. The Great Depression and WWII delayed the downward spiral of sexual education. But by the beginning of the 1950s, sex education was ready to explode onto the scene. In 1948, Alfred Kinsey published his landmark survey, *Sexual Behavior in the Human Male*; in 1953, he followed up with *Sexual Behavior in the Human Female*.

According to Kinsey, 85 percent of males had premarital sex, almost 70 percent had sex with whores, and 30 to 45 percent of husbands had affairs. Somewhere between 10 and 37 percent of men had engaged in homosexuality.[20] These statistics were debunked later on, when it was found that Kinsey had skewed his polling data by relying on the testimony of sex offenders. As Daniel Flynn, author of *Intellectual Morons*, writes, "Kinsey was a charlatan who embarked upon research to confirm his pre-drawn conclusions."[21]

Kinsey claimed that Americans were secret perverts and sex maniacs. He "concluded that generations of Americans had not simply failed to follow the accepted standard of sexual morality, but in fact had failed so spectacularly as to call into question the moral code's very validity as a social ideal."[22] This is the tried-and-true hypocrisy charge: If you've sinned, you can't advocate morality. Falsely implicating millions of Americans in immoral sexual behavior was certainly an effective way of neutralizing societal morality. The only way to alleviate guilt became abdication of moral sexual standards. And when the chief goal is erasing guilt, even for immoral actions, all that remains is narcissism.

Kinsey's view—that societal standards had to be lowered—caught on in short order. "[Our goal] is to be ready as educators and parents to help young people obtain sex satisfaction before marriage," wrote Planned Parenthood staffer Lena Levine in 1953. "By sanctioning sex before marriage, we will prevent fear and guilt...we must be ready to provide young boys and girls with the best contraception measures available so they will have the necessary means to achieve sexual satisfaction without having to risk possible pregnancy."[23]

Levine's boss at Planned Parenthood, Dr. Mary Calderone, would go on to found SIECUS, an organization devoted exclusively to "the broad aspects of human sexuality."[24] Calderone's vision was of an open sex education, a sex education that didn't view "sex as a 'problem' to be 'controlled,'" but rather as "a vital life force to be utilized."[25] Luckily for Calderone and her ilk, by the late 1960s, teen sexual behavior had escalated to such an extent that a 1968 poll showed 71 percent of Americans favoring some sort of sex education at high schools.[26] "National statistics tell part of the story," wrote John Kobler in the *Saturday Evening Post* in 1968. "Venereal diseases among teenagers: over 80,000 cases reported in 1966... Unwed teenage mothers: about 90,000 a year, an increase of 100 percent in two decades. One out of every three brides under twenty goes to the altar pregnant... illegal abortions run into the hundreds of thousands."[27] It is fascinating that Kobler dates the vast rise in unwed teenage pregnancy back to 1948. Is it any coincidence that Kinsey's seminal work premiered that very year?

The rest is history. Today's sex ed experience for members of the porn generation is wedded to the idea of permissiveness and "tolerance" for all sorts of behaviors. As "inherently sexual beings" the argument goes, our sexuality should not and cannot be contained by any system of morality. Sexuality is as much a natural characteristic as race. No form of sexual expression may be condemned, and all must be taught. Be loud, and be proud. A textbook in use at Van Buren High School in Woodland, a Midwestern city with a population of about 175,000, explains this view to ninth-graders: "Because of the strong biological urge and its association with pleasure, sexual behavior is not always easy to control. Partially for this reason, many people have tried to hide sexual feelings. Total abstinence or illicit sex may cause feelings of guilt, fear, and anxiety. Sex is beautiful and can be an essential part of the total personality of everyone. No one should be forced into a position of guilt, fear, or anxiety about their own sexuality."[28]

In the absence of traditional morality, "self-esteem" (code for narcissism) is the rule of the day. SIECUS, the foremost independent sex education organization in the United States, touts its chief goal: "SIECUS affirms that sexuality is a fundamental part of being human, one that is worthy of dignity and respect. We advocate for the right of all people to accurate information, comprehensive education about sexuality, and sexual health services. SIECUS works to create a world that ensures social justice and sexual rights."[29] Planned Parenthood, which hands out materials to thousands of school children across America each year, states that its mission is to forward "the fundamental right of each individual, throughout the world, to manage his or her fertility, regardless of the individual's income, marital status, race, ethnicity, sexual orientation, age, national origin, or residence." In the field of education, this means "educational programs which enhance understanding of individual and societal implications of human sexuality."[30]

These radical sex educators are correct in one sense: Sex shouldn't be shameful. But just because people have natural desires and drives doesn't legitimate those natural desires and drives in all contexts, especially outside the context of marriage.

The attack on abstinence

The public policy brilliance of comprehensive sex education is its self-justifying nature. Sex education has used skyrocketing rates of venereal disease, teen pregnancy, and sexual immorality as an excuse to teach its panoramic view of sexuality. Unfortunately, there's a rising threat looming on the horizon for sex educators: abstinence education. If morality can somehow be infused back into sex education, if the "tolerance for all sexual activity" mission may be discarded safely, the Kinseyans are out of a job.

So the only thing to do is rail against abstinence education. Social liberals start by claiming that abstinence education is "repressive," conjuring up purple images of religious fanaticism. "I personally feel this, that the underlying issue is sex," said Surgeon General Dr. Jocelyn Elders in 1993. "That fornication must be punished, and that teenage pregnancy and the bad things that happen after are the natural punishment."[31]

Then the social liberals claim that abstinence education doesn't work, because—of course—abstinence is impossible. "Denying our young people accurate information about sexual health will not prevent unintended pregnancies or the spread of sexually transmitted diseases. It will, however, prevent them from making responsible and informed decisions about their health and futures," growled William Smith, director of public policy of SIECUS.[32] "Personally, I don't think abstinence is going to fly at all," says Susan Foote, chairwoman of the Seabrook (New Hampshire) Planning Board. "There are other forms of pregnancy prevention than abstinence. Remember back when you were a teen; would abstinence have worked for you?"[33] (By the way, the Seabrook Commissioner's Task Force on Abstinence Education found that "roughly 60 percent of kids are staying abstinent."[34])

"Within this culture where sex sells everything from shampoo to gum, George Bush has proposed doubling the amount of federal funding for abstinence-only sex education in the classroom," states an outraged Anne Kim of the University of Washington. "[I]t's a farce to assume that exclusively teaching 'no sex is safe sex' will prevent teens from having it. This message dissolves in the real world where teens, regardless of whether they're sexually active, want to know and talk about sex."[35]

The truth is it's too early to tell whether abstinence education can work at a wide level. There have been no conclusive studies one way or another, and the studies that do exist conflict with each other. A Heritage Foundation report found that women who pledge to remain virgins until marriage are "about 40 percent less likely to have a child out of wedlock when compared to similar young women who do not make such a pledge."[36] Other research found that only 12 percent of those who made abstinence pledges fulfilled them, although those who didn't last the distance at least waited eighteen months longer on average to have sex, married younger, and had fewer sexual partners before marriage.[37] Still another study found that the rate of STDs among pledge-makers was slightly lower than the rate among those who made no pledge.[38]

Yet despite the conflicting information about pro-abstinence programs, one fact remains certain: Non-abstinence-only education programs have been a massive and complete failure. The proof is in the results.

Despite President Bush's support for abstinence-only education, the vast majority of federal and state government-backed sex education in this country remains comprehensive, non-abstinence-only sex ed. In 2002, the federal and state governments spent $1.73 billion on contraception promotion and pregnancy prevention programs, as opposed to $144.1 million for abstinence programs for teens. That's a 12:1 ratio, with abstinence programs getting the short end of the stick.[39]

Yet comprehensive sex education has done little or nothing to stanch the flow of teen pregnancy, venereal disease, and sexual licentiousness. By age thirteen, over 8 percent of girls have had sex. By age fifteen, one-third of girls have had sex, as opposed to less than 5 percent in 1970.[40] That statistic is 45 percent for today's fifteen-year-old boys.[41] In the 1970s, "39 percent of sexually active adolescent girls reported multiple partners; as of 1988 that number had grown to 55 percent. Thirteen percent of those girls reported having had sex with at least six men."[42] Two-thirds of suburban and urban twelfth graders have had sex, and 43 percent of suburban twelfth graders have had sex outside of a "romantic relationship," as have 39 percent of urban twelfth graders.[43] Meanwhile, the national illegitimacy rate has risen dramatically, from just over 5 percent in 1960[44] to 33 percent as of 2003.[45] Three to four million STDs are contracted annually by teens from the ages of fifteen to nineteen. Today, there are over twenty-five STDs of major concern, as opposed to only two in the 1960s.[46]

Arguing that it's irresponsible to try an untested regime of abstinence education is a losing argument when we compare it to our current regime of pathetic failure, and social liberals recognize that weakness. So instead of trying abstinence, most just change their colors, calling comprehensive sex ed "abstinence-plus" sex ed. It's like changing the name of South Central Los Angeles to South Los Angeles in order to prevent crime. Spin isn't very effective in either case.

But those determined social liberals continue to spin away. Nicholas Kristof of the *Times* states, without citing a single statistic, that "There's plenty of evidence that abstinence-plus programs—which encourage abstinence but also teach contraception—delay sex and increase the use of contraception."[47]

Hillary Clinton, prepping for her presidential run, is smarter. She concedes, "Research shows that the primary reason that teenage girls abstain is because of their religious and moral values. We should embrace this— and support programs that reinforce the idea that abstinence at a young age is not just the smart thing to do, it is the right thing to do." But that doesn't mean that Hillary is willing to forego comprehensive sex ed: "But we should also recognize what works and what doesn't work, and to be fair, the jury is still out on the effectiveness of abstinence-only programs...We should use all the resources at our disposal to ensure that teens are getting the information they need to make the right decision." This means backing "increasing access to family planning services," among other socially liberal programs.[48] Liberals like Hillary won't give up their self-feeding government-sponsored propaganda machine without a fight.

The president's goodnight blowjobs

Hillary's husband has played a sexual education role as well. President Clinton's impeachment scandal of 1998 had a definite impact on the porn generation, and not in a positive sense. While most liberal commentators argued at the time that Clinton didn't need to be a role model for America's children in his personal life, his actions effectively validated the worst kind of activity—both when it comes to lying about sex and on the issue of oral sex. And the kids were watching.

By February 2005, a *Seventeen* magazine poll (in conjunction with SIECUS) showed that "40% of guys have said, 'I love you,' just to get a girl to do something sexual. 31% of guys have told a friend they went further with a girl than they really did. 17% of guys have told a girl they were virgins when they *weren't* (so she wouldn't think she was at risk for STDs)."[49]

In an attempt to dodge the perjury issue, Clinton contributed to the hot new idea that oral sex wasn't real sex. Clinton claimed in August 1998 that "I said, I have not had sex with her as I defined it. That was true. And did I hope that I would never have to be here on this day giving this testimony? Of course. But I also didn't want to do anything to complicate this matter further. So, I said things that were true. They may have been misleading, and if they were I have to take responsibility for it, and I'm sorry."[50]

Despite earlier statements indicating that President Clinton defined oral sex as a sexual relationship,[51] many in the media picked up on his latter words. This scandal wasn't even about sex, they asserted—it was about fake sex!

So stated attorney W.A. Friedlander in the *Raleigh News and Observer*: "in Webster's Seventh New Collegiate Dictionary, p. 795, 'sexual relations' is defined simply as 'coitus' which, in turn, is defined as 'the natural conveying of semen to the female reproductive tract.' This would certainly exclude oral sex."[52] *Time* bought the argument as well, stating in an article titled "When Sex Is Not Really Having Sex" that Clinton had "a legal loophole narrower than the eye of a needle but considerably easier to pass through than a prison wall."[53]

Justified by Clinton, and either assented to or conveniently overlooked by his media pals, the oral sex/real sex faux distinction is now the prevailing belief among children. To be sure, the belief was prevalent even before the term Lewinsky entered common parlance, but having the president of the United States validate that belief surely didn't help matters. Ricardo Gandara of the *Austin American-Statesman* posits, "Why are kids fearless about oral sex? Perhaps former President Clinton's public distinction between oral sex and 'real' sex helped pave the way."[54]

Dr. W. David Hager, a member of the Food and Drug Administration's Advisory Committee for Reproductive Health Drugs, stated that he believed the increase in oral sex could be traced to the Lewinsky scandal and Clinton's hair-splitting.[55] And Dr. Lauren Streicher, a gynecologist from Northwestern Memorial Hospital, told the *Chicago Sun-Times* in March 2004, "There's no question that there's an increase in oral sex over the last five to seven years...One of the problems is that teenagers don't often consider it to be sex. They think that this is not the same as having intercourse."[56]

Of course, five to seven years before 2004 would be...1997–1999, precisely the period in which the Lewinsky scandal broke. Interesting how that works.

Radical social leftist and Boston University professor Shari Thurer also credits the Clinton-Lewinsky scandal for bringing oral sex into the limelight.[57] Joe McIlhaney Jr., president and founder of The Medical Institute for Sexual Health, agrees. "He said it wasn't sex," McIlhaney wrote in the *Houston Chronicle*. "Well, then how come it is causing the rampant spread of genital herpes among America's young people? The 'he' I refer to is former President Bill Clinton. And the 'it' is oral sex, which Clinton said with great sincerity, isn't sex."[58]

Kids buy into Clinton's argument. In one case, the head teacher at a school in a Washington suburb told parents that twelve girls aged thirteen to fourteen had been doing "it" with two or three boys. When one set of parents confronted their child, she quickly responded: "What's the big deal? President Clinton did it."[59]

This is a brutally harmful belief. First off, sexually transmitted diseases can easily be passed genitals-to-mouth. Second, young men and women, pressured into believing that oral sex doesn't really count, are more free to give it even if they don't really want to. According to a December 2000 study by the Alan Guttmacher Institute journal, *Family Planning Perspectives*, giving oral sex makes girls feel exploited, but they do it anyway because they want to be popular or "make boys happy."[60]

And then there's the moral aspect. Oral sex outside of marriage is still extramarital sex. Denial of that fact is simply defining deviancy down. Boys and girls degrade the sex act to the level of kissing and still consider themselves virgins, even though they have engaged in promiscuous extramarital sex. When they get married as "virgins," they breach a sacred trust between husband and wife. If the point of virginity until marriage is to keep sexual activity within moral boundaries, oral sex is a betrayal of that ideal.

Teens don't see it that way. According to a 2003 Northern Kentucky University survey of almost 600 teens who had taken abstinence pledges, 61 percent had broken them; of the remaining 39 percent, who were still in their own opinions "virgins," more than half said that they'd had oral sex. "Some people feel like they can maintain their pledge and still have oral sex, and that oral sex doesn't count," NKU researcher and psychologist Angela Lipsitz observed.[61]

On January 15, 1999, Dr. George Lundberg, editor of the Journal of the American Medical Association, published a study in which 60 percent of college students claimed that oral sex was not "real sex."[62] In July 1999, the *Washington Post* discovered an "unsettling new fad"—suburban middle school kids were commonly giving each other oral sex at parks, houses, and schools.[63] Twenty percent of teens have had oral sex by age fifteen.[64] A survey by *Seventeen* and the Kaiser Family Foundation revealed that 55 percent of teens have engaged in oral sex, as opposed to 40 percent engaging in vaginal intercourse.[65]

The *Chicago Sun-Times* termed oral sex the "new third base," while quoting sixteen-year-old John, who goes to private high school and won't have "real sex," but began having oral sex at age fourteen: "It happens mostly at parties or after school, sometimes when the girls are a little bit drunk. And these days, even the grade 7s are doing it." "People don't even think about it as bad anymore...It's cool if you do it," concurred thirteen-year-old Elissa.[66]

As for the parents, they're most likely upstairs watching *Sex and the City*, at least according to an NBC/*People* poll from 2004. Teens ages thirteen to sixteen were asked about places they received information about sex and sexual relationships; 70 percent of teens said they received either a lot or some information about sex from their parents. Yet 54 percent of the teens felt that a teenager who has oral sex is still a virgin; 57 percent felt it was okay for teens who are seventeen or eighteen to have oral sex. While only 15 percent of surveyed parents believed that their teens had gone beyond kissing, 27 percent of teens reported being with someone in an intimate or sexual way.[67]

Psychologist Dr. Wayne Warren told the *New York Times*, "I see girls, seventh and eight graders, even sixth graders, who tell me they're virgins, and they're going to wait to have intercourse until they meet the man they'll marry. But then they've had oral sex fifty to sixty times. It's like a goodnight kiss to them, how they say goodbye after a date."[68] Goodnight blowjobs? Clinton may like this world he helped build, but it's revolting for those of us with any moral standards at all.

Here's the bottom line: Without the Lewinsky scandal, millions of children would not have had to hear about this issue until reaching maturity. Instead, oral sex and masturbation with cigars became topics of conversation in classrooms and around dinner tables throughout the country. Agonized mother of four Elizabeth Avery Shelton expressed it well in her letter to the editor of the *Seattle Times*: "I would like it to be known (before her movie and book deal comes out) that I want an apology from [Lewinsky] for being solely responsible for me having to explain oral sex to my four children, ages twelve to eight." Clinton and his media cronies owe parents an apology as well. Unfortunately, an apology just won't cut it at this point. The ship has left the dock.

Parental abdication

Comprehensive sex education has taken power out of the hands of parents. The current system has the schools teaching amoral permissiveness and forcing parents with standards to un-teach their own children. And parents have become too lazy to do anything about it. Instead of opting their kids out of sex ed, it's easier for them to avoid the messy birds-and-bees conversation. Leave it to the government employees to teach the kids about standards of morality.

The social liberals who have promulgated this anti-parent system are pleased with the result. Their goal was never to allow parents the authority to teach their children; it was to shill for the god of Tolerance. Government is the most easily available tool to use toward this end—and it is certainly the most powerful. As Surgeon General Jocelyn Elders put it, "We taught them what to do in the front seat of a car. Now it's time to teach them what to do in the back seat."[69]

The callousness here is unmistakable. If government usurpation of parental authority means sacrificing some kids to the consequences of emotionally barren sex, venereal disease, and abortion, so be it. The social liberals are creating a utopian "live and let live" society, and you can't make an omelet without breaking eggs.

Social liberals can't get away with stating their goals out loud, so they hide behind the screen of youth "autonomy." They're just giving kids respect, they say. They're just providing full information. It is this perverse view of child autonomy that has led to widespread abortion "rights" for children: the kids were old enough and smart enough to have sex, and now they're old enough and smart enough to get an abortion without parental notification. Democratic Representative Jan Schakowsky of Illinois explains this view: "[O]fficials at the state and federal levels are trying to take away young people's rights to reproductive-health services, including access to contraceptives, family planning, and abortion."[70] This grants children just enough rope to hang themselves and their fetuses—autonomy in the form of a suicide pill.

The combination of parental abdication and social liberalism in our schools means that kids are easy targets for nihilism and moral subjectivism. Ironically, by destroying parental authority with regard to morality, social liberals got more than they bargained for: rampant drug, alcohol, and tobacco use. Almost three-quarters of suburban twelfth graders and 71 percent of urban twelfth graders have tried alcohol more than two or three times. Forty percent of twelfth graders in both urban and suburban schools have used illegal drugs. More than 60 percent of suburban twelfth graders have tried cigarettes, as have 54 percent of urban twelfth graders.[71]

We're now at the crisis point, and parents are beginning to wake up. A poll released in February 2003 by Zogby International showed strong support for abstinence education, and a remarkable antipathy toward the liberal social messages taught in comprehensive sex ed. For example, 71 percent of parents disapproved of teaching a middle-school child (ages twelve to fifteen) to unroll a condom and place it on a finger, banana, or wooden model of a penis. Another 71 percent disapproved of telling children (ages nine to twelve) that "Homosexual love relationships can be as satisfying as heterosexual love relationships." A plurality—46 percent to 39 percent—disapproved of telling fourteen to eighteen year-olds that "Teenagers can obtain birth control pills from family planning clinics and doctors without permission from a parent." And 70 percent disapproved of schools handing out contraception without their permission.

A full 69 percent of parents believed that nine to twelve year-olds should be taught "Sexual or physical intimacy should occur between two people involved in a lifelong, mutually faithful, marriage commitment." And 74 percent believed that fifteen- to eighteen-year-olds should be taught that they need not worry about pregnancy or STDs if they are abstinent.[72]

These parents have a reason to be angry. They've been cut out of the loop, and these explicit and ill-thought public school courses have become the primary source for their children's views about sex. After feeling the consequences of social liberalism, parents are waking up. To preserve the innocence of their children and equip them with a moral worldview, it's up to these parents to stand up for their kids, accept their responsibilities and start acting like . . . well . . . parents.

CHAPTER THREE

CAMPUS CARNALITY

"Let's not burn the universities yet. After all, the damage they do might be worse."

H.L. MENCKEN

College life for the porn generation is the social liberal's dream. In an environment dominated by secular humanism and political correctness, no one ever makes judgments about sexual activity. And the dirty little secret of the matter is: That's the way the universities want it.

Today it's the universities promoting co-ed dorms, "tolerant" speech codes, and sexual experimentation. It's the tenured hippies and their capitulating compatriots from the 1960s running the universities now. The ones who used to want a revolution are now the institution.

When they first enter college, students are thrust into an uncertain world, usually without friends or family to guide them. So they seek guidance from administrators, professors, and peer—each source worse than the last. With parents out of the picture, the universities' objections to traditional morality create a values vacuum for students.

In the context of that vacuum, the "tolerant," "live and let live" attitude of the institutional leaders filters down to the students. The common feeling is, as Elliott Davis, Cornell University class of 2004 expresses it, "People do what they want to do. It doesn't bother me."[1] And so students feel free to do what they want to do, knowing that there's no danger of stigma or condemnation.

Janie, a twenty-two-year-old UCLA student, embodies these notions. "I do whatever I want, and I've never thought twice about it," Janie told me. Janie has sex "if I've been dating a guy for a while and we say we love each other." Couldn't a guy just lie? "I've had guys say they loved me before, but I know they don't mean it. It's intuition." According to Janie, she's not a slut: "I've been having sex since I was fifteen, right? And I'm twenty-one now, so that's six years, and yet I've only had five partners. You know, that's pretty good compared to other people who started having sex when they were fifteen."[2]

With values like these, and the prevailing societal attitude of tolerance for such values, is it any wonder that 49 percent of women aged eighteen to nineteen had sex with at least two partners in the year 2002, and 81 percent of women aged twenty to twenty-four in 2002 had become sexually active before age twenty?[3]

Not only do colleges induct students into the fancy-free world of "if it feels good, do it," they subvert all opposing authorities, particularly parents. Parents drop their kids off, telling them to "find themselves." When the kids return, they haven't found themselves; they've found a substitute for the familial safety net in professors, peers, and random sex. Everyone needs a philosophical framework to justify their existence, and if parents won't provide it, the universities certainly will—and so they fill the values vacuum with a moral framework based on narcissism and hedonism. As columnist Suzanne Fields writes, "Where morality is 'dumbed down' it takes nerve to protest the tyranny of 'the student bodies.' "[4]

Sex over poker

It's Wednesday night, and a group of friends and classmates from Harvard Law are gathered around a poker table. We're in one of the dorm complexes, I'm down about $10, and everyone has had a beer or two. We've been playing for about an hour, and the conversation has revolved completely around two topics: rock music and sex. In between discussion of the best cover song ever for a rock album, A.J.[5] tells the group that he's found a sex partner online.

"She's into spanking, and I figured that sounds like it's worth a try," he says.

"Dude, that's a good way to get yourself beaten up by eight guys, meeting a girl for sex online," Jimmy[6] answers.

"I heard a story from one of my friends about a guy he knew who liked to get rough with his girlfriend," volunteers Jason.[7] "So one time they were having sex, and he just pulled out and punched her right in the crotch."

Others groan. Jimmy offers, "One time a guy I knew, his girlfriend kept asking him to hurt her, over and over, so he just grabbed a toaster and smacked her in the head with it."

"So, A.J.," Jason asks, "did you end up going out with your best friend's friend?"

"Yeah," A.J. answers, "but it wasn't really a date."

"Did you try to get some from her?"

"Nah."

"Good move."

The conversation continues like this for hours. Sex, class, rock music. Sex, rock music, sex. Sex, sex, sex.

An hour before the game, I had attended a reception for Harvard Law 1Ls (first-years) held by a major New York law firm. I was standing around with a few of the fellows from the class. "So did you hear about what happened to Adam?"[8] Jimmy asked me. "No," I said.

"Well," Jimmy explains, "Adam was in Costa Rica with a bunch of other people from our class, and they went to a bar. Some random girl approached him, and he went in the bathroom with her. She gave him a blowjob in a stall."

I make a disapproving face. "Ben, that isn't the bad part," Jimmy says.

"Oh."

"So later," Jimmy continues, "the group sees this girl being tossed out of the bar. So they ask the bartender what's going on. 'Oh, that's some guy who goes around giving people blowjobs, and we have to toss him every night,' the bartender tells them. Turns out that the girl was a transvestite."

Ugh. "It's probably not the best idea in the world to go around taking oral sex from random people anyway, if only for STD reasons," I state.

Another guy, Alan,[9] chimes in. "Well, I'll tell you, I'm usually good about making sure the girl doesn't have anything," he says. "But when a girl starts to go down on me, I'm not going to stop her."

It's worth noting that few of the people I talked to that night could be described as politically liberal. Jason is a libertarian. Jimmy is a Midwestern guy with a conservative streak on crime and economics, and a slightly conservative tinge on social issues. Still, none of these escapades triggered any moral consternation. None of these people could be described as stupid or ignorant, either. Each is a student at the top law school in the country. Yet free sex, sex that ignores both possible consequences and emotional involvement, is commonplace.

And it's not just at Harvard. "This girl who's a freshman at my school, she said she had sex with five guys in one week," 2004 American University graduate Marty Beckerman told me. "That's an extreme example, but that kind of anonymous quick, totally emotionless stuff, I don't know how many times in college I heard somebody say they had no idea the name of the guy or girl they had sex with last night."

Beckerman tells another story emphasizing his point: "I had this friend who was a seventeen-year-old junior in high school, and he was hanging out with us, and he was like 'I have to go to your college, I really wanna have sex with a college girl.' I wasn't really hot on the idea. But he was insistent. So he comes to the campus, and we're hanging out, and it's late, and we're in a friend's room, and a girl comes in who's f—ing trashed. Really, really drunk. So we're like, 'Ashley, this is our friend, he's a junior too.' Of course, he was a junior in high school, and she was a junior in college. But she didn't know that. And she's like 'Ohhhh.' Within two minutes of introducing these two to each other, they were in her room having oral sex."[10]

Check your morals at the dorm

Consider a world made up entirely of eighteen-year-old men and women, hormones raging, walk around in towels and pajamas like sisters and brothers, often sharing bathrooms and sometimes bedrooms—and, much of the time, beds. Welcome to dorm life for the porn generation.

The social situation makes for its own unique and bizarre rules and practices. Roommates are "sexiled" when their roommates are getting busy in the dorm room. Lucia,[11] a twenty-three-year-old 2004 alum of New York University, explains the basic principle of "sexiling": "I suppose at its most impolite, it is when the roommate returns home (usually late at night) and has been locked out of his/her room (whether physically by a door lock or emotionally by the potential visual of what's going on inside) because their roommate is hooking up with someone. It often happens as a stated agreement between roommates too, though. I was more than happy to vacate the room so my roommate could have it on Valentine's Day with her boyfriend."[12]

Typically, people from the same dorm don't hook up or date; that's known as "dormcest." According to Lucia, "dormcest" often leads to "sweatpant romance, which is kind of a funny concept. It's not really dating because you don't get dressed and go out of the building, you just stop by in your sweatpants and get laid or whatever, kind of the lazy man's dating. I had a friend who called off a hooking-up relationship purely out of her distaste for the label of 'sweatpant romance.'"[13]

The average college student is getting plenty of "action": an Independent Women's Forum study found that 40 percent of college women had "hooked up," and 10 percent had "hooked up" more than six times. Hooking up, for the non-porn generation readers, is "any sexual contact—ranging from kissing to sexual intercourse—in which the participants expected no further contact." Elizabeth Marquardt, who led the research team, stated that in the study, "co-ed dorms kept coming up in a negative way. They have reduced the mystery [of male-female relationships] while facilitating joined-at-the-hip relationships."[14]

Wendy Shalit, author of *A Return to Modesty: Discovering the Lost Virtue*, accurately describes the situation: "[W]hen the dorms are co-ed, and even the bathrooms are co-ed, and we're all thrown together...there's no [escape] from the culture of immodesty. When everything is integrated...there's no mystery, and there's no separation, and there's no reverence between the sexes."[15]

Rick Gabriele, a student at Haverford College in Pennsylvania, unwittingly seconds the motion: "[Co-ed] is great...You get used to being around the opposite sex. I walk into the bathroom, and there'll be a girl brushing her teeth, and then I'll jump in the shower."[16] Talk about the death of romance.

With sex readily available at every turn, it's no wonder only 38 percent of college guys are in a serious relationship.[17] "Dates and, for the most part, love affairs, are passé," writes 2001 Princeton grad Laura Vanderkam. "Why bother asking someone to dinner when you can meet at a party, down a few drinks and go home together?"[18] Princeton class of '04 Justin Johnson sums it up: "No one dates."[19]

It's not as though college administrators didn't realize that the natural result of close proximity between hormonal teenagers would lead to sex. In fact, many dorms have taken precautions to provide the students with easy access to contraceptives. At Oberlin College in Ohio, dorm bulletins announce the popular weekly Safe Sex night at the dance hall.[20] Doug, a recent NYU grad, told me, "Either the RAs [residence assistants] or Health Services would hand out condoms"—a situation that is common to many universities.[21]

UCLA's Dykstra Hall was one of the nation's first co-ed dorms, established in 1960. As early as 1994, the administration set up a dispensing machine for condoms. Nora Zamichow of the *Los Angeles Times* pronounces that the "degree of casual contact between the sexes [at Dykstra] is stunning."[22] It's not too easy to stun an *L.A. Times* reporter.

Marisa, a twenty-two-year-old UCLA senior, lived in one of the nicer dorms on campus with three roommates. She says that contraception was "definitely available," and specifically cites "a big fair at the beginning of the year in the dorms. It is mainly for freshmen to get acquainted with college and dorm life. I go every year...the Student Health Advocate [SHA] table was handing out colored condoms."[23] The SHAs, by the way, have office hours in UCLA's dorms, during which they hand out free over-the-counter contraceptives.[24] Think of it as improving convenience in an on-demand world.

Marisa also recalls a time when one of her roommates allowed her boyfriend to move into their room. "He even brought his stuff, like clothes and things," she remembers. "He slept with her, in the same bed," with three other girls in the same room.

Those who protest dorm policies that encourage this zoo-like environment are ostracized and ridiculed. In 1998, five Orthodox Jewish students sued Yale University, asking that they be allowed to live off-campus. They objected to the sexual atmosphere of the dorms; in particular, they weren't happy with co-ed toilets and showers, sex manuals and condom availability, and required "safe sex lectures" for freshmen.

Instead of accommodating their request, the Yale administration ripped into the students, stating that dorm life was "a central part of Yale's education."[25] Richard Levin, the President of the Yale Hillel (a campus Jewish organization), stated that if the students weren't willing to live in the dorms, they shouldn't have come to Yale in the first place: "Why come to a university like this one if you won't open your mind to new ideas and new perspectives?" he queried. "This is not a place where people who close themselves off to the world can thrive." In the end, the students paid for campus housing and then lived off campus.[26]

In recent years, new and more disturbing arrangements have been developing. Many campuses have created co-ed dorm rooms, where students of opposite sexes share actual living space. Haverford College in Pennsylvania has employed such a strategy; their aim is to "replicate a family situation, where students share a home with separate bedrooms," though administrators concede that boyfriends/girlfriends have taken advantage of the situation.[27]

NYU also offers co-ed space. "I think it's a valid option that should be open to consenting students," says Lucia. "I don't think it represents an oversexualization at all. It's just universities needing to keep up with the pace of social culture."[28]

This is the familiar market argument: Society is leading universities, not the other way around. There's a market for sexual freedom, so why not let the universities cater to it?

Such an argument ignores all pretense of social responsibility. If society is moving in a more and more perverse direction, is it not the job of the universities to remain a shining beacon of truth? After all, that's what the universities proclaim themselves to be. UCLA's motto is *Fiat Lux*, or "let there be light." NYU's is *Perstare et Praestare*, "to persevere and to excel." Harvard: *Veritas*, "truth."

And yet these same universities run from the idea of objective truth in pursuit of feel-good, "live and let live" morality. It is strange that in their flight from the very notion of objective truth, the universities have anointed their own version of "tolerant" truth as sacrosanct. Hence the current renaissance of speech codes designed to restrict any mode of thought other than the one promulgated by the universities. Columnist David Limbaugh reported in 2003, "Some have estimated that as many as 90 percent of American universities have adopted such codes in one form or another."[29]

Most speech codes are vague enough to sound plausibly open-minded. Still, it's hard to imagine that the tolerance espoused by the universities invariably extends to those with traditional moral views. University of Colorado at Boulder expects students "to join together to ensure a climate of diversity where everyone values individual and group differences, respects the perspectives of others, and communicates openly to attain the best education."[30] At Harvard Law, students are informed that they are joining "a community ideally characterized by free expression, free inquiry, intellectual honesty, respect for the dignity of others, and openness to constructive change. The rights and responsibilities exercised within the community must be compatible with these qualities."[31]

Standards don't come much vaguer than this. It's not difficult to see how quoting Leviticus or Saint Paul could inhibit the "dignity of others," especially in an environment where the law school dean condemns military recruitment on campus due to their "unjust" policy of "don't ask, don't tell."

Other universities are clearer about their goals. University of California at Berkeley "opposes" speech that contains "harassment, intimidation, exploitation, and other forms of discrimination that are based on race, ethnicity, sex, religion, sexual orientation, disability, and other personal characteristics."[32] Kansas State University avers, "Every person, regardless of race, color, creed, national origin, gender, sexual orientation, age or disability, shall be treated with respect and dignity."[33]

The universities have instituted a new right: the right not to be offended. When tolerance of every sort of behavior reigns, those who believe in standards and rules are destined for castigation.

Professors as parents

Universities embody another characteristic that social liberals love: replacement of parents as authority figures. And these new, improved "parents" aren't likely to give you rules to follow or goals to reach. They'll sanction whatever you decide to do. In fact, they go further than sanctioning licentious behavior: they actively proselytize for it. College for the porn generation is a whole new, fresh, exciting world—a world without rules.

Since the 1960s, the inmates have been running the asylums. When students protested administrative power during that tumultuous period, administrators and professors caved in, in some cases even cheering on the rowdy young idiots. Robert Bork, who was a professor of law at Yale during this time, recalls, "That was the pattern across the United States in the late 1960s and early 1970s: violent rhetoric and violent action from the fascists of the New Left, followed by the abject moral surrender of academic officials the public had a right to expect would defend the universities and the orderly processes of their governance."[34]

Many of the student radicals of the 1960s are now the professors and administrators at universities. Their views have not moderated. Just as

Students for a Democratic Society (SDS) proclaimed in their 1962 Port Huron Statement, the current goal of the professoriate is "finding a meaning in life that is personally authentic."[35] As Bork comments, "This translated as foul language, sexual promiscuity, marijuana and hard drugs, and disdain for the military and for conventional success."[36]

In many ways, nothing has changed. Professors are still rebelling against traditional morality—only this time, they're leading young people down the path to acceptance of deviancy and rejection of faith and family. Sexual experimentation is taught and encouraged. According to Princeton University sociology professor Patricia Fernandez-Kelly, those who are in serious relationships in college are missing out. She says that it is important for "people to protect themselves physically and emotionally," but "disagrees with moralists" who condemn sexual experimentation.[37] "I don't think we can come out and discourage sexual experimentation," agrees Elizabeth Paul, an associate professor of psychology at New Jersey College.[38]

As soon as students arrive on campus, they're introduced to the world of sexual self-awareness by the administration. "I remember very distinctly there was a sex-orientation during the orientation over the summer before entering freshman year," says a recent NYU grad, Doug.[39] "They had a professional sex therapist or something come demonstrate everything from condoms to dental dams."[40] Lucia remembers the situation as well: "I remember the whole orientation being pretty sexually charged in general, but one of the workshops towards sexual education and knowing the resources the university makes available—resources like free condoms and dental dams, counseling, crisis resources, pamphlets. At orientation specifically, we played games, watched demonstrations, and the workshop itself was conducted by the head of the sexual health center."[41]

"All that and a box of press-on nails"

At UC–Berkeley, one class involved male and female students discussing their sexual fantasies, porn star lecturers, strip-club field trips with instructor sexual demonstrations, and class exercises in which students photographed their own genitalia. This class was keeping with the students-as-teachers theme of the 1960s radicals; as columnist John Leo wrote, "A lot of educational theory says that teacher-led classes are too hierarchical. They imply that teachers know more than students. In student led-classes there aren't any teachers, just 'coordinators' and 'facilitators,' and everybody is on the same level." Everyone in the class received two credits.[42]

Courses on porn have become commonplace around the country. Universities that have offered such courses include Kansas University;[43] San Francisco State University; University of Massachusetts–Amherst; Chapman University; Northwestern University; and University of California–Santa Cruz.[44] At Wesleyan University, they describe a porn course almost as a social good: "The pornography we study is an art of transgression which impels human sexuality toward, against, and beyond the limits which have traditionally defined civil discourses and practices.... Our examination accordingly includes the implication of pornography in so-called perverse practices such as voyeurism, bestiality, sadism, and masochism."[45] The list goes on.

Other universities use their sex courses as a formula for postmodern radicalism. Women's Studies and Lesbian, Gay, Bisexual, and Transgender (LGBT) Studies departments, specifically designed to fight social traditionalism, dominate the universities. Yale has a "Women's, Gender, and Sexuality Studies Program," in which "Gender—the social meaning of the distinction between the sexes—and sexuality—sexual identities, discourses, and institutions—are studied as they intersect with class, race, ethnicity, nationality, and transnational movements."[46] And Harvard pumps as much radical social liberalism as it can into its "Women, Gender and Sexuality Department." "Cultural and historical differences in femininities and masculinities, transnational sexualities, women writers, gender and media studies, lesbian/gay/bisexual studies, transnational feminisms, gender and environmental movements, philosophies of embodiment, queer theory, women's history, transgender studies, gender and religion, the political economy of gender, feminist theory, race/class/gender politics, technology and gender, gender and science, and masculinity studies are just a few of the areas of study that fall within this concentration's purview," their website excitedly explains.[47] With this department description, Harvard actually surpasses James Joyce in the Guinness Book of World Records for the largest amount of intellectual drivel ever crammed into one sentence.

On many campuses, rabidly leftist departments like Sociology and English work in concert with the LGBT and Women's Studies departments in order to push sexual license. At UCLA, the English Department cross-lists courses with the LGBT Department and Women's Studies Department. Such courses included M101A Intro to LGBT Studies, described by the campus gay magazine as follows: "To a closeted gay boy soon to shed the cocoon and emerge a winged Nubian Princess, this class was all that and a box of press-on nails . . . The two professors were the perfect Yin-Yang combination: Professor Schultz's bright fairy flame lit the fires of pride in my soul and Professor Littleton's uber-dykey-ness slapped me with reason and political reality."[48] Apparently, singing "YMCA" in class will now move you one step closer to a university degree.

A strange new world

Surrounded by sex in the context of dorm life, campus life, and classroom life, getting sucked into the oversexed culture of the universities is easy, and it's dangerous. Still, Lucia, who lost her virginity at age twenty-one and has had two sex partners since, believes that it's good for both college guys and college girls to get their grooves on. "Sexual experiences and sex in general are great things, especially when you are young. I wish I had hooked up more. As long as a student is safe and is generally cognizant of how his/her actions may affect the people involved, I think it's a necessary thing to go through in life," she said.[49]

But that's just the problem. Youngsters engaging in sexual experimentation don't know what they're getting into. For young women, pressure to fit in often means sacrificing emotional well-being. Where once there were sanctioned excuses for upholding traditional morality—it's against university policy, men aren't allowed in the dorms, etc.—the porn generation now finds only encouragement to discard traditional morality at every opportunity.

The long-term side effects are even more disturbing. In a world of one-night stands and random hook-ups, it's only natural for young men to view women as sex objects. For young men, college is a cornucopia of illicit pleasures. "Playing the field is the norm at college," Miquel Moore, a twenty-two-year-old student at Southern Illinois University, explained to the *Los Angeles Times*: "Everyone is looking for people to hook up with at parties, and both people are content with that. A university is like a community of kids—so open, and we are free to really do what we want. I know when I got here, I thought, 'Oooohhhh, give me all the college girls!'"[50]

Lucia sees what men want as well: "I think the real difference between men and women lies in the fact that women think about these issues at all and most men probably don't. College boys are more apt to act and only think about it if it gets them into trouble later on."[51] It's notable that despite Lucia's awareness about college boys, she's still upset she didn't hook up with more of them.

Sex is considered a substitute for developing an actual relationship. For guys especially, if you're able to have sex with a good-looking girl on a regular basis, that's an excellent incentive to keep a bad, pointless, or even self-destructive relationship going. And if you're able to get several random good-looking girls to give you sex, why bother attempting relationships at all?

With the death of emotional and intellectual relationships, young people are trying to find themselves and their partners solely through physicality. Even Lucia recognizes the danger in this trend: "What I fear most is seeing young people try to figure out or articulate their emotions through sex and hooking up. I think some have the mentality of 'Oh, well I cheated on him and I don't feel bad so I should break up with him' or 'Oh, I cheated and I feel horrible so this must mean I love him and should stay with him.' You know: using others as a means to figure your own emotional relationship junk out."[52]

The saddest part of the sexual experimentation promoted by the higher education system—and by the parents who willingly and inexcusably offer their children into its clutches—is that all of these detrimental consequences are avoidable. Yet those parents and administrators who approved of the actions during the 1960s are actively seeking to pass the torch across generations, while others choose to ignore the negative consequences of their former activities, thereby allowing their children to go through an even worse chaos. Either way, this is nothing less than spiritual and emotional child sacrifice, with countless and very real Charlotte Simmons clones emerging at the end.

"If you give people more freedom, ultimately they become more responsible," says Sara Jamieson, a 2000 grad of Connecticut College.[53] That's the hope. College is supposed to be a time when young adults discover who they want to be. Self-discovery implies unrestrained freedom, trying new things, all with the hope that the identity you discover is something to aspire to, equipping you to find success and lead in the real world. But the former hippies of the 1960s have charted a different path as university leaders, and they've found the porn generation all too eager to follow, delving into sexual experimentation, nihilism, narcissism, and hedonism. Forget *Fiat Lux*, *Perstare et Praestare*, or *Veritas*—the motto of today's university is simple: "Do whatever or whomever you want."

CHAPTER FOUR

POP TARTS

OFFICIAL RECIPE for POP STARDOM:

- Start with a cute, pubescent ten- to twelve-year-old girl
- Two–three yrs. Virginal, wholesome, faux innocent play-acting (Disney Channel brand highly recommended)
- Two yrs. Ambiguous, semi-pedophilic cavorting
- Two yrs. "Sexual discovery" (dirty dancing, X-rated lyrics, and/or promiscuity)
- For extra sales, add just a smattering of bisexuality.

Voila! You've transformed yourself into a platinum-record "artist." Keep it up for twenty years, and you might even win a Madonna Award for profit-driven sluttiness!

It was the passing of the torch. On August 28, 2003, MTV held its annual Video Music Awards show. The big production number was like something out of the gay activist handbook. First, two little girls—Madonna's six-year-old daughter, Lourdes, and one of Lourdes's friends—romped across the stage, dressed as flower girls. Then, the competing princesses of pop tart whoredom, Britney Spears and Christina Aguilera, both dressed in sluttish bridal costumes, popped out of wedding cakes and began singing Madonna's 1984 hit "Like A Virgin." Finally, Madonna made her grand entrance. Dressed in a black, form-fitting S&M "groom" outfit, Madonna joined the two former Mouseketeers, and the three gyrated around the stage like hookers starved for johns. Shifting into her newest hit song, "Hollywood," Madonna began feeling up Spears and Aguilera onstage; in one especially repulsive move, Madonna snuggled up

to Aguilera's thigh and removed her garter. Then, the choreographed
moment everyone had been waiting for: Madonna lunged in at the recep-
tive Spears, who opened her mouth, and the two played a round of ton-
sil hockey.

The crowd went wild, as the on-the-spot camera panned to the
stunned face of former Britney boy toy Justin Timberlake. When
Madonna turned to Aguilera and proceeded to swap spit with the
"Dirrty" young star, it was almost anticlimactic.

The salacious kiss made front-page headlines across the United
States—and across the world. It made the top page of *USA Today*. The
Atlanta Journal-Constitution even apologized to its subscribers after it
received a wave of complaints from angry readers stunned to see the
saliva exchange on page one.

But the publicity ride wasn't done yet for the three prostitutes.
Madonna called the kisses "ironic because I was playing the groom and
I had two brides, so we were operating at many levels. It was like a passing on of the baton, so to speak."[1] For Madonna, more than one level of
meaning constitutes uncharted intellectual depths—combining the titillating and the political is quite a feat.

Here's the real irony of the situation, however: while Madonna
showed millions of little girls how to smooch other girls, she shielded her
own daughter, Lourdes, from the actual kisses, explaining: "As soon as
she got off stage she was whisked away in a car and went home. So she
doesn't know anything."[2]

The MTV awards show was a monster hit, garnering 10.7 million
viewers and the highest ratings from the twelve to thirty-four crowd of
any cable show that year to date.[3] Predictably, stories concerning lesbian
experimentation among teenage girl and articles about "bisexual chic"
began appearing in the mainstream media. A December 2003 article in
the *South Florida Sun-Sentinel* described the growing demand for lesbian
experimentation used by some as a turn-on to get guys, by others as a
journey in self-discovery.[4] Richard Luscombe of the *UK Observer* noted:
"A wave of 'bisexual chic' is sweeping the United States. Emboldened by
such images as Madonna kissing Britney Spears and Christina Aguilera

on a TV awards show, girls are proudly declaring their alternative sexualities at a younger age than ever before."[5]

As reported in January 2004 in the *Washington Post*, a Coolidge High School teacher "got so fed up with girls nuzzling each other in class and other public places that he threatened to send any he saw to the principal's office." One high-school girl interviewed, Chanda Harris, explained that she started going out with girls at age fourteen, following a breakup with her boyfriend; her mother, she says, "prefers me to be with girls than guys. She says I'm happier." What kind of boys was young Chandra dating, the illegitimate children of Charles Manson? Better question: why is she dating at all?

The *Post* piece noted that "teenagers are starting at younger ages to have same-sex sexual experiences: thirteen for boys, fifteen for girls." As the *Post* reporter triumphantly exclaimed, "Try this on, Mr. and Mrs. America: These girls say they don't know what they are and don't need to know. Adolescence and young adulthood is a time for exploration and they should feel free to love a same-sex partner without assuming that is how they'll spend the rest of their lives."[6]

Here's the question: If one prominent lesbian snog-fest—particularly an event choreographed and planned as a publicity stunt—can set off so much bisexual activity among young girls, what effect does constant promotion of promiscuity have on them?

While the world expected Madonna to do her thing—and anything—on TV, many people were shocked at the behavior of the two younger icons. After all, both Aguilera and Spears had been all-American girls next door during their days with the Mickey Mouse Club. But that's the new strategy in the pop music industry. The MTV Video Music Awards kiss merely exposed for the world what the porn generation already knew: The teen pop industry is geared and focused on sexualizing girls at the earliest possible age. Forget singing, songwriting, or even basic musical talent—sex is now the driving force in pop music. Hot young stars often begin as virgins to solidify their teen-girl base, then move on to semi-sexuality, emerge into flagrant sexuality or even promiscuity—and for that extra edgy hipness, add a tang of bisexuality. The pop tarts start with sugary descriptions of love and teen angst; then they turn dark, narcissistic, and hedonistic. And little girls go along for the ride.

The Material Girl

Madonna was really the first pop "artist" to openly advocate amorality and subjectivism to young girls. She is a heroine to the social Left and to feminists in particular—and that's no exaggeration. As *New York Daily News* writer Jim Farber wrote in 1991: "Sometimes I wake up in the morning and just think about how lucky we all are to live in the same world as Madonna. I am not being at all ironic."[7] In August 1994, even with her musical career on the rocks, Norman Mailer called Madonna "our greatest living female artist."[8]

Madonna was controversial because, in the words of *Rolling Stone* writer Mim Udovitch, "the singer was not only unapologetically sexual, but frankly horny. Where Donna Summer might talk about bad girls and loving to love you, Madonna made it clear that she was more than talk, beyond bad, and primarily interested in you loving her whether you liked it or not."[9] She has sex for her own pleasure, uses sex to her advantage, and challenges traditional morality. Instead of challenging sexist notions of morality by calling upon men to act like gentlemen, Madonna crawled into the muck with them and encouraged a generation of women to follow her, molding teenage girls into her image.

The choice of Madonna's "Hollywood" for the MTV lesbian tonguing couldn't have been more appropriate. Here's the song's key lyric: "I'm bored with the concept of right and wrong." That lyric seems to be Madonna's credo. Her purposeful degradation of morality has led to monumental success for her—and created a monumentally bad influence for her teenage fans.

It was her appearance on the first MTV Video Music Awards, September 14, 1984, that made Madonna a household name. Dressed in a white bustier (identical to those worn by Britney Spears and Christina Aguilera twenty years later) and a belt reading "Boy Toy" (identical to that worn by her daughter, Lourdes, twenty years later), Madonna burst from a wedding cake to sing "Like a Virgin." "Like a virgin/Touched for the very first time," Madonna warbled as she writhed around the stage, simulating sex. The message, according to biographer Andrew Morton, was that the notion of a virgin/whore incongruity was old-fashioned, that "it was okay to show off your body as well as your brain...Here was a woman who dressed wantonly and behaved badly, yet who, far from being punished for this behavior, was instead richly rewarded." Madonna's *Like a Virgin* album was astonishingly successful—the singer had expected the resulting firestorm, and was prepared to take advantage of it.[10]

Madonna had opened up the first chapter in the virgin/whore pop tart encyclopedia. While Madonna never claimed to be virginal, she used the imagery of virginity to contrast with her open sexuality. That's what her performance at the MTV awards was all about: exploiting the trappings of moral absolutism to promote the ends of moral relativism.

Madonna has always used the imagery of rectitude to promote degradation—simply note the Catholic (and later, faux Kabbalistic) imagery she constantly utilizes in her performances. Madonna's universe is a chaotic, existential place—but there, she is the ultimate arbiter of morality. It is that type of "live and let live" universe—in which each man/woman is his/her own god—which Madonna promotes.

Millions of young girls picked up on it. As a hot young star in the 1980s, Madonna's wardrobe—a mix-and-match garage sale outfit topped off with a large cross necklace—became her trademark. This juxtaposition of religious symbols with the attire of homelessness smacks of amorality and chaos. And it was fantastically popular. As CNN.com describes, "a fashion craze developed among teen-age Madonna fans who imitated their new idol by dressing in torn-up clothes and rubber bracelets and tying rags in their hair. The Madonna look sparked a trend of young 'wannabe' fans."[11] Madonna spawned a new generation of low-rent child prostitute poseurs, a la Jodie Foster.

In January 1985, Madonna filmed the music video for "Material Girl," again glorifying her own sexual image.[12] "Material Girl" clearly epitomizes Madonna's view of sex, as well—it's simply a conduit to something more important: money. "Some boys kiss me, some boys hug me / I think they're okay / If they don't give me proper credit / I just walk away /... Cause the boy with the cold hard cash / Is always Mister Right, 'cause we are / Living in a material world / And I am a material girl..."

Before Madonna, material girls were known as prostitutes. Afterward, they were just known as teenagers.

In May 1985, Madonna's face appeared on the cover of *Time* magazine with the headline "MADONNA: Why She's Hot." The piece describes how "hundreds of thousands of young blossoms whose actual ages run from a low of about eight to a high of perhaps twenty-five, are saving up their baby-sitting money to buy cross-shaped earrings and fluorescent rubber bracelets like Madonna's, white lace tights that they will cut off at the ankles, and black tube skirts, that, out of view of their parents, they will roll down several turns at the waist to expose their middles and the waistbands of the pantyhose." The article concludes: "Then, the Wanna Be's, to whom the war between men and women is still far less real than the eternal skirmishing between parents and children, file out of the hall, dreaming of the time when they will be able to do anything in the world they want. Like Madonna."[13]

Madonna's career has been repetition of the same theme ever since. She should have been arrested in the late 1980s and 1990s for peddling pornography to children. The music video for "Like a Prayer" was so openly offensive that Pepsi was forced to cancel its endorsement deal with Madonna in 1989.[14] Her 1990 music video for "Justify My Love" was so over the top that the liberal MTV banned it.[15] In her "Blonde Ambition" tour Madonna posed "as a modern-day Amazon, her erotic and exotic routines invariably ending with the woman on top."[16] The tour featured scantily clad men engaging in homoerotic behavior, Madonna miming masturbation, men in Viking-style pointed bras, and Madonna, the dominatrix, telling the crowd "You may not know the song, but you all know the pleasures of a good spanking."[17] She also published the photo album *Sex*, a porn book including shots of rape, homosexuality, and naked hitchhiking, as well as shots with her and other celebrities. The book currently adorns the coffee tables of hundreds of gay men and sperm banks.

Madonna is a fabulously successful musician, a failed actress, and a cultural icon. She is also a whore, selling her promiscuity for power and financial gain. Like her pop tart followers, Madonna's promiscuity has always been for a purpose. As one fellow dancer stated, "You could say she was a tramp but that was missing the point. She was never some digy white chick who slept around with the guys, she was smarter than that. All the way through her career she has been very sexy but take a closer look and she is always in control."[18]

She isn't just any whore, either. She's a whore with a microphone. And she's always willing to use that microphone to forward her message of societal amorality.

Princesses of the virgin-to-whore kingdom

If Madonna is the queen of pop whoredom, the two reigning princesses are Britney Spears and Christina Aguilera, whose careers have taken remarkably similar paths. Both Spears and Aguilera joined the cast of the "Mickey Mouse Club." Both cut hit albums, ditched their virginal, clean-cut images, and ended up exploiting their sexuality for publicity and monetary gain—and both took millions of young girls along for the ride, inducting them into a world of amorality and soft-core pornography.

Let's start with Christina. When celebrity first touched Aguilera, she posed as a clean-cut girl with a lot of talent. In 1999, she told VIBE magazine, "It's important to me to be a positive role model. Parading around in my bra and a pair of hot pants will not inspire confidence in other girls…I'm not just another bimbo. I've got a brain and a heart. And I'm not gonna let my body distract people from that fact."[19]

This moral stance lasted a couple of days. When her eponymous album broke in 1999, with the hit single "Genie in a Bottle," many (including Disney Radio) were concerned about the song's overt sexuality. The lyrics to the song: "I feel like I've been locked up tight / For a century of lonely nights / Waiting for someone to release me /…If you wanna be with me / I can make your wish come true /You gotta make a big impression / I gotta like what you do / I'm a genie in a bottle baby / You gotta rub me the right way honey / I'm a genie in a bottle baby / Come, come, come on and let me out."

The music video depicted a scantily clad Aguilera lying on a car hood, asking a male model to "let her out."[20] Aguilera defended the song, telling CNN Online, "[The song is] not about sex. It's about self-respect. It's about not giving in to temptation unless you are respected."[21] Right. And men read *Playboy* for the articles.

Christina learned her lesson well from Madonna, deriding opponents of the song as opponents of female rights: "It's really about female empowerment. When a female speaks her mind and shows a little tummy like I do, people take it a certain way. I'm a huge fan of *NSYNC, but when they're onstage doing pelvic thrusts and singing certain songs, nobody says anything negative about that."[22] Aguilera's words are a perfect illustration of feminism's flawed logic. She rightly points out that boy bands are held to lesser standards than are female pop stars, but refuses to take the high road and dives in the ditch along with them. Aguilera told an interviewer at the time: "All this do-not-touch nonsense is not me. I'm no virgin, I'm all for female sexuality and taking the sexual power away from the guys. They've had it for way too long."[23] Hey, if the boys can do it, why shouldn't Christina?

Aguilera initially attempted to downplay the sexuality creeping into her music, in order to maintain her virginal image. But in 2001, Aguilera teamed up with Pink, Lil' Kim and Mya to remix the Patti LaBelle song "Lady Marmalade" for the ridiculously stupid motion picture *Moulin Rouge*; the music video depicts all four gallivanting around dressed like prostitutes. It won an award at the MTV Video Music Awards in 2001, where the four singers reenacted the music video, which has nothing going for it besides skin and lacy under things.[24] In 2002, Aguilera took her sexuality a step further with her new album, *Stripped*, posing on the cover of the album naked from the waist up. So much for the anti-bra-and-hot-pants routine. Aguilera's comment? "I have stripped down to my inner self. I guess I've grown up in a lot of ways."[25]

Christina also dubbed herself X-tina in honor of her newfound sexuality.[26] The song "Dirrty," from the *Stripped* album, had a music video so dirrrrrrty it was banned in Thailand for promoting immodesty among young girls. The lyrics to "Dirrty" are both incomprehensible and raunchy. A sampling: "Let's get dirrty (that's my jam) ... Ah, heat is up / So ladies, fellas / Drop your cups / Body's hot / Front to back / Now move your ass / I like that / Tight hip huggers (low for sure) / Shake a little somethin' (on the floor) / I need that, uh, to get me off / Sweat until my clothes come off." As Greg Overzat of the Ft. Lauderdale *Sun-Sentinel* observed, "Looks like Xtina should change her name to XXXtina."[27]

Aguilera's development from clean-cut teen cutie to young "empowered" woman also reflects her personal and artistic descent into the world of Madonna-esque subjectivism. Aguilera promotes a world of unbridled hedonism and narcissism. She was willing to ditch traditional morality for the promise of easy money. But there's a price for this decision: Underneath all the talk about doing what she wants to do, Aguilera betrays a deep depression in her words and music. In a 2002 interview with *Rolling Stone*, Aguilera decided that she no longer wanted to be thought of as "pretty," remarking "I don't like pretty. F—the pretty," and adding that she was "showing her true colors now."[28] Aguilera also got into self-mutilation through body-piercing, explaining "There's a comfort to me in pain."[29] There's a real sickness in those words. When the world and life mean so little that only pain can prompt feeling, it's time to reexamine your philosophy of amoral freedom and "empowerment."

Like Aguilera, Spears quickly transitioned from a popular virgin into an even more popular Madonna imitator. Her first hit single, " ... Baby One More Time," moved her squarely into the realm of sexuality. The single was released in 1998, and immediately jumped to the top of the charts. The lyrics are suggestive enough: "Oh baby, baby / The reason I breathe is you / Boy you got me blinded / Oh pretty baby / There's nothing that I wouldn't do ... When I'm not with you I lose my mind / Give me a sign / Hit me baby one more time."

The video became especially popular and controversial. It depicts Spears dressed in a Catholic-school uniform with shirt knotted to reveal belly and typically short skirt. The Lolita-style video, which Britney thought up herself, prompted her to defend the semi-pedophilic content: "All I did was tie up my shirt!...I'm wearing a sports bra under it. Sure, I'm wearing thigh-highs, but kids wear those—it's the style. Have you seen MTV? All those girls in thongs?"[30] No word on whether Spears has heard of "kiddie porn."

By the end of 1999, over ten million copies of...*Baby One More Time* had been sold[31]—and Britney had posed in her nighties for *Rolling Stone* at the tender age of seventeen.[32] Still clinging to her younger audience, Britney maintained that she was happy as a role model, and implied that she was pure as the driven snow. "You want to be a good example for kids out there and not do something stupid," Spears told *Rolling Stone*. "Kids have low self-esteem, and then peer pressures come and they go into a wrong crowd. That's when all the bad stuff starts happening."[33] Just a few months later, she reiterated to *Rolling Stone* that she had "really strong morals, and just because I look sexy on the cover of *Rolling Stone* doesn't mean I'm a naughty girl."[34] Her virginity was intact as well, and she stated unequivocally that she wanted to wait until marriage to have sex: "If I did anything else, it would be a mistake, one I would regret forever." According to associates, Spears made the comment to provide support for girls feeling pressured to give sex to boyfriends.[35] While simulating sex on stage with dancers and posing for kiddie-porn for *Rolling Stone*, Spears insisted that she wasn't a sex seller: "That's the edgiest I've ever been. But it was *Rolling Stone* and it has an adult audience. The photographer explained to me what he wanted to do and I was cool about it. But it's sooo not me at all. I was playing a part, acting, and I don't regret doing it at all."[36]

Spears' 2000 follow-up album to...*Baby One More Time* was the chart-smashing *Oops!...I Did It Again*. Again, the content centered on sex. Lyrics from the title number contained this famous line: "Oops!...You think I'm in love / That I'm sent from above / I'm not that innocent."

She wasn't. Indeed, at this point Spears and her management apparently decided to leave any semblance of traditional morality behind. By May 2000, Britney had told an Australian interviewer that her favorite sexual position was "on top,"[37] and had posed again for *Rolling Stone*, this time clad in an American flag top, with the caption: "BRITNEY

WANTS YOU!" The American Family Assocation called for a ban on her music, noting "a disturbing mix of childhood innocence and adult sexuality."[38] This is the clear danger of the pop tarts: They drag their audiences from cooing their songs to imitating their dress to miming their behavior to living the lifestyle they espouse.

Britney was also recanting her desire to be a role model, explaining: "I don't like to be thought of as a role model. I'm human, I make mistakes like everybody else. I just try to be the best person I can be for me."[39] When I make a mistake, I usually don't end up on the cover of *Rolling Stone* in my underwear. Neither does anyone else I know.

By this point, Spears' career and lifestyle had become a series of hedonistic adventures, leading the *New York Times* to brand her "the postmodern virgin-whore."[40] A quick fifty-five-hour marriage, a few music videos glamorizing anonymous sex, a few more MTV appearances; over the past two years, Spears has become Madonna-lite. Like Aguilera, Spears' music has tended toward depressing nihilism as well—in one of her latest music videos, she even commits suicide.[41]

Amorality isn't a recipe for happiness, but Spears' fans keep on buying. Her popularity has hardly waned among pre-teens and teenage girls. As a *Washington Post* reporter wrote:

> Britney popularized the slut strut in music videos assembled by a former porn director and single-handedly wiped out the Spice Girls. Short skirts became known as "Britney skirts." Young girls grabbed *Teen People* off the newsstands when Britney was on the cover, packed Britney look-alike contests and Britney concerts...There's also Britney on sunglasses, handbags, bellybutton rings, video games, and of course, singing Pepsi's "Joy of Cola." Last year, according to news reports, the Britney Empire made more than $100 million US, more than the Tiger Woods machine. Is this what America means by girl power?[42]

It's important for parents to keep tabs on their children's role models before those role models "mature." Parents are continuing to buy into the cleanliness of Disney Channel stars/pop tarts like Hilary Duff and Lindsey Lohan, but each is busily transitioning from a role model to a Madonna look-alike. Duff sounds eerily like a young Spears or Aguilera when she claims "I think that I'm pretty straightforward, and I'm an honest person and if people look up to that because I'm just being myself, then that's cool. I don't necessarily feel like I have to break away or get out of this type of genre that people have put me in. I do think that I'm growing and my music, especially on this second album that's coming out, is more mature, but not so mature that it's beyond that younger audience, because I do know that I have that younger audience."[43] Duff's first album, *Metamorphosis*, sold more copies than Madonna's and Spears' last CDs combined.[44]

Lohan, who turned eighteen in 2004, started off doing family fare like the charming *The Parent Trap* and the funny *Freaky Friday*. Her most recent projects have included *Mean Girls* and *Confessions of a Teenage Drama Queen*. There's only one problem. As *Rolling Stone* describes it, "There comes a time in the life of every teenage girl who works for the Disney Corp. when that girl realizes she has suddenly— how shall we phrase this?—'broadened her appeal.'"[45] Lohan has appeared at various clubs with the Hilton sisters, drinking and smoking, as well as wearing low-cut dresses to show her newly acquired breasts, a topic that's received a gratuitous amount of discussion time among porn generation men.[46] As the *Chicago Sun-Times* correctly commented, "We're still not sure if they're real or not, but Lindsay is giving us plenty of opportunity to observe them."[47]

Shortly after turning eighteen, an event tracked and greeted enthusiastically by dozens of websites run by young men, Lohan posed sexily for the cover of *Rolling Stone*. The caption read: "Hot, Ready and Legal!"[48] This is a common porn technique. Pornographers often use stars barely over the legal age, and then pose them as young girls. If this sort of behavior doesn't constitute pedophilia, it certainly promotes it.

For more mature audiences

Among older teenagers, Britney and Christina are generally eschewed in favor of alternative rock. The floozy sexuality of pop music and early rock leads to greater and greater nihilism in "more mature" rock music. As Harvard Law student Chris Craig, twenty-five, says, "I think some of the older bands put out non-nihilistic stuff. The jaded nihilistic music is the product of the younger bands."[49] Alice, a twenty-three-year-old student at Harvard Law, agreed: "It's not cool to be happy. If you're too happy, you're looked at as illegitimate."[50]

Dr. Joan Shapiro (no relation to author), a practicing psychiatrist for three decades, summed up the situation: "Jadedness is the cool thing to do. Their peers are jaded. The media suggests that that's kind of what cool kids do. To fit in with their peers, kids are ultimate conformists, particularly adolescents."

The undisputed king of nihilism-glorifying alternative rock is now-deceased Kurt Cobain, lead singer for Nirvana. Cobain glorified the apathetic teenager and the existentialist lifestyle; the title of one of his songs says it all: "I Hate Myself and Want to Die."[51]

The voice of the lonely, existential teenager found its outlet in Nirvana, the 1990s icons that were self-absorbed to the point of complete despair. Nirvana's anthem, "the best rock song...in years,"[52] "Smells Like Teen Spirit," is an ode to nihilism and narcissism. Its dark, dingy melody growls out at the listener. Cobain follows suit, yelling at the audience: "Here we are now / Entertain us / I feel stupid and contagious / Here we are now / Entertain us / A mulatto / An albino / A mosquito / My libido / Yea." The nonsensical, Gertrude Stein-esque lyrics confuse and distance— and that's what they're meant to do. The universe is a random place, and we're stuck in it. Cobain re-emphasizes this just seconds later, gnarling "And I forget / Just what it takes / And yet I guess it makes me smile / I found it hard / It's hard to find / Oh well, whatever, nevermind."

If the world is too hard to figure out, you might as well just give up. The good news is, you get to form your own subjective system of morality. Anything goes. In "Stay Away," another Nirvana hit, Cobain screams, "Have to have poison skin / Stay away / God is gay, burn the flag." God is dead, and Nirvana put the stake through His homosexual heart.

In Cobain's own view, the past was a record of failure, and there was no point in trying to rectify it. "I like to complain and do nothing to make things better," he once stated.[53] At the same time, Cobain wasn't satisfied with his generation: "My generation's apathy. I'm disgusted with it," he famously complained.[54] Following this worldview to its logical end, Cobain blew his own brains out with a shotgun.[55]

Nirvana spawned a whole host of imitators, and the dark and dingy became the mainstream. The most extreme branch of nihilistic rock is the heavy metal/goth genre. Rock musicians rail against the very notion of a benevolent God, finding solace and rebellion in siding with Satanic imagery and messages. They take moral darkness to a whole new level. As DJ Mark Shannon told me, "Heavy metal's direction is controlled— no, dictated—by the need to increase the shock value of it, just as Hollywood has done in the movies. The problem, by the time it's gone too far, it's too late to stop it. And we've already passed that point several times."

Ozzy Osbourne, one of the more heralded members of this genre, once headlined the founding band of the heavy metal genre, Black Sabbath, spewing songs with pagan lyrics that ridiculed morality. Now, after landing a vaunted television show on MTV wherein the brain-fried former rock star babbles nonsensically to the enjoyment of his audience, Osbourne is a mainstream figure. In May 2002, Osbourne appeared at the White House Correspondents' Dinner, to the delight of reporters and politicians alike. Even President Bush paid homage to the mass murderer of morals, joking, "The thing about Ozzy is, he's made a lot of big hit recordings. 'Party With the Animals.' 'Sabbath Bloody Sabbath.' 'Facing Hell.' 'Black Skies' and 'Bloodbath in Paradise.' Ozzy, Mom loves your stuff."[56] Just over two years later, Osbourne would repay the favor by comparing Bush to Hitler during Ozzfest, a heavy metal festival.[57]

Osbourne's heirs include Marilyn Manson and morally repugnant bands like Slayer, Rob Zombie, Nine Inch Nails, Rammstein, KMFDM, and Korn—sometimes classified as goth or death metal bands, but the more accurate term is pagan. Manson, who named himself by combining the names of Marilyn Monroe and serial killer Charles Manson, is deep into a stylized form of Satanism, proclaiming himself "Antichrist Superstar."[58] His hatred for religion is monumental. In his "The Reflecting God," he christens himself a god, and then states: "When I'm god everyone dies." In Britain, one of his fans murdered a teenage girl after being influenced "by the macabre work of Manson."[59]

Manson actively opposes anything that even hints of morality. Take, for instance, his ode to degradation, "Cake and Sodomy": "I am the god of f—, I am the god of f—/ virgins sold in quantity, herded by heredity / red-neck-burn-out-mid-west-mind, 'who said date rape isn't kind?' / porno-nation, evaluation / what's this, 'time for segregation' / libido, libido fascination, too much oral defecation / white trash get down on your knees, time for cake and sodomy." Manson finishes with a slap at the religious: "cash in hand and dick on screen, who said God was ever clean? / bible-belt 'round anglo-waste, putting sinners in their place / yeah, right, great if you're so good explain the s—stains on your face."

Manson's replacement religion? You guessed it: sex. "I memorize the words to the porno movies / It's the only thing I want to believe / I memorize the words to the porno movies / This is a new religion to me," he groans in "Slutgarden."

As of 1999, the average teenager listened to 10,500 hours of rock music during the years between seventh and twelfth grades.[60] It's no surprise that today's teens feel abandoned, adrift in a sea of uncertainty and meaninglessness. As Mary Eberstadt of the Hoover Institution states:

> If yesterday's rock was the music of abandon, today's is that of abandonment. The odd truth about contemporary teenage music—the characteristic that most separates it from what has gone before—is its compulsive insistence on the damage wrought by broken homes, family dysfunction, checked-out parents, and (especially) absent fathers...Baby boomers and their music rebelled against parents because they were parents—nurturing, attentive, and overly present (as those teenagers often saw it) authority figures. Today's teenagers and their music rebel against parents because they are not parents—not nurturing, not attentive, and often not even there.[61]

Whereas oversexed pedophilia chic dominates pop music, boredom, and jadedness are the hallmarks of teenage thought. Everything "sucks," "bites," or "blows." Even if you like something, you're not supposed to get too excited about it, because nothing really means anything. We're the generation of nm (internet speak for "nothing much") and whatever. We're the generation of "I don't care." As Kurt Cobain sang, "Oh well, whatever, nevermind."

Eddie Vedder of Pearl Jam fame summed up the situation nicely in a 1994 interview: "Think about it, man . . . Any generation that would pick Kurt or me as its spokesman—that must be a pretty f—up generation, don't you think?"[62]

The fantasy world

Music stars, regardless of genre, employ sex to sell their product— whether it's the porn star stage dancers at a Kid Rock show or the dancing Lolitas of the pop circuit. But it's not just the audience that feels the effects of exploitation: Sometimes, even the pop stars themselves realize how morally and spiritually corrupt they have become.

In January 2004, Laura Sessions Stepp of the *Washington Post* wrote a piece entitled "Partway Gay?; For Some Teen Girls, Sexual Preference Is A Shifting Concept." "Move over, Ellen DeGeneres, and make way for the younger girls. Way younger, actually, and way different from what most people think of as lesbians . . . These girls pack Ani DiFranco concerts and know tATu lyrics by heart."[63]

For many readers, one question immediately arose: Who the hell was tATu?

tATu was a Russian pop group—two teen girls, in fact—who acted as though they were in deep lesbian love. The name of the group meant "this girl loves that girl" in Russian slang. The group opened its doors for business when the girls, Yulia and Lena, were fourteen and fifteen, respectively. They kissed and simulated sexual activity onstage and in music videos; they spoke about the enjoyment of lesbianism. In 2003, their single "All The Things She Said" racked up thirteen million sales worldwide.[64] tATu sold a pedophilic notion of young girls making out; the band's manager,

Ivan Shapovalov, admitted that his idea for the band originated while surfing the net and discovering the plethora of kiddie porn websites.[65]

The pair claimed to have sex three times a day.[66] Their management claimed that the pair insisted on a double bed in hotel rooms.[67] The girls managed to avoid explaining which way they swung. And Shapovalov continued to rake it in.

Everything began to crumble in 2004, when one of the girls, Yulia, became pregnant by her married lover.[68] It turns out that Yulia had already had one abortion the previous year in order to prevent public awareness of her heterosexuality. She also became suicidal, explaining "I have such thoughts that I want to die." Lena, her musical partner, says she feels "disgusted" by the way she acted. "I felt so bad about it for a long time. I realize that the time would come to pay for everything you've done in your life. And I now want to redeem my sins. I go to church all the time. I tell the priest everything about tATu. And he tries to help me. He blesses me . . . I feel I am absolutely talentless . . . I am leaving showbusiness."[69]

These gained international celebrity, but lost their innocence. They convinced thousands of young girls that lesbianism was normal, or at least valuable for titillating men. They helped define deviancy down, and promote a "live and let live" world. And they destroyed themselves.

tATu is the logical culmination of the pop tart mentality. Do anything to sell an album. Use your authority as a role model to model behavior that would make a hooker blush. Push the boundaries. Teach young girls that true strength is in bucking "old-fashioned" social convention—yet teach them simultaneously to cater to the most perverse form of male sexual fantasy.

In short, undermine traditional morality. But be careful how far you push things, since it's all about the cash and parents are the ones with the wallets. Lucky for the pop tarts that millions of parents spend less time worrying about what their kids listen to and watch than whether they should order their latte with non-fat or soy milk. Britney Spears is a morally repugnant piece of work, but she's right about one thing: "It's a fantasy world that I'm doing . . . It's up to the parents to explain that to their children."[70]

CHAPTER FIVE

WHERE PIMPS AND HOS RUN FREE

"The new trend today is depravity."

BROOKLYN RAPPER MOS DEF[1]

John Kerry finds rap "music" fascinating. At least that's what the Massachusetts senator and Democratic 2004 presidential candidate told MTV's Gideon Yago in a blatant attempt to pander to the black vote.

"I don't always like, but I'm interested. I mean, I never was into heavy metal. I didn't really like it," Kerry said. "I'm fascinated by rap and by hip-hop. I think there's a lot of poetry in it. There's a lot of anger, a lot of social energy in it. And I think you'd better listen to it pretty carefully, 'cause it's important."[2]

Believability has never been Kerry's strong point. As columnist Mark Steyn wryly noted, "Reckon if you bust into his pad and riffled through his and Teresa's CD collection you'd find a single rap album?"[3]

While Kerry was "bother[ed]" by rap lyrics advocating cop killing, and felt "that sometimes some lyrics in some songs have stepped over

what I consider to be a reasonable line," he refused to advocate government censorship of such lyrics.[4] Hey, if anyone knows what it's like to be
held down by The Man, it's John F. Kerry. He had to bus' a few caps in
Vietnam, you know, to protect the bruthas and all.

Kerry's is the politically correct view of rap, where the music is "a
reflection of the street and a reflection of life."[5] We live in a world of
multiculturalism and diversity, where every culture supposedly has its
own material to contribute to the giant collage that is America. What
pompous, wrong-thinking person would refuse to honor the gangsta art
form for its beauty (Kerry and his ideological brethren imply), or treat it
as anything less than our modern-day Gershwin or Sinatra?

That's easy: Someone who understands that this gangsta art form is
crap. There's no other way to put it. The overwhelming bulk of rap
music has no artistic value, and nearly every rap song has a negative
social value. The gangsta culture embodied by rappers and their posses
is not worthy of imitation or even exposure. It demeans women,
degrades sex, and glorifies criminal behavior.

To portray rap as vital to black culture, as Kerry did, is a subtle form
of racism. It assumes that violence and misogyny are integral to the black
lifestyle. They aren't. Black culture has contributed hugely to American
society: The civil rights movement brought meaning to American notions
of equality and freedom; black contributions to politics, science, music,
and art have helped enrich all of us. To demean these accomplishments
and contributions by listing rap among them is to demean black culture
as a whole. Even the Reverend Al Sharpton made that very point during
his presidential campaign, stating that the "music" is "desecrating our
culture; it is desecrating our race." Civil rights marchers didn't march so
that a rapper "has the right to call your mama a ho," he told a black
business group in Richmond.[6]

Truthfully, Kerry probably had no idea what he was talking about.
I wonder if Senator Kerry could name even one rap "song" he finds
enlightening, a solitary cut that illuminates life as it is. Maybe he meant
"Hotel," a single by Cassidy and accused child pornographer R. Kelly,
which hit number five on *Billboard*'s Hot Rap Tracks list the week of

Kerry's appearance on MTV[7]: "Girl you wanna come to my hotel, baby I will leave you my room key. / I'm feelin' the way you carry yourself girl. / And I wanna get with you 'cuz you's a cutie... Well if, mami is with it then, mami can give it then, mami a rider, I'ma slide up beside her. / I got a suite, you can creep on through, I know you tryin' to get your freak on too, / I'll do it all for that (lady), yeah I ball for that (lady), hit the mall for that (lady), keep it fly for them (ladies), keep my eye on them (ladies), hot tub for them (ladies), pop bub' for them (ladies), I got love for ma (ladies), yeeah!"

I'm feeling the social energy, Senator! But maybe I'm being unfair. Let's try 2004's *Billboard* leading rap single, "Lean Back," by the aptly named Terror Squad[8]: "I don't give a f—'bout your faults or mishappenin's, / Nigga we from the Bronx, New York...s— happens, / Kids clappin' love to spark the place, / Half the niggas in the squad got a scar on they face, / It's a cold world, and this is ice, / Half a mil' for the charm, nigga this is life." Other assorted curse words include multiple "s—[s]," a "faggot," and one "mo'f—ers."

Now this is more down Senator Kerry's alley. It's a reflection of street life, wherein life sucks and crime is the only way. Now that we've listened, can we call the cops on these social degenerates?

Stick with Rap Masta' B-Shap for just a bit longer. Here's *Billboard*'s number three hot rap single for 2004. This one's called "Freek-A-Leek," by Petey Pablo.[9] Parenthesis indicate background "singers" (wannabe porn stars with breathy voices). Anything outside the parenthesis is my homeboy Petey. "(How you like it daddy?) Would you do it from the front? / (How you like it daddy?) Can you take it from the back? / (How you like it daddy?) Fyna break it down like that! / (How you like it daddy?) 24, 34, 46, good and thick, and once you get it she'll work wit it. / Pretty face and some cute lips, earring in her tongue and she know what to do wit it... And she know why she came here, and she know where her clothes suppose to be (off and over there). / Sniff a little coke, take a little X, smoke a little weed, drink a little bit. / I need a girl that I can freak wit, / wanna try s—, and ain't scared of a big dick. / And love to get her p— licked, / by another b—, cus I ain't drunk enough to do that."

This verse, by the way, was broadcast live from the MTV Video Music Awards. Because of that horrific FCC censorship Senator Kerry condemns, the audience heard a series of silences where the lyrics call for obscenity.[10]

It isn't as if Petey ain't willin' to give a ho some good, clean fun in return: "Tell me what you want, do you want it missionary with your feet crammed into the headboard? / Do you want it from the back with your face in the pillow so you can yell it loud as you want to? / Do you want it on the floor? Do you want it on the chair? / Do you want it over here? Do you want it over there? / Do you want it in ya p—-? Do you want it in ya a—? / I'll give you anything you can handle!"

Petey sounds like the kind of young man a girl would want to bring home to father. That is, if her father is a drug-dealing ex-con who gets his kicks from stringing out schoolgirls and then pimping them out to his friends.

On the other hand, I'm grateful to Senator Kerry for having pointed out to me the social utility of these songs. Petey Pablo is the black Byron. Terror Squad is urban Tennyson. Cassidy and R. Kelly are the Walt Whitmans of da 'hood. The importance of these lyrics is surpassed only by Winston Churchill's "Iron Curtain" speech in the pantheon of important social statements of the last century. Censorship of this sparkling artistry would be the equivalent of banning Renoir.

The sad part is, this kind of language isn't even the most extreme—it's the mainstream. Literally millions of children are hearing this kind of garbage every day. Almost 25 percent of CDs sold in the US in 2003 was hip-hop or R&B; hip-hop is the second-biggest music genre, according to the Recording Industry Association of America.[11] You can't pull up at a stoplight anymore without hearing a booming subwoofer thumping with the sound vibrations of rap.

The rap culture is a real cancer for the black community. According to Professor Edmund Gordon of Yale and Columbia and chairman of the National Task Force on Minority High Achievement, many black males have adopted the culture of the rappers they see on music videos, and are neglecting their academic performance in order to perform rap and hip-hop.[12] Rapper Chuck D of Public Enemy told students at UCLA, "At the end of the 'hood is jail and death. And we're gonna put it to the music? That's vile."[13] A June 2003 survey by Black America's Political Action Committee (BAMPAC) found that 52 percent of black voters believe rap music is a negative influence on children, and 60 percent would support banning minors from buying sexually explicit music.[14]

The rap constituency crosses racial lines as well: Soundscan, a sales-tracking company, estimated that 70 percent of rap music consumers are white kids from the suburbs.[15] The rap culture has infested the porn generation, through and through, regardless of ethnicity. As Lori Price of the *Dallas Morning News* writes, "We—I'll say, since I'm a black hip-hop fan—demanded that nonblacks taste the raw rhythmic style and ebonic-infused, misogynistic lyrics of rap music. Accept this art form as legitimate, with its ugly epithets for women. Drink in its culture, which includes daily use of the N-word. Mainstream society accepted the invitation with a vengeance, to the point that some white fans and artists are using the same language and copping the same attitude."[16]

Walk into any high school in the United States, and you can see teenagers—black, white, Hispanic, whatever—in baggy pants, doing the "pimp roll." They imitate the dress style and the bad grammar, using phrases like "fo' shizzle my nizzle." The common high school greeting is "'Sup, biotch?" These are ridiculously stupid phrases popularized by criminal/thug/rapper/actor Snoop Dogg. Here's Snoop Dogg's explanation of his babblings: "Fo' shizzle: This has many different meanings. It means for real, for sure. I'll use it in a sentence to let you better understand, check this out: 'Doggy Fizzle Televizzle' is gonna be off the hizzle, fo' shizzle."[17]

Thanks, Mr. Dogg—that clears everything up. David Letterman put it best: "I have no idea what the fizzuck I'm talking about."[18]

Celebrating the dregs of society

One of the most important record labels in rap was "Death Row Records." Responsible for the rise of rappers Snoop Dog, Dr. Dre, and Tupac Shakur, the Death Row logo depicts a blindfolded black man strapped into an electric chair. The logo is emblematic of the sometimes fictional, sometimes all too real track of the rap industry: thugs rap, get famous, make money, and then kill someone or are murdered. Of course, it isn't the criminal justice system or the media giving rappers a bad name—it's the fact that they're criminals.

Rap is an "art form" more appropriate to the prison yard than the school yard. Snoop Dogg, the most famous rapper on Earth, stood trial for the murder of twenty-year-old Phillip Woldemariam;[19] he's also a former pornographer and a long-time druggie.[20] Tupac Shakur was murdered[21] after being convicted of sexual assault.[22] Shakur's rapping rival, Notorious B.I.G. (a.k.a. Biggie Smalls), was also murdered.[23] Death Row Records founder Suge Knight associated openly with the brutal Bloods gang in Los Angeles.[24] Known for "mixing business with violence," Knight is a convicted felon.[25] Bad Boy Entertainment founder Sean "Puffy" Combs (a.k.a. P. Diddy) was arrested in December 1999 and charged with gun possession and bribery. Victims testified that Combs had shot them, although Combs was acquitted of all charges with the help of his attorney, the late Johnny Cochran.[26]

Those criminals/rappers who are dead are often heralded as saints in the rap world and beyond. Tupac Shakur became the subject of an obsequious documentary, *Tupac: Resurrection*. "Already the most posthumously marketed music celebrity since Elvis & Jimi, rap star Tupac Shakur gets perhaps the definitive authorized-portrait-cum-sanctification treatment," *Variety* wrote.[27] The *Hollywood Reporter* lauded the movie, saying that it was "so full of his passion for life that it plays not as a grievous saga but an anthemic, inspiring example, however bittersweet," and praising Shakur's "unwavering fury over injustice."[28] Michael Medved commented cuttingly on the canonization of Shakur: "His puzzling posthumous popularity...reflects the degrading and ultimately racist notion that criminal violence represents an essential and authentic element of African American identity."[29]

Rap is inextricably linked to thuggery. We're not talking about a series of troubled artists who contributed great art to society while fighting their own demons. We're talking about a bunch of thugs who talk about their thuggery for money. As "The Boondocks" creator Aaron McGruder

states, "the gangsta image has ingrained itself so deeply into the youth culture that it just became taken for granted...[it's about] living the life you
can live once you've committed all these horrible crimes."[30]

They're thugs with regard to violence, and they're thugs with regard
to women. "Make as much money as you can and have as much sex as
humanly possible," explains Consuela Francis, assistant professor of
African American Literature at the College of Charleston.[31] Sex is never
an expression of love, but instead an expression of lust, with rappers acting as though they're dogs in heat.

In the rap view, women are all bitches and hos, and men are pimps.
It's a repulsively misogynistic view, and one that affects both boys and
girls. Boys learn that it's okay to treat women like dirt; "these contemporary buffoons, vulgarians and misogynists are defined as the purest
black young men, the ones who are 'keeping it real,'" in the words of
New York *Daily News* columnist Stanley Crouch.[32] Girls learn that boys
want strippers and prostitutes, and act accordingly; "women are defining themselves in reaction to what men want, rather than what they
want," says Touré, pop culture correspondent for CNN.[33]

The most popular rappers on earth are misogynists. Chart-topping rapper Ludacris raps dirty in "Area Codes": "I've got hos, in different area
codes...I just pick up the muthaf——' phone and dial / I got my condoms
in a big-ass-sack / I'm slaggin' this d— like a New Jack, biotch."

50 Cent, who won several "New Artist" awards for his first album,
has several songs focused on sex. In "Candy Shop," a sex-obsessed tune
which spent more than six weeks as America's number one music video
on MTV, he intones to his prostitute girlfriend: "I take you to the candy
shop / I'll let you lick the lollypop/ Go 'head girl, don't you stop/ Keep
goin 'til you hit the spot...I'll break it down for you now, baby it's sim-
ple/ If you be a nympho, I'll be a nympho...Got the magic stick, I'm the
love doctor/Have your friends teasin you 'bout how sprung I
gotcha...I'm tryin to explain baby the best way I can/ I melt in your
mouth girl, not in your hands."

Rapper Nelly, one of the most famous "artists" of his genre, has
songs entitled "Pimp Juice" ("She only want me for my pimp juice"),

"Thicky Thick Gurls" ("Lookin like a lolli-pop waitin for the lick girl"), "Wrap Sumden" ("Weed is actually a medicine for me, you know"), and "Tho Dem Wrappas" ("F—a b—- and some clothes / I gotta get rich, go platinum and do shows"), among many others.

For this wonderful contribution to society, Nelly won Favorite Male Singer at the 2004 Nickelodeon Kids' Choice Awards.[34] Yes, he's a kid-friendly scumbucket!

Essence, the most popular black women's magazine in the country, finally let loose with its frustration over the horrific depiction of women in rap in its January 2005 issue. The editors wrote:

> We are mothers, sisters, daughters and lovers of hip-hop. And today we stand at the forefront of popular culture: independent, talented and comfortable with the skin we're in. We are really feeling ourselves. Perhaps that's why we're so alarmed at the imbalance in the depiction of our sexuality and character in music. In videos we are bikini-clad sisters gyrating around fully clothed grinning brothers like Vegas strippers on meth. When we search for ourselves in music lyrics, mix tapes and DVDs and on the pages of hip-hop magazines, we only seem to find our bare breasts and butts... The damage of this imbalanced portrayal of Black women is impossible to measure. An entire generation of Black girls are being raised on these narrow images. And as the messages and images are broadcast globally, they have become the lens through which the world now sees us. This cannot continue."[35]

Of course, when confronted with female rage, male rappers claim that the demands of the marketplace give them license to do whatever they will. Ludacris protested his innocence to *Essence*: "I don't mean to depict women in a certain way. The ones who want to shake what their mama gave them are going to do that whether they're in videos or not. As artists, we explore our creativity through videos. Who sees those videos on BET, or whatever music channel is showing it, is not always up to us." Similarly, Nelly refused to take any blame for his portrayal of women: "I accept my role and my freedom as an artist. I respect women and I'm not a misogynist. I'm an artist. Hip-hop videos are art and entertainment."[36]

If a bad childhood is no excuse for awful behavior, neither is a willing market. There's no doubt that there are plenty of druggies willing to buy cocaine through dealers, but that doesn't make dealers morally blameless. Rappers need to get over their obsession with their own genitals, and start working on changing their perverse views of women, or there's no end to the damage this destructive culture can create.

The "wiggers"

"Nobody white would be allowed to get away with selling such a product," wrote *New York Daily News* columnist Stanley Crouch about the vulgarity and misogyny of rap. "It's about time we started seeing some equality."[37]

Well, we're starting to see some equality. This time, it's the white community doing for "equality" in rap what the feminist community did for "equality" in sex. The standards have been lowered for everybody—deviancy has been defined down. Young white men are so eager to take part in the rush toward musical and moral oblivion that they've begun imitating the gangsta lifestyle. Such suburban yuppies-turned-bruthas are often termed "wiggers"—white niggers. "Seriously, the clothes, the caps, the doo-rags. I'm told some whites even prefer to use black hair products, like Afro Sheen and Murray's Pomade, because it controls their tresses more securely than products intended for naturally straight hair," details Askia Muhammad of the *Washington Informer*.[38]

At my Orthodox Jewish high school, many of my classmates knew scores of rap lyrics by heart. There is very little on this planet weirder than watching a white suburban kid driving an SUV, putting on a bad "nigga" accent, pumping up the subwoofer until the car shakes—and then walking into school to study Hebrew. The closest these teens will ever come to pimps and hos is watching *Pretty Woman,* and the closest they'll ever come to "bustin' a cap" will be paintball.

Kyle Jones, a white suburbanite from Newton, Massachusetts, told FOX News "I don't want you to see me as that I'm trying to be black or I'm trying to be, like, too hard. Or I'm a white kid. I just want you to see me as me." He then proceeded to rap for the camera.[39] Adam Schneider of Great Neck, New York, explained, "It's what I am. I can relate to it. I know exactly what they're saying. It's just what it is."[40]

The *New York Times* ran a 6,597-word piece on one "wigger" who had to battle his inner white demons. The piece is worth reading simply for its tragicomic quality. "Billy Wimsatt was twenty-seven, still clinging to the hip-hop life," sniffled the *Times*. "He didn't look terribly hip-hop, and not because he was white. He was balding and brainy-looking, with an average build and an exuberant nature.... Like many young hip-hop heads, he regarded hip-hop, with its appeal to whites and blacks, as a bold modern hope to ease some of the abrasiveness between the races." Wimsatt even penned a piece for the hip-hop magazine the *Source*, critiquing "wiggers" for diluting the hip-hop culture. "Yes, Billy Wimsatt seemed about as authentically hip-hop as a white guy could get," said the *Times*. But, the *Times* concluded, "As you got older, holding onto your hip-hop values seemed a lot harder if you were white."[41]

So why are white teenagers picking up the sick stylings of rap? Selwyn Hinds, editor of the *Source*, elucidates the issue: "Black culture has always been the well of coolness. You know, if you wanted to be cool, if you wanted to be perceived as cool, you would always grab, you know, your cup and run to that well and take a drink. And in the last twenty years, that well of coolness has been hip-hop."[42] But what is cool about heavy syncopation, lack of melody and harmony, and perverse lyrics? "[W]hite kids embrace hip-hop because it's got phat beats, yes," posits Knight Ridder writer Jim Walsh, "But it also distances them from their parents, and in some sense, serves as a rejection of their parents' culture and their race itself.... Like no generation before it, the hip-hop generation recognizes that identity crisis as its own. It is the first generation to live and breathe diversity and multiculturalism, not just study it."[43]

There is a big difference between multiculturalism and the old American concept of "the melting pot." Multiculturalism is "a social or educational theory that encourages interest in many cultures within a society rather than in only a mainstream culture," according to the American Heritage Dictionary.[44] And it's a dangerous theory. It promotes moral relativism by pretending that all different cultures are equally legitimate and therefore should remain completely distinct. It says that anyone who joins the mainstream has "sold out" his roots. Multiculturalism, combined with the sharp focus on the wrongs done by the white community to American blacks, encourages white kids to hate their heritage—and mainstream culture, by extension. Rap culture provides an attractive alternative for rebellion in its hatred of mainstream culture, its focus on sex and violence, and its preening arrogance.

There are plenty of people who are pleased that young white people have begun to imitate the sick inner city culture. Dan DeLuca of the *Philadelphia Inquirer* says, "With so many hip-hop heroes living large, rapping in the dream lives of white, black, Latino, Asian, and other kids, it stands to reason that the shared culture will have its impact. Slowly, surely, incrementally, a change is bound to come...What's good for hip-hop is what's good for America."[45] Chris Cuomo of FOX News stated on *FOX Files*, "It seems black has never been more beautiful to white suburban teenagers."[46]

Many "intellectuals" love the rap culture. It is anti-establishment and "poetic," and has the romance of revolution about it. Professor Cornel West of Harvard University, who has done little of note in the past few years except to record his own rap CD, sees rap as "the raw reflection of black life in America," according to the *Washington Post*.[47] Halifu Osumare, a dance professor who taught "Power Moves: Hip-Hop Culture" at Bowling Green State University, called rap "contemporary poetry...really poignant stories even if couched in misogyny and gangsterism."[48] Full-fledged college courses on rap and hip-hop abound at highly-ranked universities around the country. "That it has reached the level of academic study is more proof of hip-hop's mainstream arrival," notes Andrew Guy Jr. of the *Houston Chronicle*.[49]

These people shouldn't be too enthusiastic about white cross-over to rap. White kids are picking up the worst of rap culture, and coming away with the false impression that it actually represents mainstream black America. And as the "wigger" market grows, "wigger" hip-hoppers have risen to the forefront of American music. They're no kinder or milder than their black counterparts.

Eminem, possibly the most despicable lyricist on the scene today, has parroted gangsta rappers to the tune of millions. His song "Kill You" speaks about murdering and raping various women, including his mother: "(AHHH!) Slut, you think I won't choke no whore / 'til the vocal cords don't work in her throat no more?!.... (AHHH!) Put your hands down bitch, I ain't gon' shoot you / I'ma pull YOU to this bullet, and put it through you / (AHHH!) Shut up slut, you're causin' too much chaos / Just bend over and take it like a slut, okay Ma? / 'Oh, now he's raping his own mother, abusing a whore, / snorting coke, and we gave him the *Rolling Stone* cover?' / You g—damn right BITCH, and now it's too late / I'm triple platinum."

In a way, Eminem is right—his status as a rap star means that he's allowed to get away with anything. He scrolls down a list of women he'd be okay with slaughtering and ends with this comforting line: "Hahaha, I'm just playin' ladies / You know I love you." It's all tongue in cheek, you see—just like Jack the Ripper loved prostitutes.

Another track on the same album, "Kim," contains an explicit, play-by-play description of Eminem cutting his girlfriend's jugular: "Ha! Go ahead yell! / Here I'll scream with you! / AH SOMEBODY HELP! / Don't you get it b—, no one can hear you? / Now shut the f—up and get what's comin' to you / You were supposed to love me {Kim choking} / NOW BLEED! BITCH BLEED! / BLEED! BITCH BLEED! BLEED!"

This guy belongs in a nuthouse, not in a recording studio. Instead, his rhythmically psychopathic CD, "The Marshall Mathers LP," sold 9.7 million copies.[50] The album also won a Grammy Award for best rap album of 2000.[51] In 2002, Eminem starred in the hit film *8 Mile*, which grossed over $100 million.[52] Eminem's success is by and large considered "a barometer...for rap in general."[53]

Even the *wimps* of the white community are buying into the rap rage. Justin Timberlake, the former Mickey Mouse Club kid—a guy about as white as Senator Robert Byrd—has found his inner gangsta as well, even aside from treating Janet Jackson like a ho at the Super Bowl. He's turned from a boy-toy into a hard-edged "urban black culture" imitator, putting him more in the realm of rap than of pop. The *Times* of London labels Timberlake "a walking clotheshorse for black urban chic."[54] Baz Dreisinger of the *LA Weekly* calls Timberlake a "[wigger] du jour."[55] Timberlake was even tapped to host the ABC-TV special Motown 45, raising the hackles of some in the black community.[56]

The only question left is which one of these white artists will go black first: Clay Aiken, Wayne Newton, Elton John, or Michael Jackson?

Playa hatas

While cultural conservatives continue to speak out against rap, the battle seems all but lost. A spokesman for Sprite tells the *Wall Street Journal* that rap "is the leader in terms of influencing pop culture today."[57] Shoe companies and cell phone makers employ many of these same rappers as part of their marketing campaigns. The NFL and NBA both utilize the rap culture to sell product; even Major League Baseball has joined in. Oxford's English Dictionary now includes an entry for "bling bling," a hip-hop term for big jewelry.

With the growth of hip-hop, can cultural conservatives win the big battles of the future if they alienate rap consumers? After Senator Kerry's silly statements about rap on MTV, he received a cacophony of catcalls from cultural conservatives. "Look, it's one thing to say you like it, but to try to pass this off as something you've intellectually examined and assigned value to? Sorry, senator," said an incredulous Rush Limbaugh.[58] "[D]oesn't Kerry recognize what so much of rap music is today—profane, sex-obsessed, selfish, greedy—in sum, the opposite of public-spirited?" asked media critic Brent Bozell.[59]

The cultural Left immediately responded by claiming that Republicans were old-fashioned, behind the times, and bound to lose votes because of it. "The animosity of culture warriors like Limbaugh...could make it extremely difficult for the GOP to court young voters," warned Salon.com columnist Eric Boehlert.[60] "When it comes to politics,

Republicans have to take hip-hop seriously," nodded Bakari Kitwana, author of *Why White Kids Love Hip-Hop*.[61] "Rush Limbaugh is like those guys who used to smash Elvis Presley records in the 1950s and said rock 'n' roll has no importance. They're just throwback people... And when you attack rap, you're not just attacking the performer but you're attacking the audience, the majority of which is white," sneered David Bositis of the Joint Center for Political and Economic Studies in Washington.[62]

Even some Republicans were wary of turning off the young rap fans. "There's no reason to perceive the Republican Party as being anti-rap or anti-hip-hop," claimed Republican National Committee spokesperson Mary Ellen Grant. "We're reaching out far and wide to youth voters regardless of their musical preference."[63]

There's no underestimating the popularity of hip-hop. Rap has functionally become the driving musical genre for the porn generation. Yet as attractive as it might seem to swim with the rap culture tide for demographic reasons alone, conservatives have no choice but to swim upstream. No, rap is not inherently rotten. It doesn't have to contain vulgarity, misogyny, and brutal violence. You could easily put the words of President Bush's State of the Union Address to a funky syncopated beat and call it rap. But there's simply no way to co-opt the gangsta rap culture that now defines hip-hop into anything that functions as a positive element in society.

CHAPTER SIX

TEENYBOPPERS

"Benjamin Franklin said that the two things you can always count on are death and taxes. I am tempted to add: You can also count on lots of boy-related articles to appear in just about any teen magazine."

KAREN BOKRAM, EDITOR, *GIRLS' LIFE* MAGAZINE[1]

Time for a quiz! This quiz has two parts. First, see if you can name the ages of the girls who submitted the following questions to advice columnists. Then, see if you can guess the advice an adult gave to these troubled females. To make it fair, we'll make this a multiple-choice test.

1. *"My boyfriend isn't affectionate. We've only kissed once in seven months—three months ago. I'm miserable with him but I know I'm going to be miserable without him. What do I do?"*
    (a) "Stop basing your relationship on physicality."
    (b) "Maybe the guy has manners. Respect his beliefs."
    (c) "Before ending it, try to kiss *him*."
    (d) "Where the hell are your parents?"

2. *"I've been developing feelings for one of my girl friends. Thing is, I'm a girl, too. I want to tell her, but I fear she doesn't feel the same way and our friendship will be ruined. Plus, students at school will harass me. (I've already been teased for liking a girl.)"*

    (a) "Sexuality is amorphous at your age. Confusion is natural. Ask your parents what they think, and about seeing a psychologist."

    (b) "Have respect for the feelings of the other girl. While you are confused about your sexuality, thrusting those confusions onto another girl is wrong."

    (c) "I hate that I can't flat out tell you to go for it...join your school's Gay-Straight Alliance, or find a local gay community center. You need more nonjudgmental people in your life."

    (d) "Where in the fiery flames of hell are your parents?"

3. *"Is it wrong that every time I think a celebrity or a guy at school is hot, I imagine myself having sex with him? Am I perverted?"*

    (a) "Those kinds of feelings are natural, but perhaps you need to focus more on your studies and extra-curricular activities and less on boys."

    (b) "Feelings are unpredictable, but as moral human beings, we can still try to control our thoughts and actions."

    (c) "Of course you're not perverted...think away."

    (d) "Where in the roasting, toasting pit of hell are your parents?"

Okay, time's up! Put down your pencils and get ready for the answers. The writer of question number one is Lauren, fourteen, from Columbiana, Ohio. The actual advice she received was (c). The columnist added: "Not to make light of this, but three months is a long time to go without a follow-up move.... Nothing says that guys are solely responsible for hooking up."[2]

Question two was from Michelle, fifteen, of Mississauga, Ontario. And yes, you guessed it, (c) represents the given advice. Explained the columnist: "The possibility of ruining the friendship is high whether you're gay or straight, but, sadly, the world is a homophobic place, and the stakes are higher in your situation. There's a chance your friend will get weirded out and tell people, and they might make fun of you again. But if it's worth the risk, there are options. Mention that you know a girl who's interested in her female friend. If she doesn't freak, it's a good sign."[3]

Question three was from Trena, fourteen, Brooklyn, New York. Again, she received (c) in response to her question.[4]

Each of these questions was submitted to the publication *YM*, aka *Your Magazine*. *YM*, according to the *New York Times Almanac 2004*, had over 2.2 million subscribers as of 2002, making it the thirty-second largest magazine in the country.[5] Other teen magazines also have gargantuan subscriber lists. *Seventeen* had over 2.4 million subscribers as of 2002 (number twenty-seven overall); *Teen People* had 1.6 million subscribers (number forty-eight); *Cosmo Girl!* had over 1 million (number eighty-three).[6] That's over 7.2 million subscribers total, from those magazines alone. That doesn't count smaller mags like *Teen*, *Elle Girl*, *J-14*, *Girls' Life* or *Teen Vogue*.

The magazines' subscribers are teenage girls, and their parents are buying them subscriptions. These magazines obsess about boys, looks, and celebrities. The teen magazines function as gateway products both for "porn lite" publications like *Cosmopolitan* and celeb-gossip magazines like *People*.

As Kathy Flanigan of the *Milwaukee Journal Sentinel* puts it, "Sex has always been a marketing tool. But who knew it would be used to sell magazines to kids as young as twelve?"[7]

"Training manuals for sex"

"A bunch of us were hanging out watching a movie when we decided to play a game of truth or dare," writes Stephanie from Alameda, California. "I whispered to my friend to dare me to kiss the boy I'm hot for. She said we had to pass candy back and forth to each other with our tongues. It worked out well and I was completely happy. That is, until I hiccupped and choked on the candy. I eventually coughed it up, but after that, the guy wasn't into kissing me anymore."[8]

The girl who wrote these inspired lines is fourteen years old. They appeared in the February 2004 edition of *YM*. Other submissions included one from a fourteen-year-old girl from California who got caught making out in the school gym with her boyfriend, his hand up her shirt,[9] and one from a fourteen-year-old girl from Virginia, who got caught kissing her boyfriend during an in-class science video.[10]

Most of the teen magazines nowadays revolve around sexual activity. "They're telling girls who read these things that everybody else out there is doing it. You could even argue that they're training manuals for sex," says Ana Garner, associate dean for graduate studies and research in the College of Communications at Marquette University.[11]

"Training manuals for sex" about pegs it. According to *YM* editors, they receive a constant barrage of letters from young girls asking about sex: "We're always receiving depressing letters from fourteen-year-old girls who think withdrawal is an acceptable method of birth control."[12] So *YM* offers information about the latest birth control drugs—"58 percent of you think the pill should be available over the counter, while 17 percent think a patient should see a doctor to get it"—and directs kids to the Planned Parenthood website for more information.[13]

Likewise, the November 2001 issue of *Seventeen* promised on the cover to answer the question: "Does Sex Hurt the First Time?"[14] The February 2004 *YM* cover offered its readers "Kissing do's and dont's."[15] *YM*'s July 2004 offered its readers advice on "How To Have The Perfect Summer Fling."[16] February 2005's *Cosmo Girl!* cover tempted buyers with an oath to reveal "5 Flirting Secrets That'll Make Him Want You BAD."[17] *Cosmo Girl!*'s "Ask College Girl" column tells readers that "No question's too heavy—or too *naughty*—for College Girl!"[18]

Seventeen's February 2005 issue answers questions from a seventeen-year-old Ohioan who "noticed some small, white bumps around the tip of my boyfriend's penis," and a seventeen-year-old Californian who had anal sex without a condom with her boyfriend in the back of his car. But the most interesting question came from one fifteen-year-old girl from Syracuse, Utah: "Me and my boyfriend had sex about three weeks ago, and he wasn't wearing a condom. He didn't come inside me, but I'm still worried—I'm having really bad mood swings, my breasts feel tender, and my stomach is, like, hard, and I can't suck it in. Do you think I'm pregnant?" "If you're pregnant, you need care and advice," the advice columnist responds, "and if you're not, you need to get birth control, so you'll avoid another situation like this."[19] Or she could stop acting like a fifteen-year-old tramp. But that doesn't seem like a viable option if she's writing to *Seventeen* for advice.

Cosmo Girl!'s February 2005 issue teaches its readers about "vulva love": "This Valentine's Day, get to know the body part that makes you so *fab!*" "If you're thinking about having sex," the magazine advises, "visit a gyno first to talk about STD prevention and birth control. If you're worried about your parents finding out, call first and ask if she can keep your visit confidential."[20] Cutting the parents out of the loop is certainly a good strategy if you attempt to replace their authority with teen magazines.

The column contains a large, graphic drawing of the genital area, complete with handy tips: "The clitoris has 8,000 nerve endings—that's more than there are in the entire head of the penis!" For further research, *Cosmo Girl!* suggests visiting vday.com/campaigns, and urges high school girls to put on their own productions of *The Vagina Monologues*.[21]

There's also a section about girls who name their vaginas. The purpose of naming genitalia remains unknown—if you lose them, will they return if you call them by name? Still, there are plenty of *Cosmo Girl!* readers willing to contribute. "Mz. Thang—because I'm a strong-minded, young, African American woman!" writes Sharmica, sixteen, Atlanta, Georgia. "Mrs. Sprinkles—it's sort of like my code word. I'll say stuff to my friends like 'Yesterday me and Mrs. Sprinkles met the hottest guy.' It cracks us up!" expounds Rachel, fifteen, of Oklahoma City, Oklahoma. "My cookie jar," explains Jessica, seventeen, of Cherokee, Alabama. "When I was a little girl, my mom used to say, 'Don't let any boys get into your cookie jar and take your cookies!' And now she calls my boyfriend of three years the Cookie Monster."[22] Boyfriend of three years—in other words, he's been going after the cookies since Jessica was fourteen. How adorable!

"Why is it that guys brag about their penises, but girls are so secretive about—even ashamed of—*their* genitals?"[23] the article asks. This is a perfect example of the "equality" sought by the women's movement. It asks the right question—why do men act like animals with regard to their genitals?—yet still gives the wrong answer: It's time for women to celebrate our vulvas like animals!

The obsession with sex is cloaked in obsession with boys. These magazines objectify boys for "liberated" young girls. *Elle Girl* prints "TOTAL BOY: THE RATING GAME," wherein "Four dashing and daring L.A. guys step out in front of a jury of L.A ELLEgirls (two of whom would like to see Alvaro lose those pants)."[24] *YM* has a "LAST BOY STANDING" contest in which readers vote on which guy is the most major "hottie."[25] *Cosmo Girl!* contains a "BOY-O-METER, asking teenage girls to rate male models on a scale of one fire ("warm") to three ("on fire!").[26] As if that weren't enough, *Cosmo Girl!* also has an "EYE CANDY" section, complete with boy-band look-alikes in fold-out shirtless poses. It's *Playgirl* lite. "Who needs a box of chocolates when you can have a cupcake like Joshua for Valentine's day?"[27] the magazine asks breathlessly.

At the same time they objectify boys, the teen magazines urge little girls to sex themselves up to attract boys. *Elle Girl*'s February 7, 2005 cover touts "SEXY JEANS FOR EVERY BODY TYPE," as well as "7 WAYS TO TELL IF HE *REALLY* LIKES YOU."[28] This kind of juxtaposition—"look better" next to "is he into you?"—directs girls toward sex.

This juxtaposition of looks to boys is ubiquitous throughout the teen mag genre. A quick survey of the teen magazines on the local newsstand shelf in mid-January 2005 reveals the pattern. February 2005's *YM* advertises "THE HOTTEST GUYS ON THE PLANET" above "40 KICK-ASS PARTY LOOKS."[29] The *Seventeen* cover promises "sweet & sexy looks inside" just above the "LOVE SURVEY: 5,000 + HOT GUYS REVEAL THEIR DEEPEST SECRETS."[30] The *Teen Vogue* offers "flirty VALENTINE'S DAY looks your date will fall for."[31] *Teen People* advertises "THE *BEST* JEANS FOR YOUR BODY" right above "*Get a date by Friday!*"[32] *Teen* proclaims "NEW YEAR NEW YOU!"—then, below,

"ALL ABOUT DATING: advice that really works."[33] The most extreme example, of course, is *Cosmo Girl!*, which carries each of these teasers on its February 2005 cover: "360 WAYS TO BE *Irresistible!*," "PLUS: 5 Flirting Secrets That'll Make Him Want You *BAD*," "Get Sexier Abs Now (The 10-Minute-a-Day Workout!)."[34] Is this the "women's empowerment" young girls were promised by the feminist movement?

While women's magazines like *Cosmopolitan* explicitly discuss sexual positions, most teen magazines stick to dating—and how to exploit the 'rents into letting you date. *Teen* explains "the dating game" by first telling teens how to sucker the adults. "Parents say, 'not until you're 18.' How do you get 'em to lighten up? Read up!" exclaims the magazine. Tips include group dating to alleviate parental fears about one-on-one contact, pushing the parents into allowing you to go to a movie with a guy, and getting around the parental strictures by running into "your cutie at school or other functions . . . Think of these as 'sorta' dates."[35] *Teen* gives other pearls of wisdom as well: "Oh yeah, don't pump him for compliments either. Of course he thinks you're hot—he asked you out, didn't he?" They also push the kissing game: "It's the end of the night—the scary moment of truth! Should you lean in and kiss him? Will he smooch you?"[36]

Here's a better question: Should parents be paying for magazines that actively seek to undermine their authority and sell their teenage daughters on sexual activity?

Star worship

The sex advice, the kissing tips, the boy fixation—all of it reappears through the vehicle of celebrity. There is probably no worse group of role models on earth than performance artists who exploit their sexuality for monetary gain. Would you trust Paris Hilton to baby-sit your kid? The teen magazines do. They spend a vast number of pages teaching Paris's life lessons to American girls. They also tout Lindsay Lohan ("Comes Clean About Her Breasts, The Breakup, And More!"[37]); the Olson twins ("Young, Famous, and Stressed-Out")[38]; Hilary Duff ("win her beauty booty!")[39]; Usher ("Confessions about sex, his soulmate, & that awesome six-pack)[40]; Chad Michael Murray ("Chad's kissing partners tell all!")[41]; Ashlee Simpson ("exclusive pics of Ashlee's home")[42] and the rest of the pathetic, talentless Pop Culture Gang. The members of the PCG are all too willing to offer their important advice to young girls. Plus cheesecake shots of themselves. And gossip. And, of course, plugs for their products.

First the advice: *YM*'s February 2004 "Feel the Love" issue announced "Kissing do's and don'ts" on its cover. The actual article contains a series of "celebrity kissing do's and dont's." Among the useful tidbits of kissing knowledge were these pearls: "DON'T use your tongue as a weapon," (Adam Levine, Maroon 5); "DO keep your mouth minty fresh," (Jessica Simpson); "DON'T invite your parents along," (Gregory Smith, *Everwood*).[43] It's a wonder that this monumental group of minds hasn't cured cancer by now.

J-14 carried a similar piece in its February 2005 issue: "stars kiss & tell." Jesse McCartney, of *Summerland* fame (or anonymity, as the case may be) told readers that he is "a big hugger. I like to wrap my arms around a girl just like a monkey."[44] All other resemblance is purely coincidental.

Orlando Bloom (*Pirates of the Caribbean*, *Lord of the Rings*) informed readers that kissing is "definitely a nervous sort of thing because you're wondering whether to tongue or not to tongue. It depends on the person you're kissing. It should be a romantic, wet kiss—nothing too intense."[45] Defying all logic, Bloom truly is more vacuous off-screen than he is on it.

Fergie from Black Eyed Peas related a personal story: "I was eleven and I had a huge crush on a guy.... Usually, people talk about their first kiss being very awkward—mine was not! We made out!"[46] At age eleven. Yes, Virginia, past behavior *is* a good predictor for future actions.

Then there are the cheesecake shots. Rating random boys through hot-meters gets old fast, so teen magazines manufacture teen idols out of male celebrities. The February 2005 *YM* dedicated eleven pages of its mag to "hot" photos of male celebrities. "We all know looks aren't everything—except when it comes to this list," *YM* pants. "Hey, every once in a while it's fun to be shallow. Check these guys out. Can you blame us?" *YM* labels R&B singer Usher "the hottest guy of the year," and carries a picture of a bathing-suit-clad Usher sitting by the pool. In his interview with *YM*, Usher talks extensively about his sex life—"The more you live, the more you learn, the more you have to say," he says—but then tells teen girls that "Virginity is something to be valued. You're not less hip if you're not having sex....Don't be pressured into it, because you never want to do something that you'll live to regret."[47] Perhaps that message would sound more sincere in a less sexualized context. As it stands, it sounds a lot like an anti-drunk driving commercial starring Teddy Kennedy filmed at the local pub.

Teen's February 2005 edition promises "Hot Celebs Inside!" Full-page "pinups" of "*Summerland* sweetie" Jesse McCartney, Adam Brody (*The O.C.*), "*Clubhouse* cutie" Jeremy Sumpter, Jake Parker (*Quintuples*), "*One Tree Hill* hottie" Chad Michael Murray, Romeo, and "*Life As We Know It* flirt" Sean Faris ensue.[48]

GL (February 2005) gets hot for Jesse McCartney—headline: "Jesse, oh yessee!!!" "We know we're always telling you to never sit by the phone and wait for it to ring," the editors drool. "But when juicy Jesse McCartney's dialing ya up, you stare at the phone and you wait. And you wait. And you wait."[49] It would be laughable if it weren't so pathetic.

Teen Vogue gets into the act, too. "The women of Wisteria Lane might be drooling over the local gardener—but they're not alone," the editors slobber about *Desperate Housewives* star Jesse Metcalfe.[50] *Teen People* (February 2005) offers two locker posters of woman-hater Eminem.[51] What a great way to promote female empowerment! But *Elle Girl* is the most obvious about its objectification of celebrities. "HOT GUYS: WE RATE 'EM, DATE 'EM AND INVESTIGATE 'EM," the magazine brags. The February 2005 issue states: "LET'S ALL OBJECTIFY...BRETT BENDER"—a seventeen-year-old snowcross racer. Editor Elizabeth Wallace asks her readers to help her in her search for a "guy who is total eye candy"—everyone is free to email her at Elizabeth@ellegirl.com.[52]

And don't forget the gossip. In reality, most celebrities are dumb as dirt, but the teen magazines encourage a sick fixation with their empty lives. They critique the clothes, agonize over the breakups, and portray them as deep personalities, suffering artists, Shakespearean tortured souls. We're supposed to cry over them, sigh over them, and buy over them.

Teen People groans with anguished sympathy for the Olson twins: "The Olsons aren't alone in their agony. More and more, young stars are raising their voices about the painful price tag attached to fame."[53] Woe to these poor celebrities! If you prick them, do they not bleed?

Cosmo Girl! gives Lindsay Lohan an outlet for her heartbreak: "I'm heartbroken," Lohan says. "Every breakup is painful—whether it's a boyfriend or your parent's marriage." *Cosmo Girl!* sympathizes. "Lindsay may be the girl everyone gossips about lately, but despite the reports that her life is all about hard partying, she has also faced hard times recently...It's been a year that has taught the eighteen-year-old a lot about herself." Ah, the slings and arrows of outrageous fortune! The magazine also makes sure to label Lohan "strong and wise" as well as "down-to-earth."[54] Yes, wearing skimpy clothing and showing off fake cleavage does take courage and wisdom.

J-14 examines "how rumors rocked Jessica's world." The Jessica of the title is, of course, Jessica Simpson. "Not long after achieving the success she's always dreamed of, Jess became the target of nasty rumors," the mag opines. "It's hard for your family and friends to hear that stuff," Simpson says.[55] Oh, that such scandalmongers could turn their eyes toward the napes of their necks, and make but an interior survey of their good selves!

Seventeen offers Jamie Lynn Spears (Britney's wannabe younger sister) an outlet for her inner turmoil. "To tell you the truth, the only reason I don't want to be too famous is because of the paparazzi," Spears states. "Somebody has got to stop them. It not only hurts my sister, but it's dangerous for *them*, too. It's getting bad, you know? They run you off the road. Why would *they* want to take that kind of risk?" *Seventeen* murmurs sympathetically, "Clearly Jamie Lynn already knows that that kind of innocent comment can easily wind up as a tabloid cover line." Fie upon the damned paparazzi! Hell is empty and all the devils are here!

Of course, teen magazine sympathy only goes so far. Just because celebrities suffer the indignities of daily intrusion upon their privacy doesn't mean that the teen magazines should stop intruding. *Teen People* makes sure photographers are present when Britney Spears and Paris Hilton reveal their thongs.[56] *Teen Vogue* grabs snapshots of Kate Bosworth and Kirsten Dunst making their daily rounds.[57] It seems that despite their protestations about the evils of mass media, the teen magazine genre doth protest too much.

Instilling social values

In supplanting parents, teen magazines encourage young girls to buy liberal social values wholesale. The first step is watering down religion. *Seventeen* does that by juxtaposing religious Christian values with secular and pagan ones, granting them all equal legitimacy. *Seventeen* asks "Does your faith affect your love life?" and then quotes a non-religious Jew, a non-religious Muslim, two pagans, and an atheist alongside four religious Christians. Of course, this being a teen magazine, all views are of equal validity. So you get quotes like this: "I am polytheist. It's hard to find a guy who shares my beliefs!" (Kelly, seventeen, Wilton, California) alongside quotes like this: "Because I am Catholic, I believe in abstinence." (Stephanie, fifteen, San Antonio, Texas) You get quotes like this: "I'm Wiccan, and all the guys I've dated have been sort of weirded out when they first see my spell books or hear me talking about tarot" (Rachel, seventeen, New York, New York) alongside quotes like this: "As a follower of Jesus Christ, I am waiting until I am ready to get married before even thinking about courtship." (Kelly, sixteen, Huntington Beach, California)[58] It's the most basic recipe for moral relativism in existence—everyone's views are equal and valid, no matter how ludicrous.

That recipe is strengthened in the following pages, as *Seventeen* presents the touching story of a girl who left her oppressive evangelical Christian upbringing for the gothic paganism of Wicca. "My religion isn't evil," the article is titled; the subtitle reads: "Jessica, eighteen, has found her faith—but lost her family in the process." What follows is a snarling rampage against Christianity. "My parents signed me up for

Bible study so I could get to know our faith better," Jessica tells *Seventeen*. "But what I ended up learning in that class was how intolerant our church was—it railed against homosexuals and taught us that people of different religions were damned. This wasn't the Christianity I'd practiced before—how could my parents really want to be a part of *this*?" Jessica goes on to describe how she wore a pentacle home, how her mother yelled at her and called the symbol "evil," and how Jessica "found such solace in Wicca that I couldn't give it up for my parents. And I hoped they'd eventually accept it—I mean, it was a part of *me*. But I was wrong." *Seventeen* directs curious readers to witchvox.com to learn more about Wicca.[59]

If you care to visit witchvox.com to learn about your inner warlock, as I did, you'll find that the basic tenet of Wicca is "An it harm none, do as ye will." Despite the appearance, this is in no way a "license to do whatever 'feels good' to the individual without accompanying responsibility. Nothing could be further from the truth. The Witches' Rede is rich with compassion, empathy and respect for others, the individual practitioner, the Goddess and God, and Mother Earth. It guides and directs our energies 'for the good of all.' "[60] Well, that's a comfort. "The other basic guideline of Witches is the 'Law of Three' or the 'Law of Karmic Return.' Witches accept responsibility for their own actions and are therefore VERY careful about how they use their magick."[61]

At this point, I decided not to become Wiccan. After all, how I use my magick is none of their business.

Once you've obliterated any idea of godly morality, it's a short step to amorality. While *Seventeen* tells girls "It's much easier to stick to your values if you and your guy talk about sex *before* things get hot,"[62] they aren't exactly conservative in their sexual mores—"It is best for you to talk to your parents or doctor about your sexual health, but if you can't do that, it's legal for you to visit a public clinic or a Planned Parenthood clinic confidentially. Call 800-230-PLAN or go to plannedparenthood.org to find a clinic near you."[63] *Cosmo Girl!* advises girls to set boundaries for their bodies. Unfortunately, those suggested boundaries are restricted to "kissing or staying above the belt."[64]

Cosmo Girl! has some advice for social activism, too. Few of their suggestions would make my list of desirable causes. Their first suggestion is "PROMOTING PEACE"; they suggest visiting websites like worldpeace.org/youth, threadproject.com, and warchild.org. Worldpeace.org/youth explains how kids can plant "peace poles" in their communities.[65] "Whatever the location, the presence of a Peace Pole announces that this is a special place, dedicated to peace on Earth,"[66] the website claims. Perhaps we should plant peace poles in Saudi Arabia, Somalia, Syria, Iran, and North Korea. Hey, for a few bucks, we can end all war! If the peace poles don't work, we can always follow up on another of *Cosmo Girl!*'s suggestions, and help create a huge "one world, one cloth" tapestry to promote world peace.[67] Tapestries. Now why didn't the Defense Department think of that one?

Cosmo Girl! also suggests "SAVING THE ENVIRONMENT." They suggest visiting globalstewards.org . . . click on 'take action.'"[68] Among the actions suggested by globalstewards.org: fighting against genetically engineered food, animal experimentation (clicking that link will get you to the psychotic People for the Ethical Treatment of Animals website), and overpopulation.[69]

Naturally, *Cosmo Girl!* wants its activist readers to aid "PROMOTING GAY/LESBIAN TOLERANCE." They list as a "success story" the Massachusetts Supreme Court decision forcing homosexual marriage onto the populace. "The ruling was historic," the magazine yelps, "the first in America to give gays and lesbians the opportunity to legally wed."[70] How nice! How about force-feeding the youngsters the right to incest or sex at any age as well? I hear the North American Man-Boy Love Association is interested in that one.

Cosmo Girl! asks readers to focus on "ENDING RACISM." Sounds good, right? Too bad that *Cosmo Girl!* considers ending affirmative action to be racist.[71] They push freechild.org, a website advocating engaging "children and youth as agents of radical democratic social change." Radical social change includes fighting for more sex education and gay, bisexual, transsexual, transgendered, queer and questioning youth rights, among others.[72] Freechild.org asks readers to engage in "hip-hop activism": "Some people refer to hip hop as a tool for social change, others see it as a degrading force that alienates communities. Young people are using hip hop culture to reach and teach their communities about social justice and taking action."[73] Perhaps I'll try some hip-hop activism right after I stop laughing, G-dawg.

For the kiddies

Avoiding the horrible advice of the teen mags can be harder than you think. Just turn to the kids section of your newspaper—if it's like most newspapers, it has advice columns from either Dear Abby or Ann Landers or both. For years, the columns have dispensed unmitigated sexual liberalism in the inches just next to the kid-friendly comics. As Robert Knight of Concerned Women for America writes, "One of the most consistent themes in Dear Abby has been the promotion of the sexual revolution in its many guises. The column consistently parrots the propaganda of Planned Parenthood, the Kinsey Institute, and the Sexual Information and Education Council of the United States (SIECUS), using loaded terms such as "sexual beings" (as in "we are all sexual beings") and bad data. Both Abby and her sister Ann Landers have relied over the years on such authorities as Dr. Judd Marmor, former president of the American Psychiatric Association, who has consistently promoted the homosexual agenda within the psychiatric profession. In column after column, Abby mocks people who resist the cultural sexual zeitgeist."[74]

Even aside from their liberalism, these advice columns are simply silly. It's as though the columnists have only three options they can dispense: (1) go to counseling; (2) visit Parents, Families, and Friends of Lesbians and Gays, or some other such liberal interest group ; (3) discuss the issues with your [fill in the blank] and see if you can come to a perspective of tolerance for their [deviant] behavior.

Here's Dear Abby doing a Type 2:

> **DEAR ABBY:** I noticed that my 16-year-old daughter wasn't her usual self. So I questioned her one night and asked if there

was anything bothering her, or if she was worried about something. She started crying and told me she is gay. I responded by
crying with her and asking her if she was sure. She said she was.
I told her she is still my daughter and I love her very much, but
that I can't help hoping she's just confused and that as time goes
on, she might see that this is not who she really is. I'm trying my
best to accept it, but it is difficult at times.—*Confused Parent in
Texas*

A proper response could have pointed out that this was a sixteen-year-
old girl, that young people are often confused about sexuality, and that
seeing someone for help might be a decent option. Instead, Abby offered
this brilliantly original response:

DEAR CONFUSED: Your feelings are normal. Most parents
have plans and dreams for their children, and your child has
turned out differently than you expected. Your next step is to
contact PFLAG. I have mentioned this organization—Parents,
Families and Friends of Lesbians and Gays—many times in my
column. It offers support groups, educational outreach and more
to families and friends of gay, lesbian, intersexual and transgendered family members. The Web site is www.pflag.org and the
telephone number is 1-202-467-8180. Please don't wait to contact them.[75]

Here's a Type 3 (complete with endorsement of pornography):

DEAR ABBY: My daughter, "Rhonda," hosts several "soft
porn" Web sites, and it upsets me greatly. She's 24 and a very
bright, sweet and loving person, which is why it's so difficult for
me to understand why she does this. Rhonda earned more than
$100,000 last year and has a sizable savings account, but her
small business is pornography! We don't discuss her occupation,
and no one but myself and my ex-husband know she's involved

in this kind of thing. As far as everyone else is concerned, she "designs Web sites." Rhonda wants me to be proud of her accomplishments, but I'm not. I love my daughter very much and keep hoping she'll grow out of this; however, I'm not sure she will. I hate lying to everyone about what she does, but I would never want anyone to know. How do I come to terms with this—or can I?—*Her Loving Mother*

A proper response might have been: "Where were you when your daughter was growing up? How about telling her you never want to hear about her business again, and make clear your disapproval?"

Instead, Abby suggested that *Mother* be Tolerant:

You and your daughter have very different moral values. While it's against your principles, what she's doing is legal. She's built a successful business and wants you to respect what she has accomplished. That said, I doubt you will ever see eye-to-eye on this issue. Love her as your daughter, try to accept that this is a choice she has made, and focus on her positive qualities: She's bright, sweet and loving—not to mention a whiz at business. At this point, I doubt you can change her.[76]

Meanwhile, Ann Landers self-righteously condemned anyone who opposed masturbation and suggested abstinence:

Well, now I am going to suggest a far more realistic solution than abstinence. The sex drive is the strongest human drive after hunger. It is nature's way of perpetuating the human race. Males reach their sexual peak as early as 17. There must be an outlet. I am recommending self-gratification or mutual masturbation, whatever it takes to release the sexual energy. This is a sane and safe alternative to intercourse, not only for teenagers but also for older men and women without partners. I do not want to hear from clergymen telling me it's a sin. The sin is making people feel guilty about responding to this basic, fundamental human drive.[77]

Parents, take comfort: if Ann Landers says it isn't a sin, it isn't a sin! When it's Ann Landers vs. God, clearly Ann takes precedence.

For "mature women" only

Ultimately, all these advice columns and teen magazines serve as gateway products for the hard stuff. Publishers have learned that you've got to prep the kiddies with *YM*, *Elle Girl*, *Teen Vogue*, *Seventeen*, *GL*, and *Cosmo Girl!* before you slip them *Cosmopolitan*. And *Cosmo* and its ilk are truly pornography; they belong behind those black pieces of plastic at the newsstands.

Cosmo has a circulation of about three million, making it number twenty-one on the magazine hit parade.[78] To make the teen tie-in clear, they often feature a teen celebrity on the cover. As of February 2005, that teen celebrity was no-talent hack Ashlee Simpson in a slinky red dress, named *Cosmo*'s "Fun Fearless Female of the Year."[79] Unlike sister Jessica, Ashlee refuses to swear off sex until marriage; instead, she says that "having sex before you're married is something that you should decide on your own."[80]

That's a terrific message for the teenagers who make up a sizable portion of the magazine's readership. Letters from readers are often from the barely legal crowd. "I was babysitting, and while the kids were napping, I decided to sit on their deck and write a note to my boyfriend, Brian. I made it really racy and described in detail how I wanted to go down on him the next time we could sneak into his shower together," writes Katie, age eighteen.[81]

Each issue revolves entirely around sex. Articles in the magazine include "BEYOND KAMA SUTRA: Advanced Sex Positions (#3 Will Have You Grinning For A Week)," "THE POWER OF *PRE*-SEX: 5 Tricks That Will Totally Rev His Engine," "Guess What He's Really Thinking in Bed," "His Butt: What Your Guy's Bum Shape Reveals About His Personality (Squeeze, Then Read)," "50 Ways to Have Fun

With Your Man," and "Hilarious Confessions of *Real* Desperate House-wives."[82]

Cosmo's sex positions include "THE *COSMO* CAT," "THE PELVIC PUSH," "THE LUSTY LAP DANCE," "THE SULTRY SPOON," "THE SLEEPING DOG," "THE BOOTY LIFT," "THE FRISKY FACE-OFF," "THE TANTALIZING TILT," "THE FLYING SQUIRREL," "THE COOTIE-HOP," and "THE PIT AND THE PENDULUM."[83] Well, actually, I just made the last three up. But since I did, can I work for *Cosmo* now?

The recommended "tricks that will totally rev his engine" are letting him see you naked ("When you finally get down to removing your panties, do it painfully slow so he feels the burn"), using your breath ("Work your way south to his package, pucker up, and blast a circle of cool air around his penis, as if you were putting out the candles on a cake"), playing a little rough ("Make him putty in your hands by phys-ically moving him into different positions, scratching your nails down his back, and being ballsy when he tries to take over"), tantalizing with touch ("Instead of heading straight for his package, mix up your sexual touches"), and bringing him to the brink ("And now for the frisky finale: Pull out the start-stop trick").[84]

Alongside the above text, *Cosmo* prints photos of polar bears in heat. I'll let this one pass without comment. Sometimes *Cosmo* speaks for itself.

Cosmo helps with your shopping needs as well with its "GUIDE TO CONDOMS." "Once you read our manual of racy roll-on maneuvers and saucy love-glove styles, no man will eschew safe sex with you again," avers the inaptly named Peter Hyman.[85]

For some hilarious hijinks, *Cosmo* gives its "Cosmo commandments: 10 Ways You Should Never, Ever Test His Love." Commandment #4: "Declare that you're taking a stand against body-hair removal of all kinds." Commandment #7: "Nickname his member The Little Engine That Could." Commandment #9: "Have dinner with your ex. Come home with a hickey...on your inner thigh."[86] That's thigh-lickingly funny!

Cosmo continues the teen trend of objectifying men; Josh Duhamel is *Cosmo's* "Fun Fearless Male of the Year." Other FFMs include David

Spade, Kevin Bacon, Simon Cowell, Carson Kressley, Bill Hemmer, Ben McKenzie, and Taye Diggs.[87] There's also the "Guy Without His Shirt" rating contest.[88] In the article "Butt Really," *Cosmo* analyzes male personalities based on the shape of their rears. Complete with half-naked pictures of male models, the magazine focuses in on the gluteus maximus, which is "a sign to behold."[89] In "WHAT HIS MOUTH MOVES REVEAL," *Cosmo* analyzes male personalities based on the way they snog.[90] It also translates the male mind: "HE SAYS: 'I love you.' (After sex) HE MEANS: 'That thing you just did with your pelvis rocked my world.'"[91] Here's a handy hint to women: Ask a guy how he feels instead of looking at *Cosmo*. We're not that hard to figure out.

And there's the requisite celeb gossip. *Cosmo* hired psychotherapist Cherie Byrd, author of *Kissing School: Seven Lessons on Love, Lips, and Life Force* to analyze pics of celebrity kisses. "Kate [Bosworth] and [Orlando Bloom's] smooch is full of heat and love, and they are both equally engaged," Byrd says. "Also, the way Kate touches Orlando's face with her fingertips is intimate."[92] Whoever said that psychotherapists were fraudulent shrinks?

Celeb gossip is a big moneymaker for other magazines as well. *People* magazine has 3.6 million readers, making it the thirteenth largest magazine in the country; their *Teen People* lead-in for teen girls was number forty-eight.[93]

Does marijuana lead to crack? Perhaps. Do teen magazines lead to *Cosmo* and *People*? No doubt about it.

The pitch

"Don't let magazines (or anybody!) try to define *love* for you," writes *Seventeen* editor Atoosa Rubenstein.[94] Yeah, right. If the teen magazines weren't trying to define love, beauty, and virtue to each and every teenage girl, who would buy their *drek*?

Girls' Life faced that very problem. "For the first eight years, *GL* barely ran any articles on crushing, dating, kissing, or anything else that smacked of guydom," admits editor Karen Bokram.[95] The magazine, designed for ten- to fifteen-year-olds, was dedicated to "features on dealing with friends and family, building self-esteem, and learning more about themselves."[96] As of 2004, they still hadn't cracked the top 100 magazines in the country, according to the *New York Times Almanac*;[97] as of 2001, their circulation remained around 400,000.[98]

In order to reach the saturated girls' market, they sold out. While remaining much milder than most of the teen magazines, they turned to boys and crushes. In August 2001, the magazine was made over.[99] "[A]fter getting letter after letter from girls asking for help and advice, we felt we needed to step up. After all, we were always saying that girls should go after their dreams. Suddenly, it seemed super-judgmental to totally blow off all girls whose dream was to have a boyfriend," Bokram explains.[100]

It's a weak explanation at best. If girls wanted boy advice, there were only a hundred other magazines from which they could choose. Finances were a motivating factor here. *Seventeen* makes over $110 million in advertising revenues each year; *YM* makes over $100 million; *Cosmo* makes over $280 million; *People* is the number one advertising revenue magazine in the country, raking it in to the tune of more than $780 million per year.[101] Why should *GL* get left out in the cold?

Once again, it's a vicious cycle. The magazines push the market ever deeper into sexuality; the market demands more; the good magazines get marginalized. Members of the porn generation keep on buying, reading, and imbibing the sweet poison of oversexed culture. Before you know it, it's the responsible folks at the teen mags that determine when, how, and why a teenager has sex.

CHAPTER SEVEN

ABERCRAPPY & BITCH

"When sex is a commodity, there is always a better deal."

JEAN KILBOURNE, AUTHOR, *CAN'T BUY MY LOVE*[1]

When Janet Jackson bared her right breast at the Super Bowl half-time show in 2004, social conservatives were justifiably enraged. But why did it take an exposed breast to cause FCC chairman Michael Powell to crack down on television sexuality and vulgarity? After all, the very same Super Bowl carried some of the most raunchy commercials in recent memory.

Budweiser ran nine commercials during the Super Bowl. In one, "Fergus, Bud Light!," two dog owners meet. The first tells his dog to fetch; the dog brings back a Bud Light. He turns snootily to the second dog owner, and asks what *his* dog can do. "Fergus, Bud Light!," the second dog owner commands. The dog immediately chomps on the first dog owner's genitals, and he tosses the beer directly to the second dog owner.

It makes you wonder whether the focus group for this ad was a group of ADD-ridden third-graders.

In another Budweiser commercial, Cedric the Entertainer visits a massage parlor. "I'm here for my massage," he tells the attractive girl behind the counter. "These big muscles need some tenderizing." "Okay, cutie, room five," she responds with a seductive smile. Cedric accidentally ends up in room four, the bikini wax room. A good-looking young black woman enters. "You're here for the body treatment?" she asks incredulously. "Oh yeah," he answers. "My body, your treatment, umm-hmm." She obliges with a bikini wax; the commercial ends with Cedric sitting beside a fellow bikini wax customer, asking "Is there a breeze in here?" Apparently the third-grade beer drinkers thought highly of this idea.

But the title for grossest Super Bowl commercial had to go to Budweiser's "Horny Talking Monkey" ad. A beautiful young woman sits on a couch, her boyfriend standing behind the couch. On the couch beside her is a monkey. "I love your apartment, Brian," she says to her boyfriend. "And Frank is so well behaved!" "Yeah, we're best buddies. I'm gonna go grab some Bud Lights," Brian responds. He exits the room, leaving the monkey alone with the girl. She turns to the monkey and coos, "You're so cute!" The monkey puts his arm around the girl and begins talking: "I think, uh, you're cute too," he says. "You can talk?" she asks. "Baby, I can do a little bit more than just talk," the monkey states. "But let's cut the chit-chat, head upstairs, or you know…" The monkey then simulates sexual motion while grunting and screeching. After Brian enters the room and then leaves again, the monkey turns to the girl and asks, "So, how do you feel about back hair?" This commercial certainly wasn't approved by the third-graders—it must have been approved by college students.

Other sexually oriented commercials included a Visa commercial about US Olympic women volleyballers playing in the snow; a Gillette commercial for men's razors containing no fewer than fourteen shots of beautiful women in a one-minute commercial, many depicting actual sexual activity; a trailer for *Starsky and Hutch* including various scantily clad women; and another Budweiser commercial joking about infidelity.

Hilariously, the most subtle commercial about sex was an ad for Levitra, an erectile dysfunction drug. The ad depicted former Chicago Bears and New Orleans Saints head coach Mike Ditka describing the differences between football ("it's fast, it's action packed, play after play") and baseball ("it's not quite the same"). Football, Ditka says, is Levitra; baseball "could use Levitra." For those who know nothing about what Levitra actually does, the references in the commercial mean nothing. Still, you wonder how erectile dysfunction commercials ever made it onto prime-time television.

"Fashionable exhibitionism"

Sex in advertising has been present for decades. In 1968, *Look* magazine publisher Thomas Shepard stated that sex in advertising was on its way out—yet as of 1999, 70 percent of respondents to an *Adweek* poll felt that there was too much sex in advertising.[2] The level of sexual explicitness has escalated over time. In its earliest incarnations in America, before World War I, sexuality in advertising was bound by the mores of the time—temptation was marketed through long skirts or subtle language, not explicit nudity.[3] In the 1920s, sex in advertising escalated; while showing the backs of women's knees remained taboo, marketing of silk hosiery helped create the "flapper" image.[4] Sex in advertising gradually escalated into the 1930s, when nudes first appeared in American advertising.[5] In the 1940s and 1950s, "the treatment of sex in advertising shifted from an almost reverent dignity to casual humor."[6] The 1960s sexual revolution opened the door the rest of the way.

Between the mid-1960s and mid-1980s, use of sexily dressed men and women in magazine advertising increased significantly; between the mid-1980s and mid-1990s, the percentage of magazine advertisements containing a man and a woman involved in sexually suggestive behavior shot from about 20 percent to over 50 percent.[7] According to Barry Gunter of the University of Sheffield, one 1998 study showed that "12 percent of advertisements from a sample of over 500 commercials recorded from one week of network television contained less than fully dressed models...One percent of the advertisements contained verbal references to sex, 7 percent contained physical references, and 8 percent contained physical contact of a sexual nature."[8] That may not sound like a lot, but when you realize that the average child watches 40,000 commercials per year, it's a ton.[9]

Sexual advertising is overwhelmingly targeted at the youth market, and has been for more than two decades. In 1981, for example, movie star Brooke Shields, who was all of fifteen at the time, starred in Calvin Klein's jeans campaign, in which she purred, "Know what comes between me and my Calvins? Nothing." Three network-owned stations in New York refused to run the ads, but sales of the jeans skyrocketed 300 percent after the first commercials hit.[10]

Advertising has only gotten worse since the arrival of the porn generation, with the rise of brand marketing like the repulsive Abercrombie & Fitch (A&F). When they're not marketing thong underwear with the words "Wink, Wink" or "Eye Candy" printed on them to seven- to fourteen-year-old girls, they're putting out pornography catalogues designed to pique the interests of teenagers. Company spokesperson Hampton Carney called the underwear "cute and fun and sweet," by the way.[11]

Illinois Lieutenant Governor Corinne Wood called for a boycott of A&F to protest its November 1998 catalogue, the cover of which portrayed four girls and a boy in bed together, with the girls triumphantly holding aloft the boy's boxers.[12] In 1999, A&F put out its Christmas catalogue, entitled "Naughty or Nice." In the catalogue, porn star Jenna Jameson was featured lying on a bed with her rear absolutely visible; she also conducts an explicit interview with the catalogue. The catalogue printed a "mock interview with a Santa Claus portrayed as a child molester" for good measure.[13]

When they're not marketing to the teeny-boppers, A&F markets to the 18–22 crowd. "Our customer is actually the eighteen- to twenty-two-year-old college student," says Carney. "We are trying to keep it as cool, editorial, edgy, and sexy as possible."[14]

The 2001 A&F Spring *Quarterly* contained an article entitled "XXX Adventure: Get Wet, Set & Go on Spring Break." The article suggested that a Catholic high school senior in love with a nun persuade her to break her vows. The issue includes an interview with a male porn star of over 1,700 films, who gives career advice. Illinois state senator Patrick O'Malley, a Republican, described the marketing strategy as "relying heavily on shock value in its advertising, using not only photos but especially narrative that is obscene." And Bill Johnson, the president of the American Decency Association, observed that "[t]heir marketing is based on the recognition that teens like edgy, line-crossing, taboo things."[15]

The 2001 A&F summer catalogue featured naked bodies galore, and required a valid photo ID for purchase. William F. Buckley Jr. commented, "[T]here was never a pitch more naked than Abercrombie's: the non-display of its products, in deference to sheer biological exhibitionism."[16]

The 2003 A&F Christmas catalogue was pulled from shelves because of the outcry it provoked (although Carney protested that A&F pulled the catalogue "because we just launched a new perfume called NOW and we had to make space on the counter for the product").[17] This issue of the catalogue included the usual nudity, as well as advice from a "sexpert" urging kids to get as much sexual experience as possible, including "sex for three." After Dr. James Dobson went on the offensive regarding the advertising/pornography, A&F removed the catalogue from its stores.[18] Carney wants to make sure, however, that no one gets the wrong idea about A&F: "Our spring quarterly will be back in stores mid-January and everyone will see that there's no change in our editorial policy," he said. "We will still have butts and partial nudity."[19]

As Joseph Sabia of the *Cornell Review* points out, A&F also markets gay sexuality like it's going out of style. They employ noted gay photographer Bruce Weber and advertise in *Out* magazine.[20] Cathy Crimmins, self-proclaimed "fag-hag" and author of *How the Homosexuals Saved Civilization*, actually writes that fraternity guys wearing A&F are imitating a gay lifestyle by buying into Weber's ideas of male beauty.[21]

Sabia concludes that "sex is all around us in advertising, but A&F's practices are particularly troubling with regard to its stealth campaign to sexualize young teenagers."[22] To that end, A&F distributes an "outta here" checklist for college life: "C is for 'condoms in ample supply.' M is 'martini shaker.' Q is for 'queen sized bed.' P is 'progressive politics.'"[23] A&F dispenses advice on sex as well. On "dorm room seduction": "it's okay to start on the sofa, but don't stay there." Other insights include "invest in a good, plush rug. The floor can be fun," and "negotiate a special group rate at a local motel, which your entire quad can take advantage of."[24] Just make sure you're not the second group to rent that room.

Then there's clothing brand FCUK. FCUK stands for French Connection, United Kingdom. But hey, kids—if you switch the U and the C, then, by golly, you've got a naughty word. So use FCUK as a brand name, and wait for the dyslexics in the crowd to figure it the coarse new brand. What a gimmick!

Thought up by advertising guru Trevor Beattie, the new FCUK brand name pushed French Connection's 1997 interim profits to an 81 percent increase.[25] Those clever marketing execs also came up with slogans (for use in Britain) like "Fcuk like a bunny" and "Fcuk for England."[26] In America, meanwhile, FCUK began advertising in Times Square, with slogans like "i you want" and "night all long"—see, the phrases are mixed up too, get it? Just like the letters in fcuk![27] Other FCUK ad campaigns have included ads for glasses, accompanied by a picture of two men and the word "homospecsuality";[28] an ad depicting a beautiful woman walking toward the camera, with the copy reading "think my clothes off";[29] an ad containing two pictures of women and the caption "yes, both."[30] When New York City banned taxi tops from carrying ads like these, FCUK countered with an ad insulting the United States—the text reads simply "brave but not free."[31]

Lynda Lee-Potter, a columnist for the *London Daily Mail*, encouraged her readers to boycott French Connection because its advertising message was "If you want to get laid, wear our clothes."[32] FCUK took retaliatory action by creating an ad campaign based specifically on that idea: Its new ads depict virile young men and women, with the word "guaranteed" plastered across them.[33]

The FCUK campaign certainly garnered a good deal of attention for French Connection. That was, after all, the goal. Beattie himself said as much: "I have two views on advertising. One is that it must always be simple with a single-minded message. Secondly, it should get noticed, because otherwise you're wasting your money."[34]

Thirty years ago, uttering the f-word in a classroom would get you suspended from school. Today, it's common to see American youths running around in sweatshirts marked "FCUK."

Why market this stuff to youth? Because the money's already there—today's parents are so afraid that their child won't think of them as a "friend" that they've stopped exercising the power of the purse. One marketing researcher refers to such buys as "guilt money": "Parents say, 'Here's the credit card. Why don't you go online and buy something because I can't spend time with you.'"[35] In 2002 alone, teenagers spent over $100 billion, and got their parents to spend $50 billion more. Alissa Quart, author of *Branded: The Buying and Selling of Teenagers*, writes that "those under twenty-five are now the fastest-growing group filing for bankruptcy"; she adds that marketing experts are now targeting nine- to thirteen-year-olds as well, "prepping the kids to be the sort of teen consumers that companies wish for."[36] Advertisers spend more than $12 billion per year on advertising aimed at the youth market.[37]

As Juliann Sivulka explains, "today's youth-oriented ads touch on every area of sexual pleasure and perversion...If today's young generation of readers are less shocked by open sexuality than their grandparent's coquettish suggestions, can culture be far from a time when any sexual inclination will be freely portrayed in advertising?"[38]

Porn sells meat

In early 2005, the fast food chain Hardee's (known in some regions as Carl's Jr.) began a marketing campaign for their "Monster Thick-burger"—an enormous greasy concoction—by running a series of ridiculously oversexed TV ads. In a spot titled "Fist Girl," a blond woman in a strapless dress and high heels sticks her entire fist in her mouth, then pulls it back out and smiles. In a companion spot, a different woman in a spaghetti-strap top crams her mouth full of plastic straws. "How do you know if you can eat the largest double burger in the country?" asks the announcer in each spot. "There's one way to find out."

Another Hardee's ad for the Thickburger was set to Foghat's rhythmic "Slow Ride," and featured model Cameron Richardson writhing around on top of a bucking mechanical bull while appearing to have oral sex with an oversized cheeseburger. The announcer says: "We could've shown you some cowboy, sitting around a campfire, eating the new Western Bacon Thickburger. But then ... who'd wanna see that?"

Writing for the online journal Slate, reviewer Seth Stevenson suggested: "I guess if the Thickburger qualifies as food porn, the Monster Thickburger is XXX hard-core food porn, with cheese bondage and underage buns and deviant bacon orgies."

The ad game is all about selling perceptions—perceptions of sex, perceptions of products. In most cases, sex is merely juxtaposed with the product, the tacit message being: "Buy our product, get laid." From cheeseburgers to razors to cars, simple juxtaposition does the trick. Britney Spears' new perfume, Curious, is marketed by selling her as a sex symbol. Commercials show Spears checking into a hotel, exchanging glances with a guy checking in to the adjoining room. The *Dallas Morning News* details what happens next: "They share a wild, pant-pant fantasy as they stand on either side of the wall, straining to hear (and feel) each other. Just when you think Britney can't get any classier, she figures out a way."[39]

In some of these cases, perceptions of sex are sold plainly, without any mention of product save a company logo. Joe's Jeans, for example, shows the naked female body in many of its ads, accompanied only by their brand.[40] That's the idea behind the Victoria's Secret advertising strategy as well: Sell the models, sell the brand. Yes, they're wearing the lingerie, but who's really looking at that? The Victoria's Secret $10 million fashion extravaganza, TV's "Sexiest Night," is all about using attractive models to drop jaws and open wallets. Scalpers were selling 2003 show tickets for upwards of $10,000.[41] The buyers certainly weren't paying all that money to see a few sets of bras and panties.

In other cases, products are sold by equating use of the product with the joys of sex. In the movie *When Harry Met Sally*, Meg Ryan fakes an orgasm while eating at a restaurant with Billy Crystal. "I'll have what she's having," a female onlooker tells her waitress. Ads have been copying the movie ever since, selling products through blatant allusions to orgasm.[42]

Herbal Essences promotes its shampoo in commercials depicting beautiful women showering and washing their hair until, shrieking, they reach orgasm. In one of their newer orgy-style commercials, "Streaking Party," a large group of men and women streak their hair while dressed in towels and robes. On their website, Herbal Essences instructs customers how to hold their own "streaking parties." Helpful tips include "Let your imagination run wild. Dare to go bare. Think bikinis, halter tops, sarongs, and terry cloth robes," "Give out 'naughty' bags," and "Satisfy your inner cravings."[43] This is innuendo taken to a whole new level. Herbal Essences spokeswoman Anitra Marsh explains that the original "Totally Organic Experience" ad "set a new bar for advertisements and pushed the envelope at the time, but in a way that stayed true to the product itself. The product is really about the experience."[44] I'm not sure that washing your hair classifies as an "experience." If it does, are you promiscuous for using Head & Shoulders some days and Herbal Essences others?

Miller Lite's infamous "Catfight" ad campaign, which ran during the 2003 NFL Playoffs, played on male fantasies about lesbians, depicting two very well-endowed, attractive women (one of them a *Playboy* girl) sitting at a coffee shop, discussing the relative merits of Miller Lite. "Doesn't Miller Lite taste great?" the blonde bombshell asks her brunette friend. "Yeah," the brunette responds, "but I drink it because it's less filling." They begin screaming at each other: "Great taste!" "Less filling!" After pushing over the table, they begin clawing at each other. They end up stripping down to their lingerie and catfighting in a pool, and then in a vat of mud. The commercial then cuts to a bar, where one guy tells another: "Now *that* would make a great commercial." The other guy responds: "Yeah, who wouldn't want to watch that?" The camera then pans to their girlfriends, who are not amused. The pitch for Miller Lite ensues. In the uncut version, one of the guys then says: "I've got an idea for the ending." Cut back to the two mud-covered women, one of whom turns to the other and says: "Let's make out!" The commercial ends with them swapping lesbian spit.

Apparently, men are so ridiculously stupid that basic juxtaposition of lesbian sex and beer is enough to sell the product. That's the joke, said Miller company spokewoman Molly Reilly: "We're making a little bit of fun of it." Oh. Too bad that according to Reilly, 30 percent of the people who saw the commercial were under twenty-one.[45]

Coors did its own version of the Sapphic sell during the same playoff season. Their commercial, "Love Songs," featured a montage of different things guys like, including several shots of two good-looking blonde sisters making eyes at the camera. As Shari Waxman of Salon.com wrote, "Besides being just plain hot, the aesthetically gifted twenty-six-year-old blondes featured in the campaign are twin sisters. Twin sisters whose four blue eyes seem always to be saying, 'Hey boys, anyone up for a three-way?' Sisters in a three-way? Gross."[46] Coors's ad company, Foote Cone & Belding, Chicago, doesn't see it that way: "Nobody would argue men love women, so why not two of them? That's why twins rings so true."[47]

Hillary Chura, a reporter for *Advertising Age*, stated that the Coors spot worked wonders: "Previously, the brand appealed to women and older men, and the problem with that is that they don't drink as much as twenty-something guys."[48] The commercials were so popular that they spawned a series of ESPN *Sportscenter* imitations, with new screaming lyrics each week, and cheerleaders as the twins. The "twins" ads were the highest-scoring spots in Coors history, according to the fortuitously named Ron Askew, marketing chief for Coors. Askew defended his use of the twins as sex objects, claiming that they were actually "leaders, not followers. The women are in control. They're the ones inviting you into the party at 4 a.m."[49]

That logic seems a bit askew; it would mean that prostitutes are not sex objects, since they are usually the ones inviting johns into entanglements.

Unintended consequences

The focus on sex in advertising shapes cultural beliefs about beauty and gender to increasing levels among the porn generation. Fifty years ago, the emaciated waifs who resemble twelve-year-old boys more than women would never have populated our billboards and our television screens to such an extent. Now, young girls are dieting in order to look like them. Barry Gunter of the University of Sheffield states: "Idealized body images in advertising may contribute to lower levels of self-esteem, especially in relation to their own body shape, among some individuals. These effects most commonly occur among young women...A number of experimental studies have indicated that exposure to advertisements containing images of alluring models with slim physiques can result in lowered body self-esteem and greater overestimation of own body size and weight, especially among young women."[50]

According to the International Journal of Eating Disorders, by fourth grade an incredible 80 percent of American girls have been, or are currently on a diet. Forty percent of six-year-old girls wished they were thinner, and half will have tried dieting by age eight.[51] According to another study, 53 percent of American girls dislike their bodies by age thirteen; that figure rises to 78 percent by age seventeen. Joan Brumberg, author of *The Body Project: An Intimate History of American Girls*, elaborates: "Although elevated body angst is a great boost to corporate profits, it saps the creativity of girls and threatens their mental and physical health."[52]

The objectified image of women in advertising damages girls on an emotional level as well. The women in these ads are sexy, risqué, and often quite aggressive. Oversexed advertising is not likely to benefit normal girls: If guys can get their rocks off just by watching a Guess? ad, how can the "normal" girl compete? The only way to compete is to imitate. The "liberated" woman model encourages girls to show off for the benefit of their male counterparts, all in the name of equality.

Meanwhile, men who used to be considered effeminate are the new standard-bearers for male beauty. Shaved pecs, toned abs, and bleached hair are all the rage in the age of the metrosexual. It was Calvin Klein who initially set the trend with his underwear ads.[53] Soon, everyone had jumped aboard. Soloflex, the exercise equipment company, put out ads with a female hand reaching out to touch muscular athletes; the caption read "A hard man is good to find." Jerry Wilson, founder of Soloflex, explained, "There's no way I can sell the product without selling sex."[54] Tom Shales of the *Washington Post* noted the new "manly" image: "It's a pecs-and-biceps world now."[55]

Gay sex/advice columnist Dan Savage was more blunt: "That our culture is now thoroughly dominated by gay men is not some paranoid Christian conservative's fantasy...but a fact of life. *Queer Eye for the Straight Guy* confirmed something everyone already knows: outside of rap and hip-hop culture, stylish gay men...are the only tastemakers. And gay men weren't content to just setting tastes in jackets and hair products and cowhide accent chairs. Hardly. We were, however subtly, setting sexual tastes as well. Out went the virile man (so long, Burt Reynolds!) and in came the vulnerable boy (hello, Ashton Kutcher!)."[56]

Men are market-oriented, and they want to provide what women want—so they allowed the gay ideal to become the reality by buying into it wholesale. The image sold by advertising becomes the goal for men and women, but the reality doesn't live up to the fantasy. Constant pornography doesn't equate to happiness or even sex appeal; ultimately, this coarseness translates to boredom.

A 1999 study published in the *Journal of the American Medical Association* found that sexual dysfunction affected 43 percent of women and 31 percent of men. Over 25 percent of women 18–29 said they didn't find sex pleasurable and younger women (18–31) were more likely to have sexual problems than older women.[57] More sexual visibility hasn't made people more happy—it's made them more critical of themselves, more unfulfilled, more unhappy. When our culture transforms a beautiful act between man and woman into a public act catering to individuals, you undermine the fundamental value of sex.

Debbie does billboards

Paris Hilton is famous for one reason, and one reason only: She's a fabulously rich slut. Hilton starred in the "sex [tape] seen around the world" with her then-boyfriend Rick Solomon;[58] she was nineteen at the time, while Solomon was thirty.[59] At least nine other sex tapes were said to be in existence as well, including a lesbian sex tape with Playboy playmate Nicole Lenz.[60] The sexually uninhibited Hilton became a target for Larry Flynt of *Hustler* fame, who released pictures of Hilton sharing some lesbian tongue at a nightclub.[61] As Conan O'Brien observed, "*Hustler* magazine announced that it will feature photos of Paris Hilton making out with another woman, while the woman fondles Paris's breasts. So the search continues for a photo of Paris Hilton not having sex."[62]

Hilton has parlayed her tramp reputation into a number of major advertising gigs. She was chosen as the Guess? jeans girl for Guess, Inc.'s 2004 "sexy fall ad campaign."[63] Although Hilton is bonier than past Guess? girls, according to the *New York Observer*, "her bad-girl image jibes with the clothing company's porn-lite ad campaigns."[64] The ads helped prompt a 13.6 percent same-store sales jump in September 2004.[65] Unfortunately for her, she was actually dumped from a planned Burger King ad campaign over her porny past.[66]

Professional porn star Jenna Jameson has made an advertising mark of her own. Jameson, who will quite literally sleep with anything that moves, posed for a billboard in Times Square in New York, promoting her website, clubjenna.com, and her filmmaker's site, vivid.com (both hardcore porn sites). Jameson stands in a mesh top, covering her nipples with her hands; the caption reads, "WHO SAYS THEY CLEANED UP TIMES SQUARE?" Vivid.com advertises on billboards along the Sunset Strip in Los Angeles, as well. One ad shows several of Vivid's porn stars, with the caption: "Look, we can even erect a billboard." Jameson has her own billboard on Sunset Boulevard for her lesbian porn flick, *Krystal Method*.

Aside from advertising her own porn videos and pictures, Jameson also represents the face of Pony sneakers, which placed her on billboards across America, as well as in the pages of *Vanity Fair* and *Vibe* magazines.[67] She does ads for Jackson Guitars as well.[68] Come Chantrel (yes, that's her actual name), vice president and general manager for Pony at the Firm, elucidated the attraction of porn in advertising: "When I grew up in the '80s in Paris, models were the ultimate feminine ideal . . . For the twenty-year-old kid, porn stars have kind of replaced what models used to represent."[69]

Youngsters across the country are catching on to the "porn as pop culture wave." "Porn Star" T-shirts for young girls are flying off shelves.[70] "Porn Star" stickers now adorn skateboards and backpacks across the nation. And that's aside from the millions of dollars in products these whores are pushing.

We shouldn't fool ourselves into thinking that the porn community doesn't understand what's happening. *Adult Video News* editor in chief Tim Connelly touts the new cross-generational marketing, averring, "There's been a glamorization, coupled with a relaxation of society's mores...It's permeating the culture now, particularly with young people. There's a whole new generation that's grown up with MTV and video porn and girls cavorting around with musicians."[71]

Buying into a fantasy

"Today, consumers don't buy products, they buy brands. They buy a lifestyle that they can wear," says Nancy Haley, co-founder and CEO of Tehama, a clothing company.[72] According to the *National Catholic Reporter*, advertising guru Leo Burnett's philosophy of advertising is "People no longer buy products; they buy lifestyles"; his clients included McDonald's, Coca-Cola, and Nintendo.[73] And there is no easier lifestyle to sell than a sexy one.

"[A]ll these sexual images aren't intended to sell us on sex—they are intended to sell us on shopping," writes Jean Kilbourne. "The desire they want to inculcate is not for orgasm but for more gismos. This is the intent of the advertisers—but an unintended consequence is the effect these images have on real sexual desire and real lives...The wreckage that ensues when people try to emulate the kind of sexuality glorified in the ads and the popular culture is everywhere, from my house to the White House. And many who choose not to act on these impulsive sexual mandates nonetheless end up worrying that something is wrong with them, with their flawed and ordinary and all-too-human relationships."[74]

We live in a consumer culture. Advertising caters to what we want. As human beings, we want sex. It's as simple as that. But by taking advantage of sex to sell us products, advertising demeans sex to the level of any other basic physical activity. It removes sex from the realm of the spiritual or the valuable. Advertisers prostitute themselves for our money, and as consumers, we play the part of the willing johns. At a certain point, it's difficult to morally differentiate between paying for sex on the street and buying a pair of jeans—the commercials have guaranteed you that in return for your purchase, you'll receive sexual attention. And that should be our goal—shouldn't it?

CHAPTER EIGHT

TV VS. VIRGINITY

"The people were cool. I wanted to try what they were doing on the show."

THIRTEEN-YEAR-OLD MANHATTAN BOY[1]

W e've been called the MTV Generation. Considering that MTV claims that 73 percent of boys and 78 percent of girls aged twelve to nineteen watch their programming, it's an accurate name.[2] A 2000 poll of college seniors at the top fifty-five U.S. universities showed that while only 23 percent could name James Madison as the father of the Constitution, 99 percent knew who the MTV cartoon characters Beavis and Butthead were.[3]

MTV sets standards in dress and in behavior, and even in thought. When Beavis and Butthead were at their peak in the 1990s, Beavis's snorting laugh was imitated ad infinitum (and absurdum) at junior high schools around the country. The show, which primarily consisted of two teenage idiots blowing snot into their sodas and lighting pets on fire, among other inane activities, became a cultural icon.[4] Why was it popular? Because these primitively drawn, headbanging, acne-ridden morons were representatives of an increasingly aimless generation. "Beavis and Butthead are regressive and proud of it; mindless role models for lethargic teens who don't want the bother of growing up," writes John Lyttle of the *Independent* (UK).[5] If Beavis and Butthead were losers with nothing better to do than sniff paint and torture frogs, what kind of losers did that make their viewers? The *Beavis and Butthead* audience was the constituency of the degraded, and *Beavis and Butthead* were their elected representatives.

Even years after *Beavis and Butthead* went off the air, they remain representative of typical MTV programming: vulgar, stupid, repulsive. MTV is morally relativist in every conceivable way. Even aside from its music videos, MTV's programming is oversexed cultural excrement targeted at kids. As media critic L. Brent Bozell states, "It's still the Temptation channel, a 24-hour hangout selling easy sex, swagger, and swearing—all aimed, directly and deliberately, at children."[6]

The Parents Television Council, run by Bozell, conducted a study of MTV during the channel's spring break raunch-fest. They found that in 171 hours of programming, there were 1,548 sexual scenes "containing 3,056 depictions of sexual dancing, gesturing, or various forms of nudity, and another 2,881 verbal sexual references. That averages out to about 18 physical and 17 verbal references to sex per hour."[7]

One of the shows that has a specifically sexual focus is *The Real World*, the famed reality TV show with a simple premise: Throw together a group of young "adults," put them in a big city, and watch the raunch develop.[8] MTV bills the show this way: "This is the true story of seven strangers, picked to live in a house and have their lives taped, and find out what happens when people stop being polite and start getting REAL."[9] The show is cast for sex appeal, chemistry, and more sex appeal. Applicants are asked questions like "How do you feel about cheating?" and "What did you do last night?"[10]

Pick an episode at random from the most recent season of *The Real World*—any episode—and you're guaranteed several instances of soft-core porn—or worse. For example, *The Real World: Philadelphia* Episode 20,

"Romantic Getaway," featured two of the female roommates, Shavonda and Sarah, losing their tops on the beach; Shavonda oiling male roommate Landon's "nice ass"; Shavonda and Sarah French-kissing each other during a game of Truth or Dare; Landon losing his shorts during Truth or Dare; Sarah asking male roommate Keramo "how many inches" he is; Shavonda making out with Landon on a bed; Shavonda and Landon going to bed together.[11] The show's producers arrange for the cast members to be surrounded by alcohol constantly to encourage hookups—in *The Real World: Las Vegas*, both a bar and a hot tub were purposefully placed in the living room. And the casting directors do their job well: *Real World* housemates have no shame, and the few who react uncomfortably to the constant sexual activity are denounced as prudes or Puritans.

MTV's goal is to get everyone laid. That's the stated premise behind their show *Wanna Come In?* "Two geeks bump greasy heads with one another to win money for a hot date with two beautiful girls," the MTV.com website eagerly explains. *Wanna Come In?* is the new show where nerds sweat through several challenges in an effort to get invited up to a babe's pad. The geeks are not alone, though, they'll each have their own personal 'stud' coach to help them hear those coveted words: 'Wanna come in?'"[12] After all, geeks need some lovin' too.

There's nothing transcendent about the MTV mindset. But why should there be, when their audience scorns transcendence in favor of materialism and physicality? MTV covers the physicality angle with *The Real World* and Co., and they push materialism in several of their other series, like *Pimp My Ride*, *My Super Sweet 16* and *MTV Cribs*. In *Pimp My Ride*, the eminently talented Xzibit, "Pimp Master of Ceremonies himself," makes over ugly cars.[13] *MTV Cribs* centers on the houses of the rich and famous. "Don't miss the only show that hooks you up with exclusive insight into your heroes' cribs," MTV.com breathlessly exclaims.[14]

MTV also glorifies the lives of the wealthy and shallow with shows like *Newlyweds*, *Laguna Beach: The Real Orange County*, and *Sweet 16*. The latter revolves around spoiled fifteen-year-olds planning their Sweet

Sixteen parties.[15] The show is really a survey in bad parenting. Natalie's "birthday wish" comes true in the form of a $900 dress and an $800 nail job.[16] Ava's becomes reality when her divorced parents buy her a Road Ranger and a custom-made beige gown that looks as though she is "wearing nothing but rhinestones." The most hilarious moment of the episode comes when Ava whines that her mother won't get her the beige dress: "If you stop whining, I'll get it for you," her father shouts. Way to impose your will, there, Dad. Ava makes her grand Sweet Sixteen entrance being carried by four members of the Loyola polo team who are "cute, sexy, and have good bodies."[17]

But the oversexed worldview of MTV doesn't stop at that channel— the same people control MTV 2, Comedy Central, TV Land, VH1, Spike TV, and Nickelodeon, among others.

Spike TV, the so-called "First Network for Men," panders to the animalistic, ridiculously idiotic side of the male mind with a veritable flood of soft-core porn and violence. "We have a phrase here: 'This channel is PG-25,'" explains Albie Hecht, Spike's president, a former exec at Nickelodeon and other MTV networks. "It's somewhere between PG-13 and R...We use the word 'raw' a lot around here...The eighteen- to thirty-four male is okay with the way life really is. They don't have a problem with words like bulls—." In a classic example of defining deviancy down, Hecht calls these viewers "the new normal."[18]

MTV also controls Nickelodeon, a channel aimed directly at children. Nick's programming has always been more edgy than its kiddie competitors. In the early 1990s, Nickelodeon aired *The Ren and Stimpy Show*, a gross-out cartoon show that targeted eight- to twelve-year-olds. While maintaining its spot on Nickelodeon, *Ren and Stimpy* became so popular that it eventually found its way to the mothership, MTV, where it aired on Saturday nights.[19]

Nick's modern programming is no better, including shows like *Zoey 101*, starring Britney Spears's little sister Jamie Lynn;[20] *Unfabulous*, a "coming-of-age" show starring Julia Roberts's niece, Emma;[21] and *All That*, the pre-teen answer to *Saturday Night Live*, former stars of which include Amanda Bynes and Jamie Lynn. Each of the shows is a kid version of something that can be found on Comedy Central or MTV, and each features a kid MTV would like to make into a cultural icon, a la Britney Spears or Christina Aguilera.

MTV's network of programming shows us what happens absent any moral grounding. Mired in nihilism, it opens a sex-obsessed world for teens who aren't interested in doing anything productive in their spare time. Killing time has become an aim unto itself. In an age of growing convenience and falling academic standards, there's more and more spare time to be had. And that means more and more time in front of the TV. As of 1999, the average seventh grader watched four hours of television per day.[22]

This boredom helps explain rapper P. Diddy's ludicrous "VOTE OR DIE" campaign, pushed heavily by MTV.[23] How else are you going to get through to teenagers who couldn't care less about life, let alone politics? The only way to get their attention is to threaten loss of life. Even nihilists are afraid of death. P. Diddy didn't have go *that* far over the top—he could have just threatened the loss of Xboxes and cable access—but somehow, "VOTE OR GO AMISH" didn't have the same ring to it.

Hollywoodites insist that they have to make their programming more edgy, since today's kids are more edgy. In the words of *American Pie* producer Warren Zide, "People need to respect the fact that kids are smarter than they get credit for. We like to speak up to kids rather than down to them."[24] American kids are not smarter than they used to be—they're more jaded than they used to be. Are kids truly "smarter" because by age twelve, they describe themselves as "flirtatious, sexy, trendy, cool"?[25] Or are they striving to imitate the "adult," "smart" behavior modeled for them by pop culture? The loss of innocence and the rise of jadedness is a direct result of negligent parenting and immersion of children into an ever-deepening pool of pop culture materialism—a trend that MTV thrives on.

Paying for sex

The only channels more extreme than MTV are the premium cable channels like HBO and Showtime. The shows aired on the pay channels are just as trendsetting among the porn generation as anything on network television.

The show that has shaped more young single females than anything else on television is *Sex and the City*, which aired exclusively on HBO and revolved around the sex lives of four young single women in Manhattan: Carrie Bradshaw (Sarah Jessica Parker), Charlotte York (Kristin Davis), Samantha Jones (Kim Cattrall), and Miranda Hobbes (Cynthia Nixon). These women act like men with regard to sex, willing to sleep with anyone at any time—and the series shows every minute of the steamy sex. They discuss sex with all the panache of a drunken sailor. They obsess over shopping, they glamorize drinking and one-night stands, and they shun all aspects that make femininity attractive—all while whining about the inability to find a nice single man with whom to have a relationship.

The glamorization of slut activity is without limit. Over the first three years of the series, Samantha has sex with forty different partners.[26] Here's Miranda on male genitalia: "Women don't care. We care about nice arms, great eyes, big dick. I have never once heard a woman say, he had such a big, full scrotum."[27] Samantha on dating strategy: "Wait a minute, you've been dating this guy for three weeks and you haven't seen his balls yet? Oh come on! Get with the program!"[28] Charlotte and Samantha discuss ejaculation:

> CHARLOTTE: "My father gave me the most beautiful pearl necklace for my sweet sixteen."

> SAMANTHA: "Actually we're talking about the other kind of pearl necklace. You know, the kind where the guy decorates your neck?"[29]

It should come as no surprise that Michael Patrick King, the executive producer for *Sex and the City*, also wrote for *Murphy Brown* and was a consulting producer for *Will & Grace*.[30] Predictably, King is a gay lapsed Catholic.[31] King describes the men on the series as "the revolving door."[32]

The creators of the show decided to make Miranda a single mother because "We thought, 'Okay, what's the worst thing we could do to Miranda?'"[33] That's the kind of moral perspective the writers bring to the series.

The show is a cultural phenomenon. "We watch it every Sunday night—we have dinner parties," explains Amber Campisi, twenty-one, of Southern Methodist University. "We sit and drink and watch the show." "We'll watch the whole DVD of the first season in one day," agrees Chevon Villaneuva, twenty-two, of SMU.[34] "Even if 'sex this good can't last forever,' at least it can be remembered that long.... Fashion trends, sexual vocabulary and dating rules established on *Sex and the City* soon found their way into mainstream fashion, sex and dating rituals," sighs Sarah Portlock of the *Washington Square News*.[35]

The *Sex and the City* phenomenon has deep societal effects. As Riley Mendoza, a twenty-two-year-old woman from Virginia and one of my classmates at Harvard Law, explained to me: "I really don't like the *Sex and the City* idea of women thinking of sex like men have thought about it for a long time. Definitely at Harvard, and I think at other colleges as well, there's this idea that feminism is about women being allowed to do whatever they want and being able to act like men. Talk about sex like it's not a big deal, talk about how to enjoy it, have one-night stands. It becomes a chatty thing to talk about. I was a part of a female social club at Harvard, and that was the topic du jour—sex. It made people feel empowered, cool. I was not used to that at all, coming from a small town, and coming from a family that didn't talk like that at all. I always thought that it was a little hollow. That in the end, women don't think about sex the way that men do, and that people get hurt a lot. But you were supposed to act like you don't care. I think that women biologically do care. And that women can't maintain these no-commitment relationships without getting hurt."[36]

Sex and the City has a substantial following among teenage girls with ignorant parents, as well. Patti Lewis of Berlin, Vermont took a *Sex and the City* bus tour with her teenage daughter, Kate, who had seen every episode of the repulsive series. "I love the show," Patti told Meena

Thiruvengadam of the *San Antonio Express-News*. 'They dare to say and do things that some women just can't say and do, and they make it so funny."[37] Julie Salamon of the *New York Times* had no problem admitting in her column that her "fourteen-year-old daughter and her girlfriends were found in front of our television giggling happily at *Sex and the City* in its unexpurgated form on HBO. Perhaps a sign of our licentious times, they didn't flinch when I sat down to join them. But I quickly left, anyway, realizing I didn't really want to encounter the show's naughtiest pleasures with my child and her pals next to me."[38]

It apparently never occurred to Ms. Salamon that her fourteen-year-old daughter and her friends shouldn't be encountering the show's "naughtiest pleasures" at all. And like a case of genital herpes, the show refuses to go away—it was recently picked up for syndication by TBS.

HBO's subscribers know what they're getting. In June 1998, HBO's top-rated show was the sex documentary *Real Sex 19*, followed by *Real Sex 20*, followed by *Pimps Up, Ho's Down*. HBO's highest-rated series was, of course, *Sex and the City*.[39]

Showtime goes even further—instead of straight promiscuity, they promote homosexuality. They have to go further than HBO, considering they've been in HBO's shadow for the last twenty years.[40] They promote the *Sex and the City* imitating, lesbian-celebrating *The L Word* with the tagline, "Same Sex. Different City," and posters of naked women. *Entertainment Weekly* describes the Sapphic lovefest: "*The L Word* is a meticulously packaged show—beautiful women; nifty fashions; slick, post-Pottery Barn furniture—that makes you say, 'Hey, I want to be a hot, successful lesbian living in Los Angeles with trendy friends and a work life that comes in short, dazzling spurts!'"[41]

While the cast maintains that they're doing the lesbian thing to bring tolerance to the world, they're not above pandering to male fantasies. "Conventionally, straight men watch lesbian sex, and there's that leering element, but we don't pander to it," insists executive producer-creator Ilene Chaiken. "But it's a sexy show and if that turns them on, I don't object to it."[42] Of course not. Even those who shill for sexual tolerance aren't above catering to males in their pursuit of ratings.

On Showtime, what's good for the goose is good for the gander, so they have a show revolving around male homosexuality as well: *Queer As Folk*. It's gay propaganda, pure and simple, with the requisite graphic sex. Even Howard Rosenberg, fanatically liberal critic for the *Los Angeles Times*, describes the show as "relentless cruising and graphically simulated sex, at the expense of character depth, in an assembly line of orgasms ultimately as tedious as it would be if the humpers and thumpers were straight instead of gay."[43]

Showtime and HBO maintain that they should be allowed license, considering that they're subscription-based. That ignores the fact that both HBO and Showtime have impacts beyond their immediate viewership. Their shows are promoted in print and on billboards. Their depictions of women and men are culturally accepted. Sarah Jessica Parker of *Sex and the City* models for GAP;[44] Kristin Davis models for Maybelline.[45] Davis and Cynthia Nixon star in an ad campaign for 7-Up. In the commercial, "Pampering," the two actresses lounge around in bathrobes as a male waiter serves them. Davis sees another male waiter coming, and says to Nixon, "Looks like our lunch has arrived." Appraising the handsome young man, Nixon quickly responds, "And he brought us grapes." The tagline: "When you add it all up, the only way to go is Up."[46]

When viewers add it all up, the only way to go is sex.

The sitcoms

Last year, the most famous television show of the 1990s came to a close. *Friends*, which centered around the lives, loves, and sexual encounters of six friends—Rachel (Jennifer Aniston), Phoebe (Lisa Kudrow), Monica (Courteney Cox), Ross (David Schwimmer), Chandler (Matthew Perry), and Joey (Matt LeBlanc).

The liberal sexual agenda pervaded the show. Sex had no consequences, and was readily available to all. According to one commentator, Rachel had twenty sexual partners over the ten-year life of the sitcom.[47] When the show premiered in 1994, even the socially liberal *Daily Variety* noted, "Moral and health issues are sidestepped altogether: *Friends* touts promiscuity and offers liberal samples of an openness that borders on empty-headedness. It's not much of a positive example for juves, though."[48]

Single motherhood was no problem. When Rachel got pregnant by Ross after a one-night stand, there was little public outcry. "I don't think the fans of the show really care that she's pregnant and not married," explained Mary Allen, director and founder of Genesis House, a Melbourne, Florida, shelter for homeless pregnant teenagers and women.[49] Even once the baby was born, the writers were careful to ensure that the baby wouldn't slow the action down. Instead, the baby simply disappeared from the screen. The same thing happened with Ross's baby (brought up by Ross's ex-wife and her lesbian lover), as well as Phoebe's surrogate triplets. Ignoring your kids is so convenient!

Homosexuality was glorified. Ross's ex-wife left him for another woman, and *Friends* became the first primetime show to broadcast a lesbian "wedding." Monica chastised Ross for initially opposing the lesbian union, arguing: "They love each other, and they wanna celebrate that love with the people that are close to them." Ross later rips into his ex-wife's parents for opposing her lesbianism, and when Ross's ex-wife has his baby, Phoebe explains that having a lesbian couple and absentee father for parents is just peachy: "Here's this little baby who has like three whole parents who care about it so much that they're fighting over who gets to love it the most. And it's not even born yet. It's just, it's just the luckiest baby in the whole world."[50]

As with other sex-filled shows, *Friends* was immensely popular among the youngest members of the porn generation. Since 2000, Phil Rosenthal of the *Chicago Sun-Times* wrote, *Friends* became "exponentially bigger in nearly every way when viewed against the changing landscape of network television, a business it helped alter through its success in attracting the young viewers advertisers covet."[51] Ann Savage, associate professor of media arts at Butler University in Indiana, teaches about *Friends* to her students. "They grew up with it," she says of her students. "They've been watching it since they were kids."[52]

The show promoted adolescent attitudes into adulthood for teenagers. *Friends* took the place of family, and lasting super-platonic relationships were unnecessary. *Friends* was essentially a ten-year-long sleep-away camp for twentysomethings, where responsibility took a back seat to fun. As Jennifer Frey of the *Washington Post* characterized it, the show is "[an] homage to endless adolescence, that fantasy world where no one has to grow up, not even when grown-up things happen to them."[53]

If *Friends* was the gold standard for 1990s sitcoms, *Will & Grace* took the silver. And this show was even more socially liberal than its birth mother. A gay man (Eric McCormack) and a straight woman (Debra Messing) lived together; the show revolved around both of their dating lives. Sample lines from the first episode of the series:

> GRACE (while lying in bed with her boyfriend): "Are you jealous?"

> WILL (while watching "ER"): "Honey, I don't need your man, I got George Clooney."

> GRACE: "Sorry, baby, he doesn't bat for your team."

> WILL: "Well, he hasn't seen me pitch."[54]

At one point in the show, Will and Grace consider having a baby together. Because, after all, what's better for raising a child than a single mother and a gay father? He's gay, of course, so she'll have to go to the obstetrician to get inseminated with Will's sperm, just like mom and pop used to do, way back when. "It's a tremendous story point and it is very complicated, obviously as in real life," Messing explained. "I think it's a very brave and exciting storyline to explore and pursue.... In New York, my dearest friends were gay men ... So probably the most gratifying part of doing *Will & Grace* is that for the first time on television there's a portrayal of a leading male gay character who is three-dimensional, complicated, humane, compassionate, loving and sensual. That's very important to the gay community, and I was insistent from the very beginning, before

I would get involved, that it be reflective of real live."[55] Propaganda in your living room, brought to you by NBC.

And Hollywood won't be policing itself anytime soon. When the Christian Action Network suggested that viewers be warned that *Will & Grace* contained homosexual content, they were given the cold shoulder. It was an "inhumane proposal that should be ignored," according to MPAA President Jack Valenti, and "outrageous" according to Norman Lear's People for the American Way.[56] "The mere idea that 'Will & Grace' could have been a mainstream hit twenty years ago is absurd," *Time* reported in December 2004. "Polls indicate that about half the population supports some form of gay union. And younger Americans (those under thirty) are vastly more accepting of gay marriage, gay adoption and homosexuality than the population in general. Simply put: While the Bush White House may be on the side of social conservatives, time is not."[57]

The vast majority of the sitcoms on network television today are immersed in sexual innuendo if not outright vulgarity. Aside from *Will & Grace*, NBC's primetime lineup includes the *Friends* spin-off *Joey*, revolving around the empty-headed, promiscuous actor made famous by Matt LeBlanc. CBS's primetime schedule carries *Yes, Dear* (two married couples, frequent jokes about sex), *Two and a Half Men* (Charlie Sheen bedding at least two and a half women per episode, plus a requisite *Friends*-style lesbian estranged wife), and *Still Standing* (a former hippie couple talking about their frisky youth), among others. On ABC, *Desperate Housewives* (glorifying all that is sleazy) is the staple of a schedule that also includes *George Lopez* (frequent sexual innuendo) and *Less Than Perfect* (the sex talk rarely stops). WB's big sitcom, *What I Like About You*, is awash in sexual innuendo.

None of these channels can touch FOX for sheer vulgarity, however. FOX's *That 70's Show* revels in its own jadedness and hedonism, and jokes about marijuana use and casual sex. *The Simpsons* helped define my generation, and it frequently engages in casual disdain for Christian values—gay marriage is legalized in Springfield in order to "strike a blow for civil rights," Reverend Lovejoy has no idea about the source for the scriptural proscription on homosexuality, and Marge (the good parent) has no problem introducing a "lesbian" couple to the children. *Malcolm in the Middle* portrays the insanely chaotic home life of Malcolm, whose parents are *very* into each other (visiting a porn store for home entertainment purposes, constant sexual references). *Family Guy* is more jaded, cynical, and vulgar than all the other shows put together. Masturbation, pornography, homosexuality—nothing is off limits.

All of this social libertinism takes place in the sitcom context, so there are never any consequences for actions taken, and everything is played for laughs. Making fun of those with traditional values is easy enough; it's always easier to satirize someone with standards than someone without them. There are two reasons for this. First, those with standards are commonly viewed as busybodies by others. External standards that apply to everyone are seen in today's society as overbearing and baroque. That's why sitcom parents are often portrayed as horrifically suppressive and oppressive—having standards is an "old folks" thing. Of course, when no one has any standards, or everyone has their own subjective standard, society decays . . . but that's beside the point.

Second, if certain people hold themselves and others to higher standards, it's more common for them to fall short and become the butt of jokes. If Jenna Jameson has adultery, there's nothing to laugh about. If Jerry Falwell does, he'll never hear the end of it. Hypocrisy as humor pushes destruction of standards.

But there's a subtext here that's important both for understanding the porn generation and understanding the reluctance of parents to criticize amoral activity. If a character is funny and likeable, it makes it tough to condemn his or her behavior. How can you reject premarital sex if your child is partaking in it? How can you condemn homosexuality if your best friend is gay? If you like Jack from *Will & Grace*, how can you say his homosexuality is sinful? If you like Rachel from *Friends*, how can you label her sexual exploits wrong?

The only danger for sitcoms comes when the laughter stops. When the jokes become stale, liberal activism isn't quite as funny as it was before—just ask the producers of *Ellen*.

Angst on Channel 11

The best way to hike ratings is to push boundaries, and television networks know it. Since 1976, the amount of sexual behavior shown during "family hour" (7 p.m. to 8 p.m.) has increased dramatically. By 1996, most networks didn't set aside the hour as "family." Professor Dale Kunkel of the University of California-Santa Barbara found that 61 percent of the shows he and his research partners watched during winter 1996 contained sexual behavior, more than doubling the amount visible in 1976. On average, a family hour of network television contained 8.5 references to or depictions of sex, over three times as many as in 1976.[58]

As Leslie Moonves, the president of CBS Television, stated, "We're competing against *Beverly Hills, 90210*, that has teenage sex every week...[My kids] know what those kids are doing on *90210*. We have stretched the envelope further."[59]

Oversexed teen angst dramas continue to make for insanely popular television and particularly dangerous values lessons. *90210* led the trend for the older members of the porn generation, giving them a show containing more sex than Amsterdam's red light district. A prom episode had the high school passing out condoms on the tables.[60] Another episode featured college students agonizing over the difficulties of abstaining from sex for twenty-four hours.[61] Another contained a college student and her boyfriend trying to have sex in an airplane lavatory; the next episode, the two were at a nightspot when the boyfriend asked, "Want to go to my place and get naked?" "So much," the girl responded."[62] *90210* was a cultural phenomenon, garnering 10 million viewers at its inception, and over half of those were teenagers.[63]

The latest incarnation of *90210* is FOX's hit show, *The O.C.* It's a soap opera about Orange County, in reality a particularly conservative part of California. But there's nothing conservative about this version of the O.C. Promiscuity, drugs, and alcohol are commonplace—in fact, they're the driving plot points. This show was designed "to retrace the boulevard *90210* tread before... *The O.C.* has set itself up to head down any number of paths that made its predecessor a camp hit."[64]

At its inception in early 2004, *The O.C.* grabbed an average of 9.6 million viewers.[65] By mid-January 2005, the show was garnering only 6.5 million viewers.[66] To reinvigorate the viewership, the creators did what they always do: push the envelope. This time, they used the tried and true shenanigan of the lesbian kiss. Marissa (Mischa Barton), the girl next door, discovers that she's in a sapphic romance with Alex (Olivia Wilde), the new-in-town barkeep. They end up making out on the beach. FOX got its ratings boost—the January 27 episode that started the lesbian relationship had 8.1 million viewers.[67] When straight sex won't do it for the viewers, going to the forbidden is always a savvy marketing move.

Of course, the makers wouldn't be as explicit about their motives as all of that. No, they're opening minds and charting new ground. "Teenagers go through this stuff," Barton told *USA Today.* "Parents need to accept it or not."[68]

Other successful *90210* knockoffs have included *Dawson's Creek* and *One Tree Hill*, both of which are based on a deep reservoir of sexuality and have promoted homosexuality to suit their ratings needs. *Buffy the Vampire Slayer* is essentially *90210* with vampire killing involved (and the requisite lesbianism as well). WB's *The Gilmore Girls* is an ode to single motherhood: Lorelai, the main character of the show, became pregnant at age sixteen and is a single mother to Rory. On these shows, virginity is depicted as loser-esque, sex is glorified, and experimentation with the same sex is considered normal. This conversation between best friends and sometimes lovers Dawson and Joey (female) from *Dawson's Creek* sums it up:

> DAWSON: "I'm the only one who has not had sex. I—I didn't plan on graduating a virgin. What—what happened?
>
> JOEY: "Best laid plans . . ."
>
> DAWSON: "This mythical college girlfriend I'm gonna have, will she have sex with me?"

JOEY: "Mm...no, sorry. She's a prude."

DAWSON: "Damn. I had such high hopes the last American virgin would fare better as an undergrad."

(The scene ends with Dawson making out with Joey.)[69]

This is the "witty," horny stuff that goes over as romance on teen television. Teens buy into it big time, and the kids on *The O.C.* and *Buffy* and *Dawson's Creek* and *One Tree Hill* set trends both sexual and ridiculous. When Seth, a lead character on *The O.C.*, started wearing an old-school "Members Only" jacket on the show, demand for the product among teens skyrocketed.

Real-life teens wish they could live like the teens Hollywood promotes. Everyone has sex, and relationships are deep and meaningful, even if they only last a couple episodes. There are never any consequences to any action, except for experiencing the angst of teenage life alongside the characters. When a generation becomes desensitized to the ramifications of the culture around them, it's natural to seek out any sort of feeling, even angst.

Uncontrollable

With the proliferation of cable channels, it becomes harder and harder for parents to monitor what is on the tube. Democrat Representative Edward Markey of Massachusetts expressed the problem well at a February 1997 congressional hearing: "We have moved from the era of *Leave It to Beaver* to the era of *Beavis and Butthead*. We have 8 million latchkey children in the United States. We have 18 million single moms. Mom is not home any longer with a peanut butter sandwich and glass of milk for Joey or Susie at noontime. Mom is working now. She's not home in most homes in America. The TV set plays the role of babysitter. That's America of the 1990s."[70]

Yet the media hates anyone who does attempt to direct television to a track that is more socially responsible. Anyone who inhibits freedom

of porn is an enemy, especially cultural conservatives like Michael Powell, the former chairman of the FCC. The *New York Times* editorial
board spoke for many other papers when it dragged Powell over the
coals after his resignation: "Mr. Powell's disappointing reign will be
remembered for the extremes to which he went to punish what he called
indecency...The broadcasts that were targeted have too often been
innocuous, such as the singer Bono's use of a single expletive after he
won a Golden Globe award, and the fines excessive, most notably the
$550,000 imposed on Viacom for Janet Jackson's 'wardrobe malfunc-
tion' at last year's Super Bowl. Media companies and artists have complained, with good reason, that the commission's indecency standards are
so vague that they are being discouraged from engaging in constitution-
ally protected speech."[71] Surely in any other context the *Times* would
never call a punitive damage award of $550,000 excessive for a corpo-
ration that earns billions of dollars a year in profits. Yet obscenity on
television is apparently a holy cause at the *Times*.

Powell is hardly the first politician to face such reaction. On May
19, 1992, in San Francisco, Vice President Dan Quayle spoke on the
topic of the Los Angeles riots. He discussed the problems of illegitimacy
and poverty, and he saved his strongest words for societal glamorization
of single motherhood. "Bearing babies irresponsibly is simply wrong,"
he averred. "Failing to support children one has fathered is wrong and
we must be unequivocal about this. It doesn't help matters when primetime TV has Murphy Brown, a character who supposedly epitomizes
today's intelligent, highly paid professional woman, mocking the importance of fathers by bearing a child alone and calling it another lifestyle
choice."[72]

The mainstream media immediately jumped on the vice president for
his statements about *Murphy Brown*. "It was a tried and true conservative tactic: when in doubt, attack the liberals," complained Andrew
Rosenthal of the *New York Times*.[73] "It isn't moral values that people
laugh at, of course—it's Mr. Quayle himself, and it isn't the elite who do
the laughing," sneered Garrison Keillor in the pages of the *Times*.[74]
Eleanor Clift of *Newsweek* launched into Quayle, snidely commenting:

"Vice President Dan Quayle went nuts ... The '50s fantasy of mom and dad and 2.2 kids went the way of phonograph records and circle pins."[75]

"[I]t is certain that television alone—or even in combination with magazines and movies—is not to blame for the decline in family values," wrote Kenneth Woodward of *Newsweek*. "Symptom it may be of deeper cultural confusions and contradictions. But as even Quayle must know, it is not the cause."[76] Of course, Quayle never claimed that television was *the* cause of moral decay—he merely claimed it was *a* cause. But straw men are easier to knock down than real arguments.

"The Murphy Brown reference was included because it was a grabby cultural thing that would illustrate the point," Quayle's speechwriter, Lisa Schiffer, told me on February 16, 2005. "This was a primetime network show. This was in its time at least as influential as *Sex and the City* became a decade later in defining the way young women thought about work norms and social norms."[77]

Both Quayle and Schiffer were correct. Television *was* promoting new, cutting-edge, anti-traditional values. A 1992 survey by the Center for Media and Public Affairs revealed that while 81 percent of the country as a whole felt that adultery was wrong, only 49 percent of Hollywood did. While only 4 percent of the country outside of Hollywood had no religious affiliation, 45 percent of Hollywood was areligious. While 76 percent of Americans believed that homosexual acts were wrong, only 20 percent of Hollywood did; while 59 percent of the American public was pro-choice, 97 percent of Hollywood was. As Schiffer stated, "We're talking about those who by self-selection and ambition run the institutions of popular culture—in contrast to a traditional cultural elite defined by erudition, wisdom, and taste."[78]

By 1998, the validity of Quayle's point was so obvious that even Candice Bergen, the actress who played Murphy Brown, felt compelled to acknowledge it. According to Bergen, Quayle's speech was "the right theme to hammer home ... family values ... and I agreed with all of it, except his reference to the show, which he had not seen ... It was an arrogant, uninformed posture, but the body of the speech was completely sound."[79]

Schiffer noted in the *New York Times* that since "Murphy Brown," television has only gotten worse. "It's clearly been one long downhill path as far as the sexualization of the culture," Schiffer says. "What's shown on TV now, you wouldn't have been able to get past anybody in 1992. The reality shows, all these teen dramas, there's nothing that shocks anybody anymore...This is a race to the bottom for ratings."[80]

The race to the bottom is having an effect on the porn generation viewers. A study published by the American Academy of Pediatrics in September 2004 found that "adolescents [twelve to seventeen years old] who viewed more sexual content at baseline were more likely to initiate intercourse and progress to more advanced non-coital sexual activities during the subsequent year, controlling for respondent characteristics that might otherwise explain these relationships."

Viewing sex on television was also likely to change children's worldviews about sex and morality: "This high-dose exposure to portrayals of sex may affect adolescents' developing beliefs about cultural norms....Social learning theory predicts that teens who see characters having casual sex without experiencing negative consequences will be more likely to adopt the behaviors portrayed. Although televised sexual portrayals can theoretically inhibit sexual activity when they include depictions of sexual risks (such as the possibility of contracting an STD or becoming pregnant), abstinence, or the need for sexual safety, this type of depiction occurs in only 15 percent of shows with sexual content. In other words, only one of every seven TV shows that include sexual content includes any safe sex messages, and nearly two-thirds of these instances (63 percent) are minor or inconsequential in their degree of emphasis within the scene. As a result, sexual content on TV is far more likely to promote sexual activity among U.S. adolescents than it is to discourage it."[81]

In the end, the proliferation of channels means that kids feel something approaching obligation about watching television. When you have three hundred channels at home, there's always got to be *something* on. Bored with homework? Grab the remote. Almost two-thirds of teens have a TV in their bedrooms, 64 percent of teens have their own TVs, and 70 percent of teenage boys have their own TVs.[82] When you're a nihilistic teen or pre-teen, the people on TV have lives much more fulfilling than your own. Why not watch? And if their lives are so much more fulfilling than your own, why not try what they're doing?

CHAPTER NINE

PORN AND POPCORN

"If motion pictures present stories that will affect lives for the better, they can become the most powerful force for the improvement of mankind"

HAYS MOTION PICTURE CODE, 1930[1]

Anne Hathaway is one of the rising young stars in Hollywood. Born in 1982, her pure acting talent and charm have already drawn comparisons to Audrey Hepburn and Judy Garland, and she's headlined major PG-rated films for the teenage set—including *Ella Enchanted*, *The Other Side of Heaven,* and the enormously successful *Princess Diaries* films. These films cater to pre-teens without crossing the boundaries of juvenile humor—and if they have any sexual messages, they are decent and restrained.

In the 2005 film *Havoc,* Hathaway's character sent an entirely different kind of message. She has sex on-screen with gang members as well as with female co-star Bijou Phillips;[2] she also goes topless.[3] Hathaway explained that she just wanted out of her clean image: "I think this whole princess thing is very much a moment in my career," she told the *Boston*

Globe. "I'm kind of ready to hang up the tiara...I don't have anything to prove, to be perfectly honest. I'm not out there to stick my middle finger up at anybody and say, 'You were wrong about me.' I just want to act, to play roles I consider interesting...Yeah, I think [*Havoc*] will change people's perception of me." She did have questions about "whether it was right for me to do the nudity," but "I realized it was the only way to make my [seventeen-year-old] character honest...I realized it was important to show she was so detached from herself that she has no problem going topless in front of guys she barely knows and exploiting her own sexuality to manipulate people...I realized that if I want to be true to the message I thought the film had, then I needed to go all the way with it."[4]

As for all of those *Princess*-loving little girls? Who cares what message you get—being true to art sometimes means not caring about your audience.

It's impossible to overestimate the amount of oversexed content coming out of Hollywood over the past decade. But it's not just the explosion in nudity among stars or the weakening of standards that have had an impact on the porn generation. There's a deeper message behind the moaning and the groaning, the games of hide-and-seek beneath the sheets, the face-licking, the half-naked groping—as Hollywood has embraced the graphic elements of pornography, the moral relativism behind these themes has become an implicit message in nearly every major mass-market film. For films targeted at youth, these messages are often explicit.

The modern Hollywood directors don't actually need to include such images or scenes for the sake of story, of course. When Ingrid Bergman goes up to Humphrey Bogart's room in *Casablanca*, you don't need full-frontal nudity to realize that they're about to sleep together. When Clark Gable carries Vivien Leigh up the stairs in *Gone With the Wind*, you don't need to be a mind-reader to figure out what's going on. The audience isn't quite as stupid as Hollywood believes they are. Hollywood may think, as H. L. Mencken said, that "nobody ever went broke underestimating the taste of the American public," but try telling that to the producers of *Showgirls*.

Somehow, filmmakers got along without topless women during the golden years of Hollywood. The greatest films ever made originate largely in the 1930s, 1940s, 1950s, and early 1960s—a period when Hollywood worked under the "heavy hand" of the Hays Production Code.

The code encouraged subtlety, especially in sexual matters. It banned explicit depiction of adultery, scenes of passion unnecessary to the plot, excessive and lustful kissing, lustful embraces, and suggestive postures and gestures, noting, "In general passion should so be treated that these scenes do not stimulate the lower and baser element." Seduction and rape were not to be shown or suggested unless relevant to the plot, and "sex perversion" was banned. Obscenity and vulgarity were forbidden, as were profanity and nudity. Since it was written in 1930, the code does have some incredibly dated and inappropriate elements—but overall, the code fulfilled its stated goal: "No picture should lower the moral standards of those who see it."[5]

After nearly half a century, it's easy to forget that the Hays Code was not some outside limitation imposed by the government. It was a content standard imposed by motion picture companies *voluntarily*. Although the code was written in 1930 in response to rising public criticism, it wasn't actually implemented until 1934. In 1933, Mae West truly provoked the implementation with her Hollywood debuts in *She Done Him Wrong* and *I'm No Angel*.[6] Her sizzling presence caused an immense public outcry, culminating in a movement led by the Catholic Legion of Decency. The Legion warned audiences of movie content, rating movies on an A-1 ("morally unobjectionable") to C ("condemned") scale. Catholics were urged not to attend any movie with a C rating.[7] During the Great Depression, moviegoers no longer had the money to support motion pictures, and those who did have the money didn't have the stomach for uncensored movies. By the end of 1932, weekly attendance figures were down 40 percent from 1929, and almost 20 percent of the movie houses in the country had closed down.[8] Hollywood had no choice but to go moral.

That doesn't mean the moviemakers were happy with the transition. Charlie Chaplin hated the Hays Code so much that he hung a pennant over the men's toilet in his studio reading: "Welcome, WILL HAYS."[9] But the code was good for movies in general, a fact that seems more and more obvious in retrospect. Many of today's critics, as open as they are about sexuality, seem to be getting that message. Steve Sailer, movie reviewer for United Press International, wrote after seeing Brian De Palma's gutter movie *Femme Fatale*, which includes a lesbian sex scene as well as graphic violence: "With the possible exception of Paul Verhoeven and Joe Esterhaz of *Basic Instinct* and *Showgirls* notoriety, no auteur would benefit more from the re-imposition of the old Hays Code censorship regime than De Palma...De Palma's tragedy has been that he was born too late to have to use subtlety and artistry to communicate."[10]

Neil Minow of the *Chicago Tribune* similarly penned, "The Hays Code said, 'The MORAL IMPORTANCE of entertainment is something which has been universally recognized. It enters intimately into the lives of men and women and affects them closely; it occupies their minds and affections during leisure hours; and ultimately touches the whole of their lives. A man may be judged by his standard of entertainment as easily as by the standard of his work.' Maybe that's not as outdated and quaint as we thought."[11]

With the death of the Hays Code, Jack Valenti of the Motion Picture Association of America quickly moved to allow more and more obscene material into films. As Valenti writes on the MPAA webpage, "From the very first day of my own succession to the MPAA president's office, I had sniffed the Production Code constructed by the Hays Office. There was about this stern, forbidding catalogue of 'Dos and Don'ts' the odious smell of censorship. I determined to junk it at the first opportune moment."[12] And junk it he did. The new ratings system is looser than Jenna Jameson after a few drinks.

It's hard for the MPAA to ruin the "General Audiences—All Ages Admitted" (G) rating, since it's restricted largely to kids' movies. But the "Parental Guidance Suggested. Some Material May Not Be Suitable for Children" (PG) rating may include "profanity" and/or "violence or brief nudity." In fact, "[t]he theme of a PG-rated film may itself call for parental guidance." As the MPAA sensitively notes, "[i]n our pluralistic

society it is not easy to make judgments without incurring some dis-
agreement. So long as parents know they must exercise parental responsibility, the rating serves as a meaningful guide and as a warning."[13] The
PG-13 rating ("Parents Strongly Cautioned. Some Material May Be Inappropriate for Children under 13") is likewise loose with language and
sex, and may also include "drug use." The Ratings Board is required to
rate a film R if the film includes more than one "of the harsher sexually
derived words," but "[t]hese films can be rated less severely, however, if
by a special vote, the Rating Board feels that a lesser rating would more
responsibly reflect the opinion of American parents."[14]

The ratings are decided by a board of members with no particularly
special qualifications, except that they "must have a shared parenthood
experience, must be possessed of an intelligent maturity, and most of all,
have the capacity to put themselves in the role of most American parents
so they can view a film and apply a rating that most parents would find
suitable and helpful in aiding their decisions about their children's
moviegoing."[15] A "shared parenthood experience"? For all the garbage
they allow under the PG-13 rating, perhaps that "shared parenthood
experience" is visiting their child in San Quentin.

There is no question that the Ratings Board is more socially liberal
than the parenting community at large—their members are drawn
entirely from the San Fernando Valley in California and its surrounding
area, where you'll find a staunchly liberal population. In fact, the Valley
itself serves as the home base of the pornography industry.

The MPAA refuses to release the identities of the people who com-
pose the board. Valenti loves the fact that the system is "subjective":
"We're dealing in imprecise boundaries here...What would you rather
have? This crazy, weird, mixed-up rating system? Or some federally
enforced one with $10,000 fines for people who would disobey it?"[16]
There's a third option: how about bringing back a slightly updated version of the Hays Code, one that could help stop the slide toward hard-
core sex in major motion pictures?

Over the decades since the introduction of the modern ratings system,
the standards for each ratings category have slipped deeper into the mire

of amorality. Bernard Weinraub noted the decline of strict family fare as early as July 1997. "The traditional family film...is quietly dying," Weinraub wrote, arguing that this was due to evolving moral standards. Today's youngsters are just more "sophisticated" than they used to be. And according to studio executives, Weinraub explained, "the film industry is, in many ways, lagging behind the tastes of children and their parents, whose appetite for more sophisticated and even violent movies has surprised even Hollywood."

Deborah Besce, then president of Nickelodeon Movies, averred: "The world is more sophisticated today. Our lives were so much simpler. And kids are demanding shows that express who they are and what they want." Jean MacCurdy, then president of Warner Brothers' television animation department, agreed: "You have to keep pushing the envelope toward more sophisticated humor and storytelling...The biggest mistake is talking down to the audience. You can't do that." Then-president of Walt Disney Pictures David Vogel told Weinraub, "it's no longer an innocent period of time...Today's eight-year-olds are yesterday's twelve-year-olds...There isn't this innocence of childhood among many children, what with broken homes and violence. We can't treat children as if they're all living in tract homes of the 1950s and everyone is happy. That is ridiculous."[17]

As L. Brent Bozell pointed out at the time, just because society is in decay doesn't mean that Hollywood should be exacerbating that decay. "Now take Vogel's argument to its logical conclusion," Bozell penned. "It is an unassailable fact (meaning: count on Hollywood to deny it) that the entertainment industry has a more powerful impact on youngsters' cultural upbringing than any other institution. To coarsen product to meet the public's lowered standards leads to an increasingly coarsened public."[18]

According to a Harvard University School of Public Health and Kids Risk Project study, objectionable material in movies increased dramatically between 1992 and 2003. Kimberly Thompson, associate professor in the Department of Health Policy and Management at HSPH and Director of the Kids Risk Project, stated that "ratings creep has occurred over the last decade and that today's movies contain significantly more violence, sex and profanity on average than movies of the same rating a decade ago."[19] The study also found that movies containing "sensuality," "sex," and "innuendo" according to the MPAA were less likely to receive a higher age-rating than those containing "sexuality" and "nudity." Conceal the sex a bit, sneak your film into the PG-13/PG range.[20]

Today's filmmakers complain even about the incredibly mild MPAA standards currently in place. Film critic Roger Ebert feels that the standard G, PG, PG-13, R, NC-17 ratings system is oppressive. He compares the MPAA's Valenti to a cruel Roman emperor: "[Valenti] said 'You compared me unfavorably with Caligula,' and I said, 'Well, that's better than comparing you favorably with Caligula.'" But Valenti himself admits that the standards admit degrading material. "When you're a First Amendment person," he says, "you have to allow entry into this marketplace that which you find squalid and meretricious and tawdry and vulgar and sometimes just plain stupid."[21]

While moviemakers and critics may complain about ratings systems and portray themselves as "First Amendment people," the reality is that Hollywood uses sex to get the glands and the money moving, not to enhance the artistic quality of its product. The simple fact of the matter is that sex sells, and subtlety doesn't. Actresses use the casting couch to get roles; directors use the sex scenes to sell tickets. In Hollywood, it's titillation for cash, highbrow whoredom. As Jane Fonda once put it, "Working in Hollywood does give one a certain expertise in the field of prostitution."

"I'll do it for art!"

There are plenty of A-list Hollywood actresses who began their careers with nudity. Whether they made their bones on the casting couch or not, they certainly made them on the film mattress. As the *Chicago Tribune* observed, "Nudity—and, often, very explicit sex scenes—is what you do if you want to go gunning for a prime spot on the A-list and be seen as a 'real' actress. Look no further than A-listers such as Nicole Kidman, Julianne Moore, and Halle Berry: When they took it off, their careers took off."[22]

When you're a toddler, your mother reminds you that you can't just walk around the house naked. When you're an actress, the critics remind you that you must.

Halle Berry is one of the most respected actresses in Hollywood. She's had a movie career spanning over fourteen years. She was the runner-up in the 1986 Miss USA contest. She starred in the successful film *X-Men*. But her movie career really took off in 2001, when she starred in the John Travolta misfire *Swordfish*. No, that movie wasn't a hit—it made under $70 million at the box office, even though its budget stood at a whopping $80 million.[23] But Berry left her mark—or, more accurately, two marks. While Berry had insisted until *Swordfish* that she would not do nude scenes, she decided to flush that principle down the toilet as soon as producers bumped her salary from $2 million to $2.5 million.[24] For those who aren't quick with the math, that's $250,000 per breast, for all of three seconds of film time.[25]

Even *Swordfish* producer Jonathan Krane felt that the topless scene was gratuitous. "I felt it was kind of like old news," Krane told the *Edmonton Sun*. "We had seen this before. But other people really wanted that. A lot of actresses turned it down on the basis of that—and they should. I didn't think it was necessary in the movie. Neither did John (Travolta). She also didn't want to do this. But, somehow, and it had to do with a number of things (including money), she agreed to do it. I was hoping she would not agree to do it and we would hire her anyway so we would not have to have that scene, but she agreed...I'm being real frank with you, I don't like it. I've made forty-three films that I have produced and I don't think I've had a naked girl in any of them until this."[26]

It wasn't about the money, Berry insisted. It was about gaining legitimacy as an artist. Because great actresses, as we all know, are defined by their lack of inhibition about nudity. "Now that I've opened the door to the sexy thing there's a whole new avenue I can travel down. It was a big step," she explained (as though her entire career were not already based on "the sexy thing"). "When I started this was the last kind of role I would have done because I came from beauty pageants and I've had to work hard to dispel the idea that I was just a pretty face who couldn't act. I felt that if I did nudity I would get typecast and prove all my critics right."[27]

Of course, the Gypsy Lee Rose of the silver screen realized that it was downright liberating to loose her breasts from the confines of her shirt for the moviegoing public. It was just those darn silly Americans who care about bare breasts! "It was the fear of allowing myself to give that much to a character [that prevented her from stripping before]," she said. "It's kind of liberating because what you discover is that they're just boobs and, in most parts of the world, it's not really a big deal. It's only in America, with our social values, that it's really hard."[28]

Why did Berry pick a terrible action flick to do her Lady Godiva impersonation? Baring all for *Swordfish* isn't exactly posing nude for Rembrandt. As Glenn Whipp of the *Los Angeles Daily News* wrote, "What does it say about the revolting new movie *Swordfish* that the biggest applause at a recent screening was prompted by Halle Berry flashing her breasts?"

Berry's answer seemed to be: Why not? "It's not really because I ever thought it was bad. I applauded the women and the men who could go there...I knew that I was doing nudity that was gratuitous. I knew that I would never be able to articulately justify why it had to be in this movie," Berry says. "I had to get over my inhibition of letting myself be exposed that way."[29]

You have to hand it to Berry—she definitely knows the game. As soon as she let her "babies" out of her shirt, Oscar came calling. In *Monster's Ball*, Berry plays the widow of Sean "Puffy" Combs, a death row inmate; she falls in love with his executioner, Billy Bob Thornton. Nowadays, love in movies can only be portrayed through graphic sex, and Berry was prepared to play the part. Berry's character decides she's really in love with the Thornton character after he gives her oral sex. Berry described her more physically demanding nude scene: "We talked about it to death, and we both agreed that we didn't want to do this too many times so let's get it right the first time."[30]

Naturally, the critics fell in love at first sight. The *Hollywood Reporter* gratuitously lauded Berry and the sex scene, writing "The collective soul-baring, which also extends to some very naked coupling, lends the film its raw, stirring power."[31] According to the critics, Berry was more than good in bed—she was "brave." Because "bravery" is measured by how many articles of clothing one is willing to discard in the name of art. Jeff Simon of the *Buffalo News* called Berry's performance "brave."[32] So did Edward Guthmann of the *San Francisco Chronicle*.[33] Mark Rahner of the *Seattle Times* explained that Berry's performance was "brave at the very least in the much-discussed raw sex scene."[34] A. O. Scott of the *New York Times* lauded Berry's screen work as "an extraordinarily brave and risky kind of performance of a kind that the Academy perhaps too seldom recognizes," and also mentioned that he believed Berry was "due" for an Oscar.[35] Yes, that absolutely masterful performance in *The Flintstones* was certainly overlooked!

It was all but a foregone conclusion that Berry would win an Academy Award. When she did, she made one of the more obnoxious speeches in Oscar history, claiming that she had overcome massive racial obstacles to reach the Oscar podium. "This moment is so much bigger than me," Berry told the audience. She stated that her win was a victory "for every nameless, faceless woman of color who now has a chance because this door tonight has been opened." As Ann Coulter bitingly observed, "Yes, at long last, the 'glass ceiling' had been broken. Large-breasted, slightly cocoa women with idealized Caucasian features will finally have a chance in Hollywood! They will, however, still be required to display their large breasts for the camera and to discuss their large breasts at some length with reporters."[36]

Berry's transformation from she-who-would-not-bare-her-babies to the Boob Queen of California isn't unique. There are countless other starlets who attempted to broaden their artistic horizons in the same manner, including Jamie Lee Curtis, who took off her shirt in *Trading Places*; Kim Basinger, who posed for *Playboy* in order to escape her Breck girl image;[37] Gwyneth Paltrow in *Shakespeare in Love*. Reportedly, Jennifer Connolly wasn't even considered for her Oscar-winning role in *A Beautiful Mind* until Ron Howard saw her in *Requiem for a Dream*, in which Connolly ends up at a sex party.[38]

Liv Tyler made the transition from clean to slutty in *One Night at McCool's*. The website for that movie featured a "provocative photo of her washing a car with the gusto of that babe who made the chain gang hot in *Cool Hand Luke*. Tyler's body is covered in a suspiciously milky film of suds. As the bubbles continue to clear, your cursor caresses three smaller pictures of the pillow-lipped actress, producing purringly suggestive sound bites ('I love it!') plus a recurring moan of pleasure. Trailers for the movie tease that her character's second favorite thing in the world is water. Her first is not tough to guess."[39]

As Brad Prager, who teaches film and popular culture at the University of Missouri-Columbia states, "An actress is now more likely to undress for a director who she feels is making a work of art."[40] Ah, the joys of "art." There's money to be made and critical praise to be garnered from dropping the robe. The virgin-to-slut phenomenon doesn't just work for pop tarts—it works for front-line actresses.

The current matriarch of Hollywood actresses, Nicole Kidman, has done dozens of feature films. Many of her major hits have involved her in the flesh. In 1986's *Windrider*, Kidman filmed a steamy shower scene. In 1989's *Dead Calm*, she bared all for her art. She dropped a towel to gaze at herself in her birthday suit in 1991's *Billy Bathgate*. She displayed her rump in *Malice* (1993). She revealed herself several times in *Eyes Wide Shut* (1999), her nipple in *Moulin Rouge* (2001), her rear again in *Birthday Girl* (2001), everything in *The Human Stain* (2003), and everything again in *Cold Mountain* (2003). She appears naked with her love interest, a ten-year-old boy, in a bathtub, in *Birth* (2004). What artistic versatility! No wonder Harvey Weinstein effuses: "She has thrown herself into the most daring kind of work, and as a result we're now seeing the celebration of one of the world's greatest actresses."[41] No wonder director Anthony Minghella labels Kidman "probably the greatest actress working right now."[42]

Julianne Moore, Kidman's co-star in the all-lesbianism-all-the-time flick *The Hours*, also rode Lady Godiva's horse to the top of the mountain. In 1993's *Short Cuts*, Moore conducted an argument while walking around a house naked from the waist down, blow-drying her skirt. Also in 1993, she did a soft-core sex scene in *Body of Evidence*, and then repeated the feat in *Boogie Nights* (1997). She went fully nude in *The End of the Affair* (1999). No wonder *New Statesman* critic Mark Kermode calls Moore "simply the greatest actress of her generation."[43]

The hottest young starlets have imitated Kidman and Moore. Kate Winslet truly began her career in Peter Jackson's *Heavenly Creatures* (1994), in which she engaged in a hot-and-heavy lesbian make-out scene. In *Titanic* (1997), which brought her fame and fortune, as well as a Best Actress nomination, she posed naked for Leonardo DiCaprio. She took off her top for *Hideous Kinky* (1998), took off the rest in *Holy Smoke* (1999), bared her breasts in *Quills* (2000), and bared it all in *Iris* (2001).

Likewise, Chloe Sevigny has done nothing in her career save getting naked and making out with members of either sex. Her genitalia are revealed while she sleeps in *Kids* (1995). She repeatedly has graphic sex with Hilary Swank in *Boys Don't Cry* (1999), revealing her breasts and earning an Oscar nomination for it. Even more horrifically (if possible), she has sex with two men at once and gives graphic oral sex in *The Brown Bunny* (2003).

This isn't to say that these actresses aren't talented. Winslet is brilliant in *Finding Neverland* and *Hamlet*; Moore and Kidman *can* definitely act. But could we *please* see that talent expressed in acting, as opposed to stripping? There used to be two kinds of actresses: those who were paid to get naked, and those who weren't. The first types were porn stars, the second were actresses. Now, it's difficult to tell the difference between call girls and movie starlets. Perhaps that's why there are now hundreds upon hundreds of pornographic web pages composed entirely of clips from mainstream Hollywood films, released and showing at your local Cineplex. The actresses do it for their "art." The directors do it for the cash. And the audience goes to get its rocks off.

Homosexuality chic

Michael Ovitz was once a member of the rich and powerful Hollywood elite. Ovitz founded the Hollywood powerhouse Creative Artists Agency, and for some time he was the number two man at Disney.[44] During the 1980s and early 1990s, Ovitz reigned over Hollywood; according to the

New York Times, Ovitz was "famously and frequently described...as the most powerful man in town."[45] He was also the most hated man in town, and when he sold his company, Artists Management Group, he was forced to take a financial hit of somewhere between $100 and $200 million.

Ovitz claimed that his fall was not the result of bad policy, but of something more dark and devious: a "gay mafia" in Hollywood. "I didn't kill anybody; I'm not a murderer," he told *Vanity Fair*. "I didn't set off a bomb in a shopping center. I didn't take off in a white Bronco. I'm an entrepreneur. The money I lost was mine. My money, my gamble, my mistake. And still they hate me. Everyone." Ovitz maintained that this "gay mafia," led by mogul David Geffen, put out a hit on his company and used *New York Times* reporter Bernard Weinraub as its publicity man.

Ovitz also labeled several other powerful Hollywood figures as members or allies of the "gay mafia," including Barry Diller, Michael Eisner, and Richard Lovett—all of whom reacted publicly with disgust. Despite the fact that Ovitz recanted the "gay mafia" comments almost immediately ("The term 'gay Mafia' does not reflect my true feelings or attitudes"[46]), the media, salivating for a juicy story, pounced. "It really reeks of the homophobia we saw in the '70s and '80s when a lot of gay execs were closeted," Gay and Lesbian Alliance Against Defamation entertainment media director Scott Seomin told *Daily Variety*.[47] "Pointing fingers at gay men and lesbians for society's ills—or for one's personal downfall—is just wrong," fumed *Philadelphia Daily News* sports desk editor Deb Woodell.[48] "He's finished," a studio bigwig told the *New York Times*. "Actually, he was finished before, but now he's really finished. I can't imagine anyone wanting to have dinner with him after this."[49] "Was it an interview or a psychotic episode?" asked Jonathan Bing and Dade Hayes of *Daily Variety*.[50] A couple of obscure filmmakers, Steve Young and Denise David, even made a twelve-minute video called "My Dinner With Ovitz," depicting an Ovitz-lookalike being shot by members of a "Gay Mafia" at a gay bar, "Mother Lode."[51]

It's too bad that Ovitz made the Hollywood "gay mafia" comments— his widespread detractors were far too quick to dispatch his comments as the result of psychosis or paranoia. Completely neglected went the fact that the term "gay mafia" has been in use for years—and with good reason. Rachel Abramowitz of the *Los Angeles Times* noted that "among a certain set of high-powered cognoscenti, the term 'gay mafia,' or 'velvet mafia,' has been used to refer to a tiny, select group of friends of which Geffen happens to be a prominent member."[52] Michelangelo Signorile, a militant gay activist famous for "outing" people, explained: "The shock and bewilderment among both journalists and Hollywood's liberals is pretty silly—not to mention a bit defensive and a tad dishonest. While Ovitz's statements certainly warranted coverage, they weren't that shocking... Truth is, many gay men will tell you that there most certainly *is* a Hollywood/media gay mafia—using that term or its synonym, 'the velvet mafia'—whether or not they are members themselves. It's made up of men such as DreamWorks co-chair David Geffen and *Rolling Stone* publisher Jann Wenner, plus many more well-known and lesser-known individuals."[53]

So is there a "gay mafia"? Not in the sense that a group of powerful Hollywood homosexuals get together at night to plot out the course that Hollywood must take. But it would be disingenuous to say that there's no "pro-gay mob" at the top of the Hollywood chain. Many powerful Hollywoodites *are* gay, but the rest are massively liberal and back the gay lobby to the hilt. How else to explain the fact that Hollywood fare has spearheaded the charge for homosexual normalization?

The death of film masculinity

Steve McQueen must be spinning in his grave. A new breed of Hollywood leading man sets the tone for the porn generation—purely metrosexual, with the old values of masculinity re-envisioned as homosexual fantasy.

As described by Manohla Dargis of the *Los Angeles Times*, "the women's and gay rights movements irrevocably altered how we look at men, on screen and off. Aided by new media outlets, these liberation movements freed the male body (or enslaved it, depending on your view), turning it into a socially acceptable field of desire and one very hot commodity. Finally, straight men could be exploited for their looks just like women by conforming to an ideal of beauty—ripped and stripped of hair—largely borrowed from gay culture. Gay or not, male actors and stars are more brazenly sexualized now, namely because they're also more feminized. In the past, Hollywood stars were unmistakably he-men; these days, they all whisper 'come hither' like hard-bodied Marilyns."[54]

The gay movement took the initiative in shaping perceptions of male beauty because women are far less focused on male beauty than gay men are. Yes, women want a guy who doesn't look like Michael Moore. But women typically focus on a man's physical appearance as part of the whole, while men focus on physical appearance first and foremost. Because the gay movement defined male beauty, young women began identifying that vision with their own vision, and gay standards of beauty were accepted as normal. Hence Brad Pitt, Ben Affleck, and the other girly-men who permeate the silver screen (a six-pack and shaved chest do not a male make).

These feminized male stars are expected to be "comfortable with their own sexuality"—so comfortable, in fact, that they can't make their bones without playing a homosexual. In 1951, Humphrey Bogart said: "The only honest way to find the best actor would be to let everybody play Hamlet and let the best man win." Today, that might read: "The only honest way to find the best actor would be to let everybody play Richard Simmons and let the best man win."

Actors can't wait to imitate Tom Hanks, who leapt to true glory in 1993 when he played AIDS-stricken gay attorney and victim of homophobia Andrew Beckett in *Philadelphia*. Kevin Kline attempted to match Hanks' homosexual hamming in the 1997 comedy *In & Out*; in 2004's *De-lovely* he tried again, playing gay songwriter Cole Porter. Leonardo DiCaprio took one for the team in *Total Eclipse* (1995), and Russell Crowe got some man-lovin' in *The Sum of Us* (1995). Dennis Quaid went gay in 2003's *Far From Heaven* and garnered great reviews. Robin Williams hooked up with a transvestite-ing Nathan Lane in *The Birdcage* (1996), and they both patronized Gene Hackman's conservative senator to the tune of millions.

The newer faces are ready and willing to hop in the sack with a guy to boost their acting chops. Colin Farrell, best known as a wild party-boy, played a homosexual who goes straight in *A Home at the End of the World* (2004), but it's his bisexuality in the epic *Alexander* that is bound to raise a few eyebrows. *Alexander* isn't just an art-house pic; it's directed by Oliver Stone and stars Oscar-winners Anthony Hopkins and Angelina Jolie alongside Farrell. Nothing like some good, old-fashioned fun with pagan morality! According to reports, *Troy* star Brad Pitt wanted to play Farrell's gay lover, but wife Jennifer Aniston told him to reject the part.[55] That homophobe!

Jake Gyllenhaal is slated to play a gay cowboy (yes, a gay cowboy—can it be long before we get *Lone Ranger and Tonto: A Biracial Love Story?*) alongside fellow young up-and-comer Heath Ledger in Ang Lee's *Brokeback Mountain*. Ledger plays a ranch hand and Gyllenhaal plays a rodeo cowboy; they fall in homosexual love on the plains of Wyoming and Texas in the 1960s. The Gay and Lesbian Alliance Against Defamation has already lauded the film, saying "If what we are hearing about this film is true, this is a significant and groundbreaking step for Hollywood in terms of mainstream movies." Apparently, Ledger and Gyllenhaal weren't the only Hollywood stars hot for a chance to bugger on the prairie—Farrell, Josh Hartnett, and Billy Crudup were interested in doing the movie as well. Hartnett is the only one without a gay project on his plate right now, since Crudup plays a gay Elizabethan actor in *Stage Beauty*.[56] Jude Law, nominally heterosexual gay icon, will join Paul Bettany in a jaunt into the world of gay flirting in *Brideshead Revisited*. Brendan Fraser, last seen playing in *George of the Jungle* and *The Mummy*, will take up the part of James Bond's homosexual alter-ego in *Gay Secret Agent*.[57]

Established actors, too, want to revitalize their careers by playing "friends of Dorothy." Hot competition broke out for the part of sexologist Alfred Kinsey in 2004's *Kinsey*. Russell Crowe, Tom Hanks, Kevin Spacey, and Harrison Ford (Han Solo and Chewbacca—more than meets the eye?) all considered taking the part of the bisexual doctor.[58] Liam Neeson got the role, and made out with Peter Sarsgaard; Sarsgaard, meanwhile, revealed his genitalia for the film. Laura Linney, who plays Kinsey's wife, Clara, sums up the reaction to the film: "People just flip out. They feel like the fabric of American society is coming undone."[59]

It is. The standards of the audience are being lowered. Hollywood has enormous propaganda power; it can paint homosexuals as saints, and intolerant moralists as sinners. It can paint amoralism as a "tolerant" standard, and traditional morality as close-minded. And that's exactly what it does.

When girls go wild—with each other

While male homosexuality has become an almost constant presence in film, lesbianism has become even more popular as filmmakers seek to cater to the porn generation. The market for male homosexuality is limited— some women, a few men, the gay community—but the market for lesbianism is much broader. Hollywood filmmakers have churned out hundreds of films with lesbian content within the last decade. Of late, actresses appearing in these films often make sure to mention that they enjoy their lesbian encounters, just to heighten their sex appeal.

One of the most common types of lesbian-content movie is the "sexual experimentation" film. Generally, this stuff is soft-core pornography masquerading as art. One example is *Cruel Intentions* (1999), in which Sarah Michelle Geller plays the stepsister of Ryan Phillippe. When Geller's boyfriend dumps her for Selma Blair, Geller wants revenge, so she goes after Blair herself, telling her that most girls learn to kiss by practicing with other girls. A long, wet, tongue exchange ensues between the two girls, with Blair realizing—surprise, surprise!—that she likes kissing girls. Audiences loved the lesbian titillation so much that Hollywood concocted *Cruel Intentions 2* (2001), a prequel. And not only is there lesbian action, there's "every man's fantasy": lesbian action, in a shower, with a guy in the middle.

Wild Things (1998) tried both the lesbian discovery angle and the ménage-a-trois angle. First, Denise Richards and Neve Campbell discover lesbian love in the pool. Then, both of them hop in the sack at the same time with Matt Dillon. Like *Cruel Intentions*, *Wild Things* also spawned

an atrocious quickie sequel with requisite lesbian action and threesome—
it still ended up in the bargain bin.

Just as with male homosexuality, showing lesbian behavior on screen
in any context desensitizes the audience to lesbian behavior. The most
obvious brand of these "agenda" flicks is the "lesbian normalization content movie," which simply purports to show how lesbians are just as normal, loving, and/or socially valuable as straight couples.

This is the *Kissing Jessica Stein* (2002) model. That movie centers on
Jennifer Westfeldt's character, a straight woman, who responds to a per-
sonals ad from a bisexual woman, Heather Juergensen, on a whim. The
two women immediately fall into lesbian love, complete with graphic
make-out scenes. Westfeldt's character is embarrassed about the affair,
and reluctant to have sex with a woman, but she eventually gives in. The
two women eventually split up after Juergensen's character gets fed up
with her partner's lack of sex drive and commitment to the relationship.

The issue in the movie isn't whether this is right or wrong—it's
assumed that either way Westfeldt's character decides to swing is right.
Amoralism is the standard. The basis for the movie is that any type of
relationship, straight or gay, is legitimate.

Hollywood also pumps out movies with "lesbian moments" in order
to turn on male viewers; these are typically raunchy comedies, bad action
flicks, or cheesy horror films. In the hit movie *American Pie 2* (2001),
one of the characters presumes two women who live with each other are
lesbians; he goads them into making out with each other. Later in the
movie, he winds up in bed with both of them. The PG-13 rated *Anger
Management* (2003), starring Adam Sandler and Jack Nicholson, contains a scene where two porn star lesbian lovers passionately exchange
spit.

Titles in this "lesbian moment" category are too numerous to list
anywhere near comprehensively. A very sparse sampling: *40 Days and
40 Nights* (2002), *Bowfinger* (1999) starring Eddie Murphy and Steve
Martin, *Bram Stoker's Dracula* (1992) starring Winona Ryder, *Book of
Shadows: Blair Witch 2* (2000), *Almost Famous* (2000) starring Kate
Hudson, *The Devil's Advocate* (1997) starring Keanu Reeves and Al

Pacino, *Dodgeball* (2004) starring Ben Stiller, *The Fast and the Furious* (2001) starring Vin Diesel, *Femme Fatale* starring Rebecca Romijn-Stamos, *The Girl Next Door* (2004), *From Hell* (2001) starring Johnny Depp, *The Haunting* (1999) starring Catherine Zeta-Jones, *The Hot Chick* (2002) starring Rob Schneider (this somehow received a PG-13 rating—someone had to have been drunk), *Not Another Teen Movie* (2001), *The People vs. Larry Flynt* (1996) starring Woody Harrelson, *Nurse Betty* (2000) starring Rene Zellweger, *Romeo Must Die* (2000), *Rock Star* (2001) starring Jennifer Aniston, *The Salton Sea* (2002) starring Val Kilmer, and *Starsky and Hutch* (2004) starring Ben Stiller (yup, PG-13!), among many others.

Actresses realize that a quick way to the top is titillating the male audience with lesbianism, so they've adopted bisexuality in their everyday lives. A few tabloid photos never hurt the market price! As nut job Angelina Jolie explained, "Whether I'm loving a man or a woman, it makes no difference to me."[60]

Of course it makes no difference. That's Hollywood. In reality, actresses aren't necessarily straight or gay or bisexual: They're simply sluts. The stories about Hollywood casting couches are true, and sex has no meaning for many actresses. Meanwhile, the Hollywood pro-lesbian lobby continues to churn out legitimizing lesbian films. By producing mass quantities of lesbian exposure, films lauding lesbianism as equal or superior to heterosexuality, Hollywood prevents moral outrage against lesbianism. And then Hollywood pats itself on the back and says it's doing the right thing.

Oscar and Steve

Gay men and women aren't just portrayed sympathetically on screens across America—critics around the country are lapping it up. Take the Oscars, for example. Play a gay man, receive an Oscar nomination. Play a lesbian, receive an Oscar nomination. Make a film celebrating homosexuality, receive an Oscar nomination (or at least get great reviews). Virtually every film with gravitas that depicts homosexuality in a positive light becomes "important."

In the last decade especially, Oscar has found a special place in his heart for homosexuality. In 1994, Tom Hanks won an Oscar for his portrayal of a gay man dying of AIDS in *Philadelphia*. In 1998, *As Good As It Gets* swept into the Academy Awards—the movie revolves around an obsessive-compulsive, homophobic writer (Jack Nicholson) who falls in love with a waitress (Helen Hunt), and learns to accept an openly gay artist (Greg Kinnear) severely beaten during a robbery. Another 1998 Best Picture nominee was the silly, if likeable *The Full Monty*, about six out-of-shape English fellows who decide to go nude to raise some cash. Two of them are closet homosexuals.[61] In 1999, Ian McKellen grabbed a nomination for his role as the gay director James Whale in *Gods and Monsters*, and Kathy Bates received a nomination for her role as a lesbian political guru in *Primary Colors*.

In 2000, films with major homosexual plot points—including *Boys Don't Cry*, *The Talented Mr. Ripley*, and *Being John Malkovich* were all nominated for awards. The cliché-ridden *American Beauty* won Best Picture and Best Director for Sam Mendes. The film was an attack on the "dark underside of suburbia" written by a gay man; the only normal people are a gay couple, and a closeted homosexual military colonel kills the main character because of his own homophobia. The main character himself re-enacts a thinly veiled "coming out" story—he find fulfillment by discovering "forbidden love" with a teenager (yes, that's statutory rape, folks!).[62]

In 2002, David Lynch's *Mulholland Drive* earned the director a Best Director nomination, while Kate Winslet and Judi Dench snatched nominations for the film *Iris*, playing the young and old versions of bisexual author Iris Murdoch, respectively. The 2003 Oscars found films like *The Hours*, *Far From Heaven*, and *Frida*—all of which were enveloped in the issues of homosexuality and sex—literally drowning in nominations.

The bottom line: Since 1994 and the "landmark" film *Philadelphia*, actors and actresses playing non-straight characters have been nominated for seventeen Oscars; they have won four Oscars. Clearly these films are not being made for financial gain—none of them have broken the list of historical top one hundred grossers,[63] and only *As Good As It Gets* and *American Beauty* earned over $100 million in the year following their release.[64]

These movies are being made by a cadre of elitists, specifically for a cadre of elitists: the critics. Audiences are not turning out in huge numbers to see these propaganda pieces. But if Hollywood can keep churning them out, and the critics can keep on praising them, maybe their message will seep into the minds of Americans as a group.

No wonder young girls are experimenting with lesbianism and bisexuality. If movies can drive kids to have sex, they can certainly drive kids to have sex with partners of either gender. Jane Ganahl of the *San Francisco Chronicle* notes that the bisexual or lesbian-chic fad skews young: "I've noticed that whether you've had the experience is somewhat determined by age: Many of my friends under thirty-five have had them; women closer to my age have not. Even those of us who won Purple Hearts in the sexual revolution. I guess that means that young women today are all about openness and exploring, and it probably goes hand in hand with the later marrying age." As for Hollywood's overload of lesbian action, Ganahl—no pre-teen herself—notes that she feels pressured: "It's enough to make you think you have a weird life because you don't go around casually exploring your girlfriends' tonsils."[65]

One movie in particular provides an insight into the issue of pop culture promoting homosexuality. In 2004, Holly Hunter was nominated for a Best Supporting Actress Oscar for her part in the extremely telling film *Thirteen*. Hunter plays the mother of a thirteen-year-old girl, Tracy (played by Evan Rachel Wood), who falls in with a popular bad girl, Evie (played by Nikki Reed). Tracy is quickly seduced by the fast-living Evie and becomes a sexually promiscuous, drug-using criminal; one scene features the two young girls kissing each other, with Tracy lying on top of Evie. During this scene, Evie goads Tracy into kissing her, taunting her with the claim that she doesn't know how to kiss. Tracy insists that she does indeed know how to kiss, citing the fact that she has practiced kissing while watching the lesbian kissing scene from the Sarah Michelle Geller movie *Cruel Intentions* "like fifty times." *Thirteen* is accurate in this respect: pop culture and bad parenting are a very dangerous combination. *Cruel Intentions* is rated R—but how many kids under seventeen have seen it?

Even for those of my generation who do not experiment with homosexuality (generally, same-sex experimentation seems to be less common among boys because of the social stigma attached), Hollywood skews our views toward the "gay rights" side of the fence and away from Judeo-Christian standards of morality. An MTV/Zogby International/Hamilton College poll in 2001 showed that two-thirds of recent high-school graduates supported gay marriage, including 80 percent of Catholics and 46 percent of non-born again Protestants. A shockingly low 39 percent of grads said that they believed "gay lifestyles are morally wrong." This opposes 2001 statistics among older audiences, who are against gay marriage by a margin of two to one.[66]

The homosexual community cannot argue that pop culture has not had a hand in promoting its agenda—after all, the Gay and Lesbian Alliance Against Defamation routinely condemns films it considers "homophobic" as the cause of violent activity. For example, in 1991 GLAAD sent out a press release announcing that according to its Los Angeles Executive Director, "GLAAD sees a definite connection between the negative images films convey to impressionable young people and the increasing incidents of violence against gays and lesbians around the country."[67]

So while the hubbub over Michael Ovitz's "gay mafia" remark was partially understandable, there should be no controversy about this statement: There is a Hollywood pro-gay, non-organized mafia. Hollywood is run by political leftists, moral relativists, and Judeo-Christian valuephobes. Hollywood is putting out a pro-gay product. And film does have an effect on its viewers—an effect that is even more significant for the youngest members of society.

Of standards and sexuality

The Hays Code went out of use completely in 1968. With it went the idea of Hollywood as a purveyor of moral standards. Films were already raunchy in the 1960s and 1970s, but by the 1980s, all standards had left via the emergency exit. Gone were the days of inspirational movies and heroes. There was no longer any good and evil. There was no longer any sin. Moral relativism and amoralism had conquered Hollywood.

Portrayal of sexual activity onscreen is not simply about telling a story or enlightening viewers—it's about legitimizing the behavior. When increasingly younger teens are exposed to soft-core pornography on the big screen, there is a cultural result. When the hottest actors in Hollywood are making out with other guys, when the hottest actresses are claiming to be attracted to other girls, when tough guys onscreen are portrayed as macho jerks and heroes are portrayed as feminized, homosexual fantasies, those who back Judeo-Christian morality are in serious trouble. It's no wonder that in a 1996 poll, 62 percent of children aged ten to sixteen said that sex on TV shows and movies influences kids to have sex when they are too young.[68]

Here we stand, almost forty years into the new era of filmmaking. We traded the old morality for a new, more permissive, more open, and more arbitrary ethic. Sexual activity and homosexuality in the movies gets more and more prominent with each passing year. By promoting the idea that anyone—anyone!—could be gay, Hollywood hopes to force acceptance of a homosexual lifestyle. By pushing warped views of sexual activity into the mainstream of pop culture, kids begin experimenting with their sexuality at earlier and earlier ages.

In the early pre-teen or teenage years, sexuality is a new phenomenon, and as such, tends to be rather undirected. By forcing homosexuality onto the table and claiming equal legitimacy with heterosexuality, kids are forced to confront their sexuality before they have had a chance to come to grips with it.

The Hays Code stated: "When right standards are consistently presented, the motion picture exercises the most powerful influences. It builds character, develops right ideals, inculcates correct principles, and all this in attractive story form. If motion pictures consistently hold up for admiration high types of characters and present stories that will affect lives for the better, they can become the most powerful force for the improvement of mankind."

When, as a society, we decided that standards in movies no longer mattered, we sacrificed something great—the popular requirement that filmmakers strive to enrich society and uphold traditions of American morality. We sacrificed the idea that there's any kind of responsibility by our cultural authorities to think about the effect of their work, not just cater to the lowest common denominator. It's a sad commentary that we sold that goal for a few feet of dirty film.

CHAPTER TEN

THE LOTION PICTURE INDUSTRY

"Jim Haynes and Germaine Greer had just published the first issue of a newspaper that All London was talking about. It was called 'Suck.'...[Jim Haynes] went on with a discourse about the aims of 'Suck.' To put it in a few words, the aim was sexual liberation, the liberation of the spirit of man. If you were listening to this speech and had read 'Suck,' or even if you hadn't you were likely to be watching Jim Haynes's face for the beginnings of a campy grin, a smirk, a wink, a roll of the eyeballs—something to indicate that he was just having his little joke. But it soon became clear that he was one of those people who exist on a plane quite...Beyond Irony. Whatever it had been for him once, sex had now become a religion, and he had developed a theology in which the orgasm had become a form of spiritual ecstasy."

—TOM WOLFE, *NEW YORK MAGAZINE*, AUGUST 23, 1976[1]

He could have been the boy next door. Smart, handsome, outgoing, Ted Bundy was the picture of a man on the way up. But Bundy was no ordinary young man on the make. He was a serial killer, and he murdered dozens of young women, sexually assaulting many of them as well.

Dr. James Dobson interviewed Bundy just hours before his execution. The man with nothing to lose opened his dark soul before Dobson. The day after Bundy was electrocuted, Dobson released the tape of his talk with the mass murderer. The transcript is chilling—and the insight of the killer is far too matter-of-fact to be ignored.

Bundy insisted that his home life in early childhood was normal. "[T]hat's part of the tragedy of this whole situation," he explained. "Because I grew up in a wonderful home with two dedicated and loving parents, as one of five brothers and sisters, a home where we as children were the focus of my parents' lives, where we regularly attended church, two Christian parents who did not drink, they did not smoke, there was no gambling, no physical abuse, no fighting in the home."

So when did the young man with a future become a man with brutal rape and murder on his mind? "This is the message I want to get across," he said, "that as a young boy...I encountered, outside the home again, in the local grocery store, in a local drug store, the soft-core pornography that people called soft core...And from time to time we would come across pornographic books of a harder nature than...of a more graphic, explicit nature than we would encounter at the local grocery store. And this also included such things as detective magazines."

Bundy described the pornography he encountered: "this is something I think I want to emphasize is that the most damaging kinds of pornography, and again I'm talking from personal experience...are those that involve violence and sexual violence. Because the wedding of those two forces, as I know only too well, brings out the hatred that is just, just too terrible to describe."

Like most addicts, after a certain point, the dosage needs to be raised in order to achieve the same effect. When the effect of hard core porn is minimized, the addict needs to do more to get the same thrill—and when that thrill can no longer be attained from paper filth, the addict must move on to higher forms of perversion.

"[I]t happened in stages, gradually," Bundy related. "My experience with pornography generally, but with pornography that deals on a violent level with sexuality, is once you become addicted to it—and I look at this as a kind of addiction like other kinds of addiction—I would keep looking for more potent, more explicit, more graphic kinds of material.

"Until you reach a point where the pornography only goes so far, you reach that jumping off point where you begin to wonder if maybe actually doing it would give you that which is beyond just reading it or looking at it."

And then Bundy snapped. "It's a very difficult thing to describe, the sensation of reaching that point where I knew that, that something had say, snapped." Bundy described it as "a compulsion...a building up of this destructive energy. What alcohol did in conjunction with exposure to pornography is alcohol reduced my inhibitions at the same time the fantasy life that was fuelled by pornography eroded them further."[2]

So Ted Bundy raped and murdered. Other sources—particularly porn industry sources—would later question whether indeed Bundy had been a boy-next-door type turned maniacal killer. Al Goldstein, a contributing editor for *Penthouse* magazine and publisher of *Screw*, wrote a piece for the *Los Angeles Times* in which he claimed that the anti-porn cause would lead to the repeal of the First Amendment: "The implicit message of the Dobson-Bundy interview is that we should censor adult material. But censorship, once embarked on, has a way of growing out of control. Look to Iran, or the Soviet Union, to see about that."[3]

Playboy repeatedly attempted to blame Bundy's evil on sexual repression rather than sexual excess. A piece by "anti-repression" crusader Philip Nobile, co-author of *The United States of America vs. Sex*, appeared in the July 1989 issue of *Playboy*; Nobile quotes Meese commission member Dr. Park Dietz praising soft-core *Playboy* erotica as "among the healthiest sexual images in America."[4]

In July 1990, *Playboy* reiterated its pro-porn propaganda in an interview with Dr. John Money of Johns Hopkins University School of Medicine. The interview reads like a direct transcript of Tom Wolfe's conversation with Jim Haynes. "In the sixties," Money says, "America experienced what the media called a sexual revolution. However, if we wanted to be accurate, we would call it a reformation. Like all reformations, it was spontaneous rather than planned...Historically, all reformations are followed by a backlash, a counter-reformation. We are currently in a sexual counter-reformation.

Money continued: "Essentially, some people are taking everything that is sex-positive and labeling it sex-negative. Today's witch-hunt goes after women's liberation, gay liberation, sex education, contraception, teenage pregnancy, abortion and pornography...When you criminalize pornography, you criminalize sex."

According to Money, not only is pornography not immoral—pornography actually prevents sex crimes. Noting that he sees "many" positive benefits of pornography, Money stated: "I have one patient who, when he is exposed to normal erotic images such as you find in *Playboy*, has normal sexual fantasies. In the absence of healthy erotica, he has sadistic, brutal fantasies about bondage, rape and death." Nods the interviewer: "Close a newsstand, create a killer."[5]

No wonder Hugh Hefner expressly requested that *Playboy* interview Dr. Money.[6]

The hard, cold truth of the matter is that pornography is addictive. It's addictive because the male mind is hard-wired to crave sexual imagery. Where pornography differs from "checking out" a woman is the extent shown. Soft-core pornography and cheesecake photos are all less dangerous by degrees than harder stuff. And the Ted Bundy-like progression from soft-core to hard-core to obscenely violent porn to murder is extremely rare.

All the same, the idea that sex fiends become sex fiends because of lack of sexual knowledge or exposure to sex is a self-serving lie. A Los Angeles Police Department study spanning ten years found that pornography was a factor in 62 percent of child molestation cases. An FBI study of serial killers found that 81 percent reported hard-core porn to be their "highest sexual interest."[7] As Dr. Dobson explains, "You don't have to be a psychopath to become desensitized to violence and harm to other people. You can show statistically that exposing young boys to certain kinds of sexual experience in early adolescence produces a rather high probability of sexual problems later on."[8]

Dr. Kelly Hollowell, founder of Science Ministries, Inc., explains that there is a biological predilection toward pornography. Once the switch is turned too many times, it's tough to turn off. Writes Hollowell:

> Simply said, the more pornography is viewed the more distorted one's views of sex become. This is called desensitization. For example, when one study group was exposed to as little as five hours of non-violent pornography, they began to think pornography was not offensive and that rapists deserved milder punishments. They also became more callous and negative toward

women and developed an appetite for more deviant or violent types of pornography...Researchers now link this change in behavior to the startling discovery that when people indulge in pornography, they release powerful chemicals that actually change the structure of the brain and body creating a physical and chemical addiction. This addiction is so powerful it is being likened to cocaine, alcohol, and heroin. And like any drug addiction, once hooked, addicts need harder and more perverse images to achieve the same "high."[9]

Even in the most "innocent" cases, pornography is still, in Dr. Dobson's words, "damnable." It implicitly teaches men—and I speak here almost exclusively about men because the market for porn is overwhelmingly male—that women have no dignity.

The feminists are right when they say that pornography debases women. It provides a false standard for female sexuality, because it teaches that women are as sexually driven as men. It provides a false standard for female beauty, because normal women don't have boob jobs and liposuction (unless you're in Los Angeles). It's no wonder, as Professor James B. Weaver of Virginia Tech explains, that the use of pornography leads to "sexual callousness, the erosion of family values and diminished sexual satisfaction."[10] And the sexual imagery doesn't simply dissipate once men stop looking at it—it sticks in their memory. As Mary Anne Layden, co-director of the Sexual Trauma and Psychopathology Program at the University of Pennsylvania, testified before Congress, pornography is the "most concerning thing to psychological health that I know of existing today."[11]

There is a connection between mainstream porn and kiddie porn as well. Much of what passes for soft-core pornography is schoolgirl porn, passing models off as high school cheerleaders ready for some action. Vincent Golphin of the *Syracuse Post-Standard* explains: "One of the students—I won't use her name—was shown fully clothed with an armful of books, leaning against a tree with the college's Ivy League-looking, Hall of Languages in the background. Next to that shot was a photo of the same girl wearing only tennis shoes, sitting legs wide open in what looked like a dorm room.... In one photo the young woman looked like a bobby-soxer. Virginal. Innocent. Is that reality? In the nude photo she sat brazenly, hair swept back, looking too worldly. Is that reality? Maybe that's why Bundy said the person hooked on pornography looses [sic] grip on reality."[12] Is it any wonder that virgin-slut characters like Britney Spears are the most-downloaded figures on the Internet?

Yet we're told that to pass laws against porn means infringing upon basic American freedoms. The Supreme Court has repeatedly ruled against Internet pornography laws. The ACLU routinely stands with the pornographers in their fight against morality—under the guise of free speech, of course.[13] Labeling obscenity a right that the Founding Fathers sought to protect is, in and of itself, an obscenity.

In the end, it's all so indescribably selfish. One of the most sickening aspects of pornography is its narcissism, a narcissism so deep and broad that it approaches theology of the self. Because looking at naked people in the sexual act is really about getting *your* rocks off. It's about leaving the real world and entering a sick fantasy world where everything revolves around the penis, the vagina, the breasts, and the anus— and all of those sexual organs revolve around you. As Tom Wolfe puts it, "It is merely an example of how people in even the most secular manifestation of the Me decade—free-lance spread-'em ziggy-zig rutting—are likely to go through the usual states...Let's talk about Me...Let's find the Real Me...Let's get rid of all the hypocrisies and impediments and false modesties that obscure the Real Me...Ah! At the apex of my soul is a spark of the Divine...which I perceive in the pure moment of ecstasy (which your textbooks call 'the orgasm,' but which I know to be heaven)."[14]

The biz

Jaz McKay is a conservative/libertarian talk show host from Fresno, California. His show, broadcast from six to nine p.m. every weeknight on 580 AM, covers politics and pop culture. I met Jaz after he invited me on his show to promote my first book. We've been friends ever since, and I participate in his radio program each Thursday night and discuss the issues of the day.

Jaz is an interesting fellow. A staunch fiscal conservative, a foreign policy hawk, and a social libertarian, he's been in radio all his life. But for a few years, he had a side career as well: Jaz started as a DJ for the "gentlemen's club" chain Déjà Vu, and worked his way up to management of several of the Midwest clubs. Déjà Vu has dozens of outlets around the country; they're famous for their dancing strippers and their no-alcohol policy.

Déjà Vu is known in the porn community for its responsible business practices (in the rest of the community, of course, they're known only for their porn). The front page of their website carries only a bikini-clad blonde and a disclaimer: "The materials which are available within this site may include graphic visual depictions and descriptions of nudity and sexual activity and should NOT be accessed by anyone who is younger than eighteen years old or who does not wish to be exposed to such materials."[15] It also includes a link away from the site, which directs you to a search engine.

Jaz is no whistle-blower. He enjoyed working at Déjà Vu. "It was a very professional organization. When they started, they made most of their money off of book and tape sales and sex toys. Now, most of their business is made in the gentlemen's club. A typical Déjà Vu has three sections. There's the real moneymaking section—the dancers with the stage and all that. There's the porn shop. And then there's the booths, where the customers go in, put some money in the slot, the curtain goes up, and they get a private show."

According to Jaz, he once took a group of Christian protesters through one of his clubs (after first "telling the girls to tone down the raunchy stuff"), and they gave it a clean bill of health. His typical ploy with community protesters was to kill them with kindness, bringing them coffee in the snow, bringing out the girls to meet the protesters. "It worked like a charm," he told me.

Jaz is an open porn advocate. "There's nothing wrong with adult entertainment. Look, you and I, we believe that there's something more to sex than just the physical act. There's emotion there too. But the physical isn't bad either. It may not be something you are into but others are. And I believe it's harmless. There have been countless studies done and I don't know of any that can prove any harm to anyone. And let me tell you, sexual experimentation can really be good thing. My first marriage, my wife and I were swingers. The first time we swung, we took home this guy named Jon my wife had known most of her life. It was a fantasy my wife wanted. I loved her, I wanted to give her that fantasy, so I said okay to it. It was one of the most moving nights of my life. After the two of us had pleasured her several times, I turned over to go to sleep; I wasn't really out yet, but they thought I was. I heard Jon tell my wife, 'I've always loved you,' and then—and this still makes me cry—she said to him: 'I love you too, but I'm in love with Jaz, now go to sleep.'" When I ask him why he broke up with his wife, Jaz tells me that that's a long story. He had had an affair several years after the swinging days had ended.

I ask Jaz whether he thought the porn and swinging led to the marriage's breakup. "Not in the least, it was because of a long series of events that had absolutely nothing to do with the swinging, or porn. Hell, porn wasn't even something either of us watched in those days," he says. I explain that from a Jewish perspective, sex within the confines of marriage should have an intensely spiritual element; if a man is even thinking of another woman, he is forbidden from sleeping with his wife. The respect for the woman is tremendous, and the idea of opening a marriage to the slings and arrows of an oversexed society, let alone to a third party, is abhorrent. Jaz disagrees. "Porn has never once had any negative effects on any of my relationships," Jaz states.

A porn connoisseur, Jaz owns over three hundred vintage porn videos, from the "bad old days of one-camera, stationary shots" to slick, thinly woven porn movies ("where there'll be a group of guys staring at two girls making out on a beach, and devise a way to get in on the action"). Jaz made his own, low-budget amateur porn flicks for awhile in the late 1980s: "I'd ask the girls from the club to come to my house. I'd pay them $50 bucks to do a solo act or $100 each for girl on girl action." He also claims to be one of the first people to come up with the idea of using regular people to make porn—"real people, not professional actors or actresses. I submitted the idea to some people in the business, but they basically said 'Thanks but no thanks.' Then a few months later, the amateur adult film becomes a huge part of the adult industry."

Isn't porn exploitative of women? "That's feminist bulls—," he growls. "These women are making a living for doing something they enjoy. And men and women are watching something they enjoy. What's the problem? Look, this whole exploitation thing is garbage. Of the millions of adult movie rentals every year, studies show most were watched by two people. Forty-seven percent of these rentals are made by women in couples or women alone. The overall stat shows that 500 million videos are rented each year. If 47 percent are rented by couples that means nearly 250 million are being rented by women or couples. Well, Reagan's 1984 election was considered to be a landslide with 54 million votes. And these figures don't include adult video sales, cable TV viewings, Internet sales, or adult theatre attendance."

Jaz dismisses the idea that a skewed vision of male patriarchy plays a negative role in pornography. It's interesting to note that the feminist movement has become increasingly schizophrenic on this issue. For some, the porn industry is pure exploitation. For others, the newly found women-for-porn fad is merely female sexuality leaping out of the closet. I'm of the mind that porn is exploitative for different reasons. Some girls unify the two views, as does "Sarah," a former University of Washington student. Sarah says that if a man thought less of her for stripping, he'd be a "real asshole"—yet she admits that "I'm always in the position of feeling objectified. Why shouldn't I get paid for it?"[16]

Porn says women are the embodiment of sex—but the best relationships are supposed to be about more than sex. As "Max," Sarah's University of Washington boyfriend, told the campus newspaper, "There's a tension between my appreciation [of watching Sarah's naked cavorting] and the dehumanizing aspect."[17] Porn degrades the men who view it, and the women who allow themselves to be degraded by it.

I ask Jaz what he thinks of youngsters being exposed to sexual images. "I don't think it's incredibly damaging for young people to see 'adult material' within reason of course. I first saw *Playboy* magazine, which I do not consider porn, by the way, at ten years old and it didn't screw me up. Look, seeing images you're already imagining isn't damaging, is it? For instance, you can't tell me—not you, or any other straight guy—that you don't dream of having two women in bed at the same time. So what's wrong with seeing that happen? . . . But in any case, porn isn't being marketed to kids, and I'll say this, that the Internet is pretty loose, which needs more policing."

What are the girls like, I ask? Why do they get into the business? "Most of them are pretty typical girls. At one time in the seventies they used to be aspiring actresses who couldn't make it in the legit film business, but now they're drawn by the allure of the cash. As a stripper, they walk into the club, get naked, and get $500 the first night. But that's also part of the problem. With all that expendable cash, lots of young strippers get into drugs. When I was managing the clubs, I would toss a girl at the first sign of drug use."

I ask what seems to me to be one of the more important questions: What do these girls think about sex? If they're willing to sell their bodies and souls for some easy money, what does "making love" really mean to them?

"It's a job, with the added benefit of living out a fantasy of making men take on the role of the subservient. It's nothing deeper than that," Jaz explains. "But that's the life of the stripper, nothing whatsoever to do with the 'porn star.' Porn actors are another animal. Like apples and oranges they are nowhere near the same. The truth be told, porn actors and actresses are doing what they love and earning a paycheck, paying taxes, et cetera. They are public fornicators make no mistake about it. Period, paragraph, end of story. And who are you, or anyone for that matter to pass judgment on them? You don't know them or the reasons why they do what they do. As I said, I'm no mind reader, so I can't answer for them. But I will say they are enjoying their jobs. As I would too, if I could do it." This isn't any surprise to me by this point in the conversation; after all, I've just been informed that these talented men and women are all about "c—ing on cue."

The porn industry is skewing younger and younger. It's the college-aged who are being targeted by the porn industry—and used by it. *Girls Gone Wild* is a symptom of a larger disease. At Indiana University, a film crew from the California-based Shane Enterprises taped several students engaging in sex acts with porn actresses. Between twenty and thirty students signed releases to appear in the film—and according to Shane Enterprises, university students invited the company there to film.[18] The artistic masterpiece: *Shane's World No. 32: Campus Invasion.*

Larry Flynt went so far as to start a whole magazine, *Barely Legal*, devoted to photographing girls just over eighteen. One click into the site, the viewer receives titillating pictures of teenagers in lesbian poses, with the captions: "From the homeroom to the bedroom, these young cuties are eager to please and try everything," "Sweet and cute but not innocent," and "Barely eighteen and ready for some action."[19] The viewer also gets an unending stream of pop-up ads leading to various teenage porn sites. Some of the girls in the pop-ups don't look more than sixteen—and even if they're overage, they're certainly not telling viewers to lay off the youngsters.

"Certainly the porn industry is geared more toward college students these days," Jaz says. "Poor old fat, ugly Ron Jeremy wouldn't last ten minutes in today's porn industry. When an actor hits forty, he's through, and that's if he's lucky. The strippers and actors are all in their early twenties."

The Britney Spears phenomenon came about because of her Catholic schoolgirl, faux virgin routine. And though Jaz and other industry spokesmen maintain that no underage girls slip through the cracks—even if these girls aren't underage, they pose as if they were. Aren't there guys looking at fifteen and sixteen year old girls as sex objects now?

"Yeah, I guess it happens," Jaz admits. "I'm no pervert but I do date younger women, all of legal age by the way. I feel I have to say that because your readers may misconstrue my statements. One friend of mine is Hyapatia Lee, who is today in her mid-forties. As I understand her story she started at the age of sixteen or seventeen. She has controlled her entire career, like the vast majority of adult film stars, and today is retired with a huge bank account, and no desire to suck off the government tit of welfare or Medicare."

I ask him whether the porn honchos are driven by profit, or by something deeper. "I'd say it's 90 percent profit," he explains, "but for many of them, the cause goes along with it. They have to justify themselves somehow. If you're a prude or a moralist, this ain't your business. Or maybe it is but you just don't know it yet."[20]

The net

The Internet is easily the most prolific porn producer in the world, even if the quality of the porn is "low-class" in Jaz's words. Even as a porn proponent, he admits that the Internet porn industry needs more regulation.

As of 2002, the National Research Council reported that there were 400,000 sexually explicit websites on the net. N2H2, a Seattle-based software company, reports far more: 1.3 million, 1800 percent more than in 1998.[21] The Internet Filter Review places the number at 4.2 million websites encompassing 372 million web pages, constituting 12 percent of the total number of websites on the internet.[22] Type in the term "porn" on Google.com, and you'll get a nearly infinite number of 149,000,000 hits. Easy misspelling of search terms often leads straight to porn. If you type "teen" into a search engine, you'll get teen magazines. If you type in "teeen," you'll get porn. Type in "Hun," as in Attila the, and you'll likely get thehun.com, a yellow pages for porn. More famously, if you type whitehouse.gov into your search engine, you'll get the White House. Type in whitehouse.com, however, and you'll get a porn site.

Online porn is certainly a moneymaker. The National Research Council report stated that cyber-porn garners over $1 billion per year, and could soon grow to $5 billion.[23] The porn industry in general takes in $57 billion worldwide and $12 billion in the United States per year—more than all the combined revenues of pro football, basketball, and baseball franchises, as well as the combined revenues of ABC, CBS, and NBC.

Kiddie porn generates $3 billion each year.[24] There are at least 100,000 child pornography websites available on the Internet.[25] Also available: incestuous porn, bestial porn, and with extreme commonness, "virgin" porn—for those guys who like to pretend that their fetish girls really haven't done anything before taping a hard core sex video. "Schoolgirl" porn is especially typical—from "first-time lesbian" school-girls to "orgy" schoolgirl porn. The "college roommates" idea is also big; lesbian porn between co-eds is insanely popular. The idea that the porn industry doesn't push men to look at fifteen- to eighteen-year-old girls as sex objects is ridiculous.

Unfortunately, the Internet isn't just the most prolific porn producer—it's also the easiest place to find porn. Registering for nearly anything on the net guarantees that you'll have porn spam in your e-mail box—including everything from "WANT A BIGGER PENIS?" to "ASIAN SCHOOL-GIRL FUN!" There are 2.8 billion daily pornography e-mails circulating around the Internet, 8 percent of the total number of daily e-mails.[26]

Here's the newest weapon: Instant Messenger (IM). You can be sitting online on AOL, MSN, or another IM service, when suddenly you receive an instant message from some gal asking you to check out her webcam (a camera set up to film people, often in compromising positions). With e-mail spam under attack, the IM spamming, also known as "spimming," is the new wave. As *PC World* reported, "The number of IM spam messages will triple [in the year 2004], from 400 million to 1.2 billion, according to the research firm the Radicati Group...IM spammers are developing sophisticated software which automatically sends messages—which are mainly touting pornography—to millions of users, and which can automatically change screen names when the user blocks an IM attempt."[27]

Think your child is safe from online porn if you don't give him a credit card? Try again. Hard-core porn pictures are available all over the Internet, and children don't even have to pretend to be eighteen to see them. Over 70 percent of porn sites offer free images and stories to draw people into the site, and there are any number of search engines that will help kids find these pictures.[28]

If you spend any amount of time on the Internet, it's difficult not to find yourself in the midst of a hard-core porn site—and if you do, you can't easily leave. A practice called "mousetrapping" means that by clicking out of the site, you'll be hit with a virtually endless series of pop-up ads for other porn sites, and the only way to stop the flood of pornography is to shut the window or turn off the web browser.[29]

More and more people—specifically men (72 percent of visitors to porn sites are male[30])—are being drawn into the world of web porn. Whereas the non-Internet porno man would have to go to the darkened section of his local video store, or stroll to his nearest newsstand to browse the blacked-out magazine section, it's oh-so-easy to simply click on a web link. All it takes to stash the porn is a quick minimization click. You can do it from work or from home.

And they do. According to 2003 IFR statistics, there are 72 million worldwide visitors to porn websites annually. Twenty percent of men admit to accessing porn at their place of employment; forty million U.S. adults regularly visit porn sites. Ten percent of adults admitted to internet sexual addiction. Most shockingly, religious communities have been hard hit by the problem of Internet porn. A full 53 percent of Promise Keeper men stated that they had viewed porn in the last week, and 47 percent of Christians said pornography was a major problem in their home.[31] In a 2003 poll, 34 percent of Today's Christian Woman's online newsletter readers admitted to intentionally accessing Internet porn.[32] A Zogby International poll conducted for Focus on the Family in 2000 showed that 25.9 percent of American men and 16.7 percent of American women said it was either very or somewhat likely they could find sexual fulfillment online. 18.68 percent of Christians said the same thing.[33] A survey by Christianity Today magazine found that 37 percent of pastors admit to struggling with pornography.[34]

Internet porn doesn't only affect adults. Kids are the hardest hit by the Internet porn hurricane. The average age of first Internet exposure to pornography stands at eleven years old. The largest consumers of Internet porn are kids aged twelve to seventeen. The statistics are incredible: 80 percent of fifteen- to seventeen-year-olds report having had multiple exposures to hard-core porn, and 90 percent of eight- to sixteen-year-olds report having viewed porn online, most while doing their homework.[35]

Kids are victims of sexual aggression online, as well. Nearly 24 million children aged ten to seventeen were online regularly in 1999; one in four had an unwanted exposure to pictures of naked people or people having sex in that year. Seventy-one percent of those kids experiencing unwanted exposure found it while surfing the web, and 28 percent received it while opening e-mail or clicking on links in e-mail or IMs. Only 17 percent of incidents occurred wherein the youth knew he or she was entering a porno site.[36]

A full 89 percent of sexual solicitations toward youths are made in chat rooms; 20 percent of youths have received sexual solicitations.[37] One in thirty-three children aged ten to seventeen received an aggressive sexual solicitation (a solicitor who asked to meet them somewhere, called them on the telephone, or sent them regular mail, money, or gifts); one in seventeen was threatened or harassed.[38] Many of these "sexual solicitations" were propositions for "cybersex," wherein participants describe various sex acts, often while masturbating.[39] The National Center for Missing & Exploited Children stated in a June 2000 report that in the year 1999, there were at least 785 "traveler" cases, where a child or adult traveled to physically meet with someone he or she had first encountered on the Internet.[40]

The kids aren't telling their parents, either. Only a quarter of youths who encountered a sexual solicitation or approach told a parent, and only 40 percent of those who experienced "an unwanted exposure to sexual material" informed a parent.[41]

Online porn is the direst threat to moral attitudes toward sex today. Availability has thrust perversion and depravity onto computer screens around the country, free of charge—and those weak enough to click once may end up refreshing their screens rather often. As Dr. Kerry Hollowell puts it, "what was once a rather isolated problem has become a widespread crisis based on three factors uniquely related to Internet use: accessibility, affordability, and anonymity."[42]

The cheap and easy porn found online means setting unattainable standards for real-life sex. It means devaluing sex to a merely physical act. As Dr. Ursula Ofman, a Manhattan-based sex therapist, told NewYorkMetro.com, "It's so accessible, and now, with things like streaming video and Webcams, guys are getting sucked into a compulsive behavior. What's most regrettable is that it can really affect relationships with women. I've seen some young men lately who can't get aroused with women but have no problem interacting with the Internet. I think a big danger is that young men who are constantly exposed to these fake, always-willing women start to have unreal expectations from real women, which makes them phobic about relationships."[43]

Without any leadership or restriction by society, the situation spirals ever downward, with no end in sight.

Porn in the public square

Porn has hit the mainstream—and hit it big. In 1953, Hugh Hefner sprung onto the scene with *Playboy* and a nude Marilyn Monroe centerfold. In the words of Professor Jeffrey P. Moran of the University of Kansas, "More literary and mainstream than cheap 'girlie' magazines, more overtly sexual than its ancestor, *Esquire* magazine, *Playboy* sprang from Hefner's conviction that millions of American men, at least, were ready for a more public expression of sexuality. Hefner's creation was to have the same ripple effect as [Alfred] Kinsey's books in shifting public discussion toward greater sexual frankness... Even as the public culture grew more overtly sexual, the moral unity among family sociologists, family life educators, sex educators, and other authorities on sex was beginning to crumble."[44]

Now, of course, Hefner is hailed as an influential mainstream figure. The *Washington Post* calls Hefner an "icon."[45] Anderson Cooper of CNN lauds Hefner as "the granddaddy of all playboys, the seventy-seven-year-old who still puts the play in player."[46] He's a "champion of free speech" according to the *New York Post*,[47] a "sexual pioneer" according to the *Boston Herald*.[48] Hef is so mainstream that in 2003, he even did a raunchy commercial for burger chain Carl's Jr. The aging

Hefner, bearing a strong resemblance to the Crypt-keeper in silk pajamas, looks directly into the camera and tells the audience: "People always ask me: 'Hey, Hef. Do you have favorites?' I tell 'em, 'No—It's not about that.'" Three young hotties then explain Hefner's philosophy. "He can have anything he wants. I don't know how he makes the choice," says Side O' Beef #1. "I feel for Hef. It's so hard to choose," avers Side O' Beef #2. "I don't know how he does it," marvels Side O' Beef #3. Cut back to Hefner: "I love 'em all. It just depends on what I'm in the mood for." The commercial then pictures Hefner biting into a burger while the announcer intones: "Because some guys don't like the same thing night after night."

The president and CEO of Carl's Jr. parent company CKE, Andy Puzder, justified the Hefner commercial to shareholders, writing: "Who better to deliver the message of variety than Hugh Hefner? We're appealing to an audience of young, hungry guys who expect a quality product, but want to have something different from time to time... As a pop-icon, Hefner appeals to our target audience and credibly communicates our message of variety."[49]

Fellow porn enthusiasts like Larry Flynt have also been enshrined in the popular culture. Flynt, who ran for California governor during the Gray Davis recall, was also deified by Hollywood in *The People vs. Larry Flynt*. Woody Harrelson played the porn magnate, a fun-loving, free speech–pushing dude. It's no wonder that Jaz cites Flynt as one of his personal heroes.

The court system has ensured that people like Flynt and Hefner are seen not as dirty old men but as purveyors of free speech, implying that our founders laid down life, liberty, and property for the sake of naked pictures. The latest decision to support the pornographers concerned Internet porn, in *Ashcroft* v. *American Civil Liberties Union* (where porn is in danger, the ACLU is just a phone call away!). The Supreme Court ruled on June 29, 2004 that a law created to punish pornographers who push their wares to web-surfing children is probably unconstitutional. The Child Online Protection Act was passed in 1998, signed by President Clinton, and backed by the Bush administration. It would have authorized fines of up to $50,000 for the crime of placing material "harmful to minors" within the easy reach of children on the Internet, and also would have required adults to use access codes and/or other registration means in order to see porn online.[50]

A 5–4 court decision upheld a lower court decision declaring the law a violation of the First Amendment. Justice Department officials derided the decision as a step in the wrong direction, but ACLU lawyers were happy as could be. As Ann Beeson, one of those righteous attorneys, told the Associated Press: "We're very pleased with the decision. The status quo is still with us and the court made it safe for artists, sex educators, and web publishers to communicate with adults without risking jail time."[51]

A whole new generation of porn icons is on the way up. In 2004, widely known (yes, that includes the biblical sense) porn star Jenna Jameson put out her memoir/advice book, *How to Make Love Like a Porn Star*. It immediately slept its way to the top of the bestseller lists. The *Los Angeles Times* characterized Jameson as an advocate for feminist ideals, explaining "Conventional forms of self-improvement will never catch on with some people, a fact that troubles many feminists, and this porn diva wants to remind them of it."[52] *Publishers Weekly* described the 577-page ode to porn as brimming with "wit," noting "the book is dedicated to Onan."[53]

Fifty years ago, masturbation was taboo. Nowadays, mention masturbation and receive literary praise for your wit. As Jameson's website touts, "Jenna Jameson has made the transition from adult star to mainstream personality... *Revolver* magazine chose her at the 2003 "Girl of the Year" ... recently the FOX News Networks carried three separate programs profiling Jenna in a space of four days ... and Entertainment Tonight featured her in three back-to-back segments within a week's time."[54]

Jameson represents a new wave of porn hitting the bookshelves disguised as mainstream literature. In fall 2004 alone, the following titles had entered or were scheduled to enter bookstores across the country: *XXX: 30 Porn-Star Portraits* (with introduction by Gore Vidal), *The*

Intimate History of the Orgasm (has the orgasm evolved over time? Pick up this book to find out!), *Star* (the fascinating life of Pamela Anderson's breasts), as well as a history of prostitution and one of the porno film industry. As even the lusty, heavy-breathing *New York Times* was forced to note, "A wave of confessionals and self-help guides written by current or former stars of pornographic films is flooding bookstores this year, accompanied by erotic novels, racy sexual-instruction guides, histories of sexual particulars and photographic treatments of the world of pornography... rarely have [such] books been as prominently positioned as some of the current crop, which have been elbowing their way onto display tables at the front of the major chain bookstores."[55]

Generation Porn

Porn serves to desensitize, to rev up the sexual instinct for no real purpose, to separate sex from love and spirituality. There's absolutely nothing spiritual or loving about logging on to jennajameson.com and downloading videos of Jameson's "cum shots." And for today's generation, porn has become just another perfectly acceptable portion of the public square.

So where is all the condemnation? Many of those on the side of traditional morality ignore the problem of porn, hoping that it will go away. We let those who degrade and destroy the concept of spirituality within sexual relationships win. Unless we're willing to throw away our computers, televisions, and library cards for the sake of raising children in a safe and healthy environment, we can't afford to let the porn-pushers win. As Professor James B. Weaver of Virginia Tech told a Senate subcommittee, "We're so afraid to talk about sex in our society that we really give carte blanche to the people who are producing this kind of material."[56]

Others are simply afraid of frank talk—not about sex, but about morality in general. Morality is passé in today's society. Even if you oppose pornography, you're not supposed to take a stand against it. As Paige Messec, a twenty-four-year-old Harvard Law student, explained, "There are plenty of things about pornography that make me uncomfortable,

but I would be much more uncomfortable with those things being pro-
hibited."[57]

Standing up for morality means facing loud derision, especially for
children of the porn generation. Those of my age group may hold a quiet
admiration for the sexually moral among us, but it's hidden beneath a
façade of cynicism. We grew up in an age of Hugh Hefners and Jenna
Jamesons who no longer have to fight the moral establishment, but are
instead hailed as heroes. We grew up in an age where acquiring pornographic material doesn't involve anything more strenuous than a few key-
strokes at your laptop. We've been told there's nothing wrong with
homosexuality and premarital sex—so what's so bad about checking out
a few dirty pictures? Or visiting the local strip club? Or even signing a
release to appear in the new *Girls Gone Wild: Mardi Gras* video?

Our parents' generation smoked grass and listened to psychedelic
rock while making love, not war. We're not doing anything nearly that
drastic—we're only watching two girls get it on. So what's the problem?
As Amber Madison, formerly of Tufts University (and star of *The Real
Cancun*) explained in her *Sex and the City*-style column, "I've come to
the conclusion that maybe porn isn't that bad after all...Nudy [sic] flicks
may not be your thing—they're not mine either—but they're also not the
downfall of healthy sexual relations."[58]

Hugh Hefner would agree. Ted Bundy wouldn't. Neither would his
victims.

CHAPTER ELEVEN

TAKING A STAND

"No period of history has ever been great or ever can be that does not act on some sort of high, idealistic motives, and idealism in our time has been shoved aside, and we are paying the penalty for it."

ALFRED NORTH WHITEHEAD

After looking at the social breakdown of the porn generation, we are left to wonder: Where does America go from here?

Reversing the tide of our "live and let live" culture won't be easy. I know. I'm twenty-one years old, a heterosexual red-blooded American male, a graduate of University of California at Los Angeles, a student at Harvard Law School, a nationally syndicated columnist, a bestselling author…and a virgin. And I'm proud of it.

I am proud of my choice, a decision that the amoral political Left ridicules and cannot understand. I'm not a virgin for lack of easy girls—in college, they aren't hard to find. I'm not a virgin because I lack a sex drive, either. I'm a virgin because according to Jewish law (halacha), men and women must remain virgins until marriage.

The amoral Left and our oversexed culture cannot comprehend abstinence as a choice. If you're a post-teenage virgin in the porn generation, you're weird at least, and probably demented. There's a high probability that you're deformed, either mentally or physically, because dude, you couldn't "get any." Virginity is a barrier to knowledge, according to the sexual activity advocates, and only those who are sexually active are bestowed with ultimate wisdom—which is, of course, why gigolos and prostitutes are among civilization's leading thinkers.

Because of my vocal advocacy of abstinence until marriage, I've been reviled by leftists and labeled "The Virgin Ben." The Internet is riddled with writing like this: "In [Ben's] case it is helpful to remember that some people choose celibacy, while others have it thrust upon them. Poor Ben. He no more chose abstinence than Clarence Thomas chose to be black."[1] "The Virgin Ben also apparently has never had a really great Saturday night."[2] "The Virgin Ben judges college-age fornicators. Who could have guessed this was coming?"[3] "The Virgin Ben, indeed. This guy's 'interview' so completely reeks of repression that I almost feel violated having read it. Like I stepped into someone else's wet dream. It's freakin' eerie, man."[4] "You know I'm starting to feel sorry for this kid. I look into his future and I can see that *not once* is he ever going to get to have really good hot sweaty sex with Miss Scarlet in the parlor with a bottle of lube. That kind of sex may not approach godliness, but for a few brief moments and a lifetime of memories it sure feels like it."[5]

Whether these Internet denizens recognize it or not, they are representative of a larger anti-virtue demographic. My own experience is representative of what many members of the porn generation endure in their own high schools and on their college campuses every day. We're forced to undergo this experience because, in the twisted view of the sex-obsessed moral relativists, abstinence before marriage is a demented way of life, and virginity itself is seen as some sort of strange plague. In a world where deviance is praised, purity is the new sin.

So the question of where we go from here—for those who care about their future, the future of their children, and the future of our country—

becomes a simple one to answer. We must recognize how bad things have truly become, and act in response to it.

In order to prevent the porn generation from plunging into the cultural abyss, we need to strengthen ourselves, our families, and our children. Parents must stop and pay attention to what's going on in our culture. They must equip their children with the moral compass that will guide them through life as a member of the porn generation. And strong young men and women must be prepared to stand up to the cultural intimidation and peer pressure of an oversexed society.

By rebuilding a culture founded on strong moral standards, we can heal the porn generation from within. Ultimately, our generation will not be led by the oversexed pop stars, the sex educators, the celebrities, or the blind followers of "live and let live"—it will be led by those brave enough and dedicated enough to climb their way out of the morass, to return our country to the ultimate truth of its moral heritage— to a place that honors and cherishes all that once was good, and can be again.

Solving the problem

Laws and regulations cannot, by themselves, stem the tide of societal amorality. When a society is absolutely determined to poison itself, mere legislation cannot stop it. So the first job is to raise the level of personal adherence to traditional morality. Parents must teach their children traditional standards, and they must live by those same standards themselves. Sometimes this means turning off the television, throwing out the CDs and DVDs, and canceling subscriptions to teen magazines. Sometimes it just means talking to your kids.

But this isn't enough. Libertarians and social liberals would have us believe that as long as those of us who adhere to traditional morality do so, we should allow opponents of traditional morality to live life their way, without consequences. This ignores the fact that these actions are social, not individual. The direction of our culture has ramifications for society. Tolerance of all behavior leads to societal immorality, and societal approval of immoral personal behavior has vast externalities. Just as a manufacturing plant that produces toxic waste may affect others by poisoning a river, so too may the immoral among us affect others by poisoning the culture.

This means that we should not hesitate to move forward in protecting our culture collectively. Here, then, are some collective, practical solutions we should enact in order to protect our culture from further anti-traditional assault:

- *Abstinence-only education*: We must tell our elected representatives to make abstinence-only education the primary course across America. We know that the comprehensive sex education has failed miserably in curbing teen sexual voraciousness—it's time to try a path that actually values chastity.

- *Faith-based initiatives*: We must adopt faith-based community initiatives to revitalize traditional values among students. Abstinence-only education can only be truly successful in the context of a full set of values, taught by parents and religious communities. Thankfully, the Bush administration is dedicated to slowing the indoctrination of children into the lifestyle of sexual permissiveness and moral relativism. This goal is well within reach.

- *School vouchers*: It's time to take our schools back. We can do this by pushing for school vouchers, allowing parents to make informed decisions about the values they wish schools to teach to their children. Competitive pressure can only help move public schools away from teaching amorality.

- *Dress codes*: Public schools should begin (and have begun) instituting dress codes. Permissiveness in dress is an early and important step toward permissiveness in values.

- *Single-sex dorms or living at home for college students*: In higher education, parents should demand that their children live in single-sex dorms (or at least in dorms with single-sex bathrooms) or get apartments. Sending young adults to local universities is also a good move—at eighteen, teenagers aren't ready to face the pressures they will encounter at a college hundreds of miles from home. Even religious teenagers may be converted by the temptations they see on university campuses and the ridicule they encounter there.

- *Monitoring alumni funding for universities*: Alumni and donors should consider directing their funding to universities where traditional values are still part of the curriculum. In my first book, *Brainwashed: How Universities Indoctrinate America's Youth*, I advocate what I call "start-up universities."[6] Conservatives should begin a movement to open politically balanced universities. Competition is the ultimate equalizer.

- *Using the Federal Communications Commission*: The Federal Communications Commission has some authority to control obscenity and indecency. The FCC requires written complaints from viewers in order to invoke its powers. To that end, here is the contact information for the FCC:

    FCC
    Enforcement Bureau, Investigations and Hearings Division
    445 12th Street, SW
    Washington, D.C. 20554
    EMAIL: *fccinfo@fcc.gov*
    TELEPHONE: 1-888-CALL-FCC (1-888-225-5322) or
                        1-888-TELL-FCC (1-888-835-5322)

    Still, the FCC doesn't have enough power to limit obscenity, pornography, or indecency. Considering the overwhelming saturation of cable and satellite TV, its current power should be extended to cable channels as well as networks.

- *Governmental censorship*: As Robert Bork puts it, "Without censorship, it has proved impossible to maintain any standards of decency."[7]

We must press for government to use the force of the law against pornography, obscenity, and indecency across the board, from Howard Stern to Larry Flynt, from TV to radio to the Internet, from music to movies. To do this, we must first address the issue of the judiciary, which has removed the ability of communities to set social standards against the mainstreaming of pornography, an area that should not fall under the protection of the First Amendment.

- *Reining in the judiciary*: Several interesting suggestions have been voiced with regard to reining in an overreaching judiciary. Judge Bork has proposed "a constitutional amendment making any federal or state court decision subject to being overruled by a majority vote of each House of Congress."[8] Mark Levin, in *Men in Black*, proposes amending the Constitution to "limit judges to fixed terms of office," or alternatively, "a constitutional amendment limiting the Supreme Court's judicial review power by establishing a legislative veto over court decisions—perhaps a two-thirds vote of both houses."[9] Paul Carrington and Roger Cramton suggest appointing one justice or chief justice per term of Congress, allowing each appointee to serve approximately eighteen years, and creating a regular rotation of justices far more responsive to the American people.[10] Each of these proposals would work wonders over the current system.

- *Non-governmental censorship of film*: There's plenty we can do to re-infuse society with traditional morality, even aside from government action. All it takes is coordination to build public and financial pressure on propagators of moral relativism and social immorality. The Hays Code of the 1930s, '40s, '50s and early '60s was brought about solely through public pressure. Similar public pressure should be created through active and organized boycotts of movies we know to be obscene or indecent. The website screenit.com does a wonderful job of evaluating the content of today's films.

- *Cleaning up music*: Communities should boycott companies that carry obscene CDs. In 1985, the Parents Music Resource Center forced the Recording Industry Association of America to adopt warning labels for recordings containing explicit and/or offensive lyrics.[11] Wal-Mart refused to market any product with the parental advisory label, prompting the usual critics to whine about market pressures. Similarly aggressive strategies should be adopted today.

- *Boycott advertising*: Some of the companies Americans should boycott include but are certainly not limited to: FCUK, Old Spice, Axe, Abercrombie and Fitch, Joe's Jeans, Herbal Essences, and other companies that use oversexed content to make a sale. Polluting the airwaves shouldn't be consequence-free.

Saving ourselves

It's no easy task to save the porn generation from nihilism, narcissism, and hedonism. But preventing today's teenagers and their children from growing up in a society that values "tolerance" above virtue is well worth the effort. This country cannot afford to continue defining deviancy down while simultaneously defining it up. What makes this country great is its adherence to moral principle. Our drive to spread liberty across the globe and protect liberty at home, to ensure equal opportunity for all of our citizens—all of it springs from our adherence to moral principles. Without a clear moral vision, we devolve into moral relativism, and from there, into oblivion.

In 1630, John Winthrop stood on the deck of a ship off the Massachusetts coast, and spoke to his congregation. "[W]e shall be as a City upon a Hill, the eyes of all people are upon us; so that if we shall deal falsely with our God in this work we have undertaken and so cause Him to withdraw His present help from us, we shall be made a story and a byword through the world, we shall open the mouths of enemies to speak evil of the ways of God and all professors for God's sake," Winthrop thundered. "Therefore let us choose life, that we, and our seed, may live; by obeying His voice and cleaving to Him, for He is our life, and our prosperity."

On January 11, 1989, over 350 years later, President Ronald Reagan invoked Winthrop's wordage in his farewell address. "I've spoken of the shining city all my political life, but I don't know if I ever quite communicated what I saw when I said it," Reagan explained. "But in my mind it was a tall proud city built on rocks stronger than oceans, wind-swept, God-blessed, and teeming with people of all kinds living in harmony and peace, a city with free ports that hummed with commerce and creativity, and if there had to be city walls, the walls had doors and the doors were open to anyone with the will and the heart to get here. That's how I saw it and see it still."

Reagan concluded: "After two hundred years, two centuries, she still stands strong and true on the granite ridge, and her glow has held steady no matter what storm. And she's still a beacon, still a magnet for all who must have freedom, for all the pilgrims from all the lost places who are hurtling through the darkness, toward home."

Today, our city is under attack from within. Temptation surrounds us: temptation to eroticism, temptation to hedonism, temptation to egoism. Most of all, we face the temptation of liberal tolerance, allowing immorality to grow like a cancer, disguising itself as a "new morality." The porn generation remains lost in this maelstrom of temptation, and they cannot see the consequences of giving in.

Yet I have faith that we will not give in. We will stand strong and we will stand fast against the forces that seek to destroy our basic American values. With the strength of dedicated families and the help of God, we *will* save our shining city on a hill and pass it on to our children, so that they may once again carry the torch of American greatness with pride.

CHAPTER TWELVE

ROUNDTABLE

"The central conservative truth is that it is culture, not politics, that determines the success of a society."

SENATOR DANIEL PATRICK MOYNIHAN

For this concluding chapter, I asked a group of individuals with interesting perspectives on the issues at hand to weigh in on the critical questions facing the porn generation.

Michelle Malkin was an editorial writer and columnist for the *Los Angeles Daily News* and the *Seattle Times* before becoming a nationally syndicated columnist with Creators Syndicate. Her witty, mordant, and hard-hitting column appears in nearly 200 papers nationwide. She has written two books: the *New York Times* bestseller *Invasion: How America Still Welcomes Terrorists, Criminals, and Other Foreign Menaces to Our Shores*, and more recently, *In Defense of Internment: The Case for Racial Profiling in World War II and the War on Terror*. She is a graduate of Oberlin College and a contributor to the FOX News Channel. She lives with her husband and two children in Maryland.

Rod Dreher is a columnist and editor of the Sunday opinion and commentary section of the *Dallas Morning News*. Dreher previously worked as an editor for *National Review* and chief film critic for the *New York Post*. He is currently writing a book on "crunchy conservatism." A native of St. Francisville, Louisiana, he graduated from Louisiana State University with a Bachelor of Arts degree in Journalism. He lives in Dallas with his wife and two sons.

Father C. John McCloskey, III, STD, is a priest of the Prelature of Opus Dei and the former chaplain at Princeton University. He received a degree in Economics from Columbia University in 1975, and worked on Wall Street prior to joining the priesthood, where he has converted many to the faith. He served for five years as the Director of the Catholic Information Center of the Archdiocese of Washington, and his articles and reviews have appeared in a wide range of publications, including the *Catholic World Report*, *Crisis Magazine*, the *Washington Times*, the *Wall Street Journal*, and the *New York Times*. He is native of Washington, D.C., and is now based in Chicago.

David Limbaugh is a lawyer, a nationally syndicated columnist with Creators Syndicate, and the author of two *New York Times* bestsellers, *Absolute Power* and *Persecution: How Liberals Are Waging War Against Christianity*. He attended Southeast Missouri State University and the University of Missouri–Columbia, where he graduated cum laude with a Bachelor of Arts degree in Political Science. He lives in Cape Girardeau, Missouri, with his wife and five children.

1. Why do you think today's young people are so jaded? Do you feel that the "live and let live" culture has corrupted our moral system? Why do you think American society rejected traditional moral values—the values our founders believed were necessary for our national survival—in favor of moral relativism? How much do you feel our cultural institutions—Hollywood, academia, public schools, and the mass media—are complicit in lowering societal standards?

MALKIN: More than a decade ago, the *Wall Street Journal* published a famous editorial titled "No Guardrails." It identified the 1968 Democratic National Convention as the pivotal moment when American society began to veer off its moral and emotional tracks. Restraint, accountability, and reverence for first principles went out the window. The public schools abandoned prayer, civics, and assimilation in favor of condom instruction, America-bashing, and glorification of diversity above all else. Hollywood championed Jane Fonda and Murphy Brown and "Sex in the City." Academia ditched Shakespeare for Rigobeart Menchu, and replaced Plato's *Dialogues* with the *Vagina Monologues*. "Live and let live" gave way to "Just do it" and, yes, "Drive outside the lines."

Why did the nation abandon the traditional moral values that the founders believed was integral to our survival? Because relativism feels good. Because sex without consequences is easier. Because self-control takes self-sacrifice.

DREHER: It seems to me that being jaded is the most rational response to the decadent culture we've created. Ours is a popular culture suffused with radical doubt, intense sensuality and ironic detachment. Why are we surprised by the jadedness of youth? As C.S. Lewis wrote, "We make men without chests and expect of them virtue and enterprise. We laugh at honour and are shocked to find traitors in our midst. We castrate and bid the geldings to be fruitful."

We threw out tradition in the name of liberation, and find that liberation has condemned the young to lives that are rootless and full of despair. The Bible says, "Man cannot live by bread alone," which is to say that materialism—whether manifested in the form of lust or greed—will kill a society if it becomes the highest aspiration of that society. That's where we are today. George Weigel has said that we are now engaged in a grand experiment to see if civilization can survive luxury. I think that is exactly right.

I feel our cultural institutions are the agents of this civilizational demoralization. Hollywood, academia, public schools and the mass media are guilty, but they are also easy targets. What about big business? It is inconceivable that they could profit without exploiting sexuality and envy. What about the political parties? The Democrats are the party of lust, the Republicans the party of greed. Both are deadly sins.

And what about the country's religious institutions? As a practicing Catholic, I learned more about the teaching of Pope John Paul II from reading the *New York Times* than from going to Mass. By and large, America's churches and synagogues have failed to oppose this culture of death in any meaningful way, and have made their peace with it.

MCCLOSKEY: Young people are jaded for many reasons—among them is the fact that young people today have generally had to suffer no hardship. There have been no serious economic troubles, no major war, nothing that has required selfless sacrifice on their part. Affluence undreamt of by their ancestors also has been a weakening influence on their character. It is one thing to work hard to take care of your family; it is quite another to work so as to amass more or more goods that in many cases are totally unnecessary. A comfortable life with no sacrifices and few ideals would leave anyone jaded.

When you grow up in a culture where people flee commitments, how can you trust anyone, or for that matter any institution? When you have tried drugs, alcohol, become sated with pornography, and have experienced promiscuous sex at an early age, you have suffered shattering and destructive blows to both your physical and mental health. Life becomes a boring pursuit of ephemeral pleasures that never satisfy.

When it comes to evaluating whether the "live and let live" culture has corrupted our moral system, I believe that our moral system is only effective if it is based on either the natural law or the common wisdom of human nature that is fortified by the Revelation of orthodox religion, whether it is Christian or Jewish. Forgiveness and mercy are essential for a healthy society, but there must be an admission of sin and true repentance in order to change, to convert. There must be accountability both in this life and the next.

American society has rejected traditional moral values for fairly simple reasons. One reason that isn't always acknowledged is the gradual decline of absolute norms of moral conduct—based on the Bible for Christians and Jews—and the corruption of moral theology in seminaries by heretics, whose views spread down to the people in the pews each

Sunday. In all these cases, the religious instruction of young people both in the family and from the church and synagogue has faltered significantly. Ultimately, I place the blame for moral decline and the lowering of social standards on the decline of orthodox religious belief and practice on the part of both Jewish and Christian families. Too many of them reflect the general beliefs and practices of the public, instead of standing out as a model of action.

One solution to reverse the decline is giving parents choice—and responsibility—in education. Public education at every level is completely corrupt and should be abolished to leave room for and require parental authority. Whether it be via vouchers, tax exemptions, or some other system, parents should be responsible for choosing their children's education and not deferring that responsibility to the state religion of radical secularism that inculcates vice and destroys virtue.

LIMBAUGH: First, I'm not sure to what extent kids today are jaded, but I do think they are significantly more so than kids in my day. To the extent they are jaded, though, I think several factors are involved, all related to the steady coarsening of our culture. They are inevitably influenced by this coarsening through television, the Internet, movies, the mainstream media, public schools and academia, all of which, on the whole, exude a disdain for religion and traditional values and promote narcissism, hedonism and licentiousness. Even children from faith-based homes are inevitably exposed to these influences, some earlier and more intensely than others, depending, in part, on whether they attend public schools.

There is little doubt that secularists dominate our major cultural institutions. They often exhibit open contempt for Judeo-Christian values, mocking all who espouse them. In place of moral absolutes, they promote moral relativism and sometimes even question the very existence of truth and reality. To them truth and reality are what we subjectively perceive them to be. Such psychobabble can be disorienting even to a college student whose worldview is still being shaped. It's difficult for parents to insulate their children from such insidious and destructive notions.

The education establishment, especially, denigrates Western civilization and the prospect of a unique American culture. It depicts Western values and the white males largely responsible for promoting them in American history as intolerant, bigoted, homophobic, sexist, and racist. It decries capitalism as exploitative and greedy and glamorizes socialism, preaching that it is government's responsibility to provide for the people. Truth be known, many of the professorial elite view America as an avaricious, world resource glutton. They are hostile to national sovereignty, especially where America is concerned, and would probably be quite pleased if America would just wither away and merge into an idealized, global community where economic misery can be more equally distributed to all the "world's citizens." A kind of peer pressure emerges on our university campuses, making it uncomfortable for students who believe differently to express their views.

I am not prepared, however, to conclude that American society has affirmatively rejected traditional moral values. But at the very least traditionalists have surrendered leadership to secularists. There are still huge numbers of people, perhaps even a majority, who nominally embrace traditional values and claim to be Christians. Whether their concept of moral absolutes is completely clear is another matter. With secular influences seeping into every crack of our society it is difficult to avoid a dilution of the ideas and values that once informed our culture. So even many who profess an allegiance to moral absolutes are, on closer inspection, deeply conflicted and confused and their views lack the consistency that inheres in a more fully developed worldview. With secular intellectuals mocking our traditions every day and constantly undermining the sacred it is no surprise that we've seen a disintegration of our values and intellectual chaos surrounding them.

Fortunately, there are those fighting against this values upheaval and the moral nihilism it has ushered in. Practicing Christians and observant Jews, along with other social conservatives, are fighting back to restore traditional values. It is hard to tell what the outcome of this culture war will be, but it is certain that if social conservatives opt out of the war, traditional values will degenerate at an even quicker pace. This is because secular forces are relentless in their determination to supplant traditional values with their seductive, distorted concept of morality where their glorified idea of tolerance—which is actually a grossly selective tolerance—is touted as the highest good.

If traditionalists have any hope of preserving the America they adore for their children and grandchildren—morally healthy and politically free—they have a duty to engage in the Culture War, no matter how distasteful they might find it to be.

2. Is there anything parents can do to shield their children from our oversexed, tolerance-of-all-behavior culture? Do the state and/or federal governments have a role in upholding moral standards? If so, what can we do to stop an overreaching judiciary and other anti-values institutions while getting our elected representatives to act with moral conviction? Outside of government, what can we do to revitalize proud belief in traditional morality?

MALKIN: There are so many things parents can do—and we have reached the point where they are now things we *must* do. Support home schooling and educational choice. Turn off the television. Limit your children's exposure to the Internet. Say "NO" without apologies. Defend the Boy Scouts. Volunteer at a crisis pregnancy center. Vote out spineless lawmakers who refuse to rein in our reckless judiciary. Pray. Live what you teach. And most of all, do not depend on government to do your job.

DREHER: Yes. Be a revolutionary: kill your TV. Getting rid of television—by which I mean its unrestricted use—is non-negotiable. Mind you, we still have a TV in our house, because we like to watch the news and videos from time to time. But our children are learning that TV is a special thing. It is not the family hearth.

In general, though, it's clear to me that a family has to be consciously countercultural if they're going to survive with their moral sanity intact. You have to know what you believe, and be willing to live by those beliefs, and make sacrifices for their sake.

My wife and I have chosen to home school, for example, not because we're religious separatists, but because we know that the care and custody of our sons' character is our sacred obligation, the most important thing we are asked to do. We do not want our boys raised by the culture. Nor do we want them to grow up fearful of "contamination." Rather, we want them to be joyful kids with strong minds and stronger backbones.

My wife and I make family the center of everything we do, and at the center of our family is faith in God, and the practice of our religion. I do think the state has a role to play; I am a conservative, not a libertarian. But if we wait for state officials to get their act together, our kids will be grown and gone. Nobody is coming to rescue any of us. We've got to do it ourselves.

This is not grim work. It is a joy to celebrate life, and tradition, and to participate in the drama of teaching your children wisdom. But to do it right requires a level of commitment, spiritually and emotionally, that cannot be sustained on a casual basis. You have to mean it, and you have to be smart about it, and you have to stick with it, no matter what. It can seem daunting. It *is* daunting. But what choice do we have? If we love our kids, we know what we have to do.

MCCLOSKEY: People's hearts have to change in order to change their minds and behavior; and that's obviously made easier when society encourages virtue and the building of strong character. Ultimately the changing of hearts has to come from a "New Evangelization," such as John Paul II preached to Catholics and from an orthodox Jewish and evangelical Christian equivalent.

Ultimately, only religion can transform a corrupt and decaying culture, such as we live in. It may take decades or centuries as it did in the time of early Christianity but it can be done. Pornography was rampant in ancient Rome. Only a society that respects the indissolubility of marriage, the equality of women, and the good of having children can have a proper attitude towards the body.

LIMBAUGH: Parents cannot, obviously, entirely shield their children from the pervasive secular influences in our culture. But there are constructive steps they can take. Those able to afford private schools can avoid much of the destructive message being advanced by the public education establishment. Others, if they are in a position to do so, can home school their children. As for parents who find either option unfeasible or undesirable, they should actively monitor the curricula and activities at the public schools they attend. They should participate in the PTA and otherwise demand accountability from their schools and teachers and strenuously object when indecency rears its head or when secular values are promoted.

I believe that whether we personally participate in home schooling or enroll our children in private schools, we should do what we can to encourage and protect the home schooling and school choice movements. If nothing else, the robustness of these movements will force public schools to compete and improve academically.

The government definitely has a role in upholding moral standards. Regulating obscenity and profanity is certainly compatible with conservative governance, provided the regulators don't use "decency" as an excuse to suppress speech they find politically objectionable. So while these regulations are fine in theory it is sometimes difficult to maintain a balance and the government should always be scrutinized against overreaching, which could be worse than the harm they seek to regulate.

It is also proper, indeed imperative for the government to advance moral standards through the laws it promulgates. The conventional wisdom dictating that we must not legislate morality is patently absurd. As I (and others) have written elsewhere, almost all of our laws, both criminal and civil, are grounded in morality. We outlaw certain behaviors on the criminal side, or make certain civil wrongs actionable, primarily because they violate our moral code. Our government is perfectly within its proper purview to sanction certain behaviors and discourage others. It is appropriate, for example, that government places its imprimatur on traditional marriage and refuses to recognize same-sex marriage, if for no other reason than heterosexual marriage is a profoundly important institution that lends essential stability to our society.

Generally, those who argue against legislating morality are opposed not to our legislatures injecting their moral values into the law, but to the type of morality that is legislated. The radical homosexual lobby, for example, is quite comfortable with laws that force the government to recognize, officially, homosexual marriage. Political liberals are all too happy with the state enacting hate crime legislation on mostly moral grounds. Affirmative action laws are similarly rooted in moral concerns. Some liberals opposed the Iraq War resolution on moral grounds. On a host of other issues, liberals are insistent on using the law to enforce their version of morality. Sadly, all too often, they are perfectly happy with the judiciary imposing those laws when they can't elect legislatures willing to legislate in accordance with their worldview.

Under our constitutional separation of powers, it is improper for the judiciary to "legislate." Conservatives have long decried judicial activism because they believe that judges are required to honor the plain meaning of the text of the Constitution and the framers' original intent concerning it. When judges make policy they are usurping the constitutional authority of the legislative branch, whose members were duly elected by the people and are politically accountable. It is one thing for the courts to interpret the Constitution and to exercise judicial review—to pass upon the constitutionality of laws—but it is not proper for the courts to rewrite the Constitution or otherwise to legislate from the bench.

Conservatives need to continue to push for the election of executives who will appoint constitutionalist judges and legislators who will confirm them. We need to encourage the Senate—if it hasn't already done so by the time this book is published—to change the Senate rules to outlaw filibustering over judicial nominees to ensure that the minority cannot thwart the president's constitutional judicial appointment power. We have co-equal branches of government, but that doesn't mean they have co-equal authority over every governmental function within their sphere. The Senate has an advise and consent role on judicial appointments, not the power to veto any appointment for any reason. The Senate should pass on the competency and character of the nominees, but beyond watch-dogging those threshold qualifications, the Senate should recognize that the judicial appointment power resides in the executive—the president—who is elected by the people and the states, democratically. Under Article III of the Constitution, Congress can take other actions to rein in an abusive judiciary, such as limiting the courts' jurisdiction over certain matters.

While the courts and to a lesser extent the legislative branch has contributed to the pollution of our moral fabric, most of the decay has occurred outside government at the level of our culture. If traditionalists want to reverse this trend they must be willing to engage in the culture war and try to take back our culture from those who have systematically degraded it. Christians, for their part, should try to clean up their churches, eradicating the corruption that has infected their hierarchies and diluted their biblical message.

But Christians or not, all who care about restoring overall decency to our culture need to do what they can to positively influence society, by raising their children on the values they believe in and by standing up for and defending those values in the public square and promoting them through the government officials they elect.

ACKNOWLEDGMENTS

This book is a tribute to the greatness of American values and traditional morality. Those who have helped shape this work are embodiments of all that makes this country great.

First and foremost, I must thank David Limbaugh. David is a true gentleman, a man of true discernment, and a touchstone during difficult times. It is about people like David that Jethro spoke of in Exodus 18:21-23 when he informed Moses to find "men of accomplishment, God-fearing people, men of truth."

I must also thank the wonderful people at Regnery. The faith in me shown by Jeff Carneal and Harry Crocker has been incredibly gratifying and humbling. Thanks to my editor, Ben Domenech, for honing this work and pushing me to greater clarity and concision.

Thanks to Rick Newcombe and all of the folks at Creators Syndicate, who gave me the opportunity to grow both in my writing and in my vision. Thanks in particular to Katherine Searcy, my former editor, and Ashley Daley, my current editor, for their invaluable input and guidance.

Thanks to Jon Garthwaite and Jennifer Biddison of Townhall.com, who provide Americans with an everpresent source for conservative thought and news—and who provide me with friendship and guidance. Thanks also to David Horowitz and the people at Frontpagemag.com, as well as the people over at WorldNetDaily.com, all of whom are fighting the good fight every day in the culture wars.

Thanks to Ann Coulter for her constant humor, wisdom, support— and, of course, her biting wit. Thanks also to Andrew Breitbart, who has been a source of knowledge and advice since I first met him four years ago. Thanks to Michelle Malkin, Rod Dreher, and Father C. John McCloskey III for their help and their brilliance in completing this work. Thanks to Sandy Schulz for her tremendous aid in navigating the waters of the publishing and publicity world.

Thanks to all of my friends in talk radio and column-writing—without all of them, this country truly would be doomed to the slow decay of moral relativism.

Thanks to my three younger sisters—they are all shining examples of purity on earth. It is people like them who will bring this culture back from the brink.

Finally, thanks to Dad and Mom. God commands all of us to "honor your father and your mother, so that your days will be lengthened upon the land that Hashem, your God, gives you."(Exodus 20:12) Never has a child been able to fulfill a commandment with such ease. My parents are truly righteous people—in Hebrew, *tzadikkim*. It has been a privilege— a true blessing—to grow up in their house. May every child be blessed with such parents.

And lastly, I must thank God, both for the opportunities He has granted me, and for granting all of us the priceless gift of His morality. Without Him, we would be lost to chaos, nihilism, narcissism and hedonism. With Him, we can—and we *will*—cross over to the promised land.

NOTES

CHAPTER 1: A GENERATION LOST

1   Interview, 19 February 2005
2   Leland Elliot and Cynthia Brantley, *Sex on Campus: the naked truth about the REAL SEX lives of college students* (United States of America: Random House, Inc., 1997), 5-19
3   Tom Wolfe, *I Am Charlotte Simmons* (United States of America: Farrar, Straus, and Giroux, 2004), 156
4   Ibid, 150
5   *Griswold v. Connecticut*, 381 U.S. 479 (1965)
6   Daniel Patrick Moynihan, "Defining Deviancy Down," *The American Scholar*, Winter 1993
7   Charles Krauthammer, "Defining Deviancy Up," *The New Republic*, 22 November 1993
8   Ben Shapiro, "The radical homosexual agenda and the destruction of standards," Townhall.com, 9 March 2005
9   Paddy Chayefsky, *The Collected Works of Paddy Chayefsky: The Screenplays Vol. II* (New York, NY: Applause Books, 1995), 251
10 Kaiser Family Foundation, "Generation M: Media in the Lives of 8-18 Year-olds," March 2005, http://www.kff.org/entmedia/loader.cfm?url=/commonspot/security/getfile.cfm&PageID=5 1805
11 "Urban, suburban students engage in similar bad behaviors," *Today's School Psychologist*, 25 February 2004
12 "Survey: Parents Blasé About Kids' Drug Use," NewsMax.com, 22 February 2005
13 *The Today Show*, NBC, 27 January 2005
14 *The Today Show*, NBC, 26 January 2005
15 Rhonda Bodfield Bloom, "Safer choices: Sex can wait," *Arizona Daily Star*, 27 January 2004
16 Associated Press, "Report: Suburban schools not safe havens," CNN.com, 29 January 2004
17 Meg Meeker, *Epidemic: How Teen Sex Is Killing Our Kids* (Washington, D.C.: Regnery Publishing Company, 2002), 12
18 Cassie Wolfe, "*SEX, ETC.*: Young People's Sexual Choices: Hot News, Hot Topic," MTV.com, March 2004
19 Robert E. Rector, Kirk A. Johnson, and Lauren R. Noyes, "Sexually Active Teenagers Are More Likely to Be Depressed and to Attempt Suicide," Center for Data Analysis Report #03-04, June 3, 2003

20   The National Campaign to Prevent Teen Pregnancy, "America's Adults and Teens
      Sound Off About Teen Pregnancy: An Annual National Survey," December 2003
21   Michelle Malkin, "The new youth craze: Self-mutilation," Townhall.com, 23 February
      2005
22   Laura Vanderkam, "Hookups starve the soul," *USA Today*, 26 July 2001
23   Anne Jarrell, "The face of teenage sex grows younger," *The New York Times*, 2 April
      2000
24   Dr. James Hitchcock, "Limits of Tolerance," WF-F.com, 24 March 2005

CHAPTER 2: FUN WITH BANANAS

1   "Dr. Laura Considers Presidential Run," NewsMax.com, 3 June 2002
 2   Name changed to protect personal privacy
 3   Interview conducted 28 February 2005
 4   Kay S. Hymowitz, *Ready Or Not: What Happens When We Treat Children As Small
      Adults* (San Francisco, California: Encounter Books, 2000), 165
 5   Wolf Blitzer et al, "Should Iraqi Elections Be Postponed?; Are Police Close to Catching
      BTK Killer?," *Wolf Blitzer Reports* (5:00 PM EST) on CNN, 2 December 2004
 6   John Gibson, "Back of the Book Abstinence-Only Programs," *The O'Reilly Factor*
      (20:45) on Fox News Network, 9 August 2001
 7   David Campos, *Sex, Youth, and Sex Education: A Reference Handbook* (Santa Bar-
      bara, California: ABC-CLIO, Inc., 2002), 9
 8   As quoted in Ibid
 9   Name changed to protect privacy
10   Interview, 18 March 2005
11   Name changed to protect privacy
12   Interview, 18 March 2005
13   http://prochoiceaction.org/campaign/real_choices_keystone
14   Robert H. Bork, *Slouching Towards Gomorrah* (New York, New York: ReganBooks,
      1997), 159
15   Kay S. Hymowitz, *Ready Or Not: What Happens When We Treat Children As Small
      Adults* (San Francisco, California: Encounter Books, 2000), 172
16   Robert E. Rector, "When Sex Ed Becomes Porn 101," The Heritage Foundation Press
      Room Commentary, 27 August 2003, http://www.heritage.org/
      Press/Commentary/ed082703b.cfm
17   Ibid
18   Jim Brown and Jody Brown, "Parents Generally Unaware What 'Comprehensive Sex
      Ed' Entails," AgapePress News, 21 April 2003,
      http://headlines.agapepress.org/archive/4/afa/21003e.asp
19   C.W. Eliot, "The Pioneer Qualities of Dr. Morrow," *Social Diseases* 4 (July 1913), 135
20   "OBSESSED WITH SEX," WorldNetDaily.com, 18 November 2004
21   Daniel J. Flynn, "Kinsey revisited," Townhall.com, 17 November 2004
22   Jeffrey P. Moran, *Teaching Sex: the Shaping of Adolescence in the 20th Century* (Cam-
      bridge, Massachusetts: Harvard University Press, 2000), 135
23   Samual Blumenfeld, "Sex ed and the destruction of American morality," WorldNet-
      Daily.com, 18 January 2003
24   Jeffrey P. Moran, *Teaching Sex: the Shaping of Adolescence in the 20th Century* (Cam-
      bridge, Massachusetts: Harvard University Press, 2000), 161
25   Ibid, 167

26 Ibid, 168

27 Ibid, 167-168

28 Bonnie Nelson Trudell, *Doing Sex Education: Gender Politics and Schooling* (New York, NY: Routledge, 1993), 104

29 SIECUS Homepage, http://www.siecus.org

30 Planned Parenthood, "Planned Parenthood Federation of America Mission and Policy Statements," http://plannedparenthood.com/pp2/portal/files/portal/aboutus/mission.xml

31 Philip J. Hilts, "Blunt Style On Teen Sex And Health," *The New York Times*, 14 September 1993

32 "SIECUS to Address the Failings of Federal Abstinence-Only-Until-Marriage Programs at March for Women's Lives in New York," U.S. Newswire, 28 August 2004

33 Clare Kittredge, "BENEFITS OF ABSTINENCE STRESSED," *The Boston Globe*, 22 April 2004

34 Ibid

35 Anne Kim, "Garden of abstinence," *The Seattle Times*, 18 April 2004

36 Cheryl Wetzstein, "Pledge seen reducing out-of-wedlock births," *The Washington Times*, 30 March 2004

37 Ibid

38 Suzanne Goldenberg, "US study of teenage sexual disease destroys basis of virginity crusade," *The Guardian*, 10 March 2004

39 Melissa G. Pardue, Robert E. Rector, and Shannan Martin, "Government Spends $12 on Safe Sex and Contraceptives for Every $1 Spent on Abstinence," The Heritage Foundation Policy Research and Analysis, Backgrounder #1718, 14 January 2004, http://www.heritage.org/Research/Family/bg1718.cfm

40 Mary Eberstadt, "Home-Alone America," *Policy Review*, 1 June 2001

41 Sharon Robb, "FAT STAT: 1 IN 4 GETS ENOUGH EXERCISE," *Sun-Sentinel*, 18 March 2001

42 Kay S. Hymowitz, *Ready Or Not: What Happens When We Treat Children As Small Adults* (San Francisco, California: Encounter Books, 2000), 173

43 "Urban, suburban students engage in similar bad behaviors," *Today's School Psychologist*, 25 February 2004

44 Robert H. Bork, *Slouching Towards Gomorrah* (New York, New York: ReganBooks, 1997), 155

45 Jim Hunter, "Stronger marriages are worth working for," *The Commercial Appeal*, 11 February 2005

46 Dr. Joe S. McIlhaney, "Q: Should Congress stay the course on education for sexual abstinence until marriage?," *Insight on the News*, 20 May 2002

47 Nicholas D. Kristof, "Bush's Sex Scandal," *The New York Times*, 16 February 2005

48 Hillary Rodham Clinton, "Remarks of Senator Clinton to NYS Family Planning Providers," 24 January 2005

49 "guys' love & sex secrets," *Seventeen*, February 2005, 66-67

50 Henry Hyde, Chairman, House Judiciary, "Report on the Impeachment of William Jefferson Clinton: President of the United States—Part 1 of 6," Congressional Press Releases, 16 December 1998

51 Ibid

52 W.A. Friedlander, "Clinton's distinction," *News and Observer (Raleigh, NC)*, 26 September 1998

53 Walter Kirn, with reporting by Jay Branegan, James Carney, J.F.O. McAllister/Washington and Victoria Rainert/New York, "When Sex Is Not Really Having Sex," *Time Magazine*, 2 February 1998

54 Ricardo Gandara, "What isn't sex to teens really stuns parents," *Austin American-Statesman*, 4 February 2001

55 Mary Meehan, "New study raises questions about abstinence pledges," *Ventura County Star*, 9 November 2003

56 Donna Nebenzahl, "The new third base," *Chicago Sun-Times*, 25 March 2004

57 Steve Wernick, "Boston U. prof examines sexuality, society," University Wire, 4 October 1999

58 Joe McIlhaney Jr., "Your teenagers may be doing 'it,' so warn them," *The Houston Chronicle*, 18 August 2002

59 Damian Whitworth, "Oral sex becomes the norm among US teens," *The Times (London)*, 9 July 1999

60 "Troubling teen-sex trend," *USA Today*, 27 December 2000

61 Mary Meehan, "New study raises questions about abstinence pledges," *Ventura County Star*, 9 November 2003

62 "Medical journal raps AMA editor firing," United Press International, 10 February 1999

63 Ricardo Gandara, "What isn't sex to teens really stuns parents," *Austin American-Statesman*, 4 February 2001

64 Kate de Brito, "How times do change," *The Sunday Telegraph*, 1 September 2002

65 Saundra Smokes, "ORAL SEX INVADES TEEN SCENE," *The Post-Standard*, 12 May 2002

66 Donna Nebenzahl, "The new third base," *Chicago Sun-Times*, 25 March 2004

67 Princeton Survey Research Associates International, "NBC/People: National Survey of Young Teens Sexual Attitudes and Behaviors," 4 September 2004—7 November 2004

68 Anne Jarrell, "The Face of Teenage Sex Grows Younger," *The New York Times*, 2 April 2000

69 Philip J. Hilts, "Blunt Style On Teen Sex And Health," *The New York Times*, 14 September 1993

70 Rep. Jan Schakowsky, "Q: Do parents always have a right to know when their teen is seeking birth control?," *Insight on the News*, 29 October 2002

71 "Urban, suburban students engage in similar bad behaviors," *Today's School Psychologist*, 25 February 2004

72 Zogby International, "Parents' Reactions To Proposed Sex Education Messages In The Classroom," Coalition for Adolescent Sexual Health, 3 February 2003

CHAPTER 3: CAMPUS CARNALITY

1 Interview, 4 March 2005

2 Interview, 1 March 2004

3 Ben Shapiro, "Sex too young: Janie's story," Townhall.com, 3 March 2004

4 Suzanne Fields, "Co-ed life at Yale," *The Washington Times*, 25 September 1997

5 Name changed to protect personal privacy

6 Name changed to protect personal privacy

7 Name changed to protect personal privacy

8 Name changed to protect personal privacy

9 Name changed to protect personal privacy

10 Interview, 4 March 2005

11 Name changed to protect personal privacy

12 Interview, 6 March 2005

13 Interview, 6 March 2005

14 Tarleton Cowen, "Fling or forever?," *The Daily Princetonian*, 8 October 2001

15 Aaron Brown, "LET'S GET MODEST," *ABC GOOD MORNING AMERICA SUN-DAY*, 14 February 1999 (10:00 am ET)

16 Stephanie Cook, "This isn't Ally McBeal. It's the college dorm.," *Christian Science Monitor*, 3 October 2000

17 "the truth about college guys," *Seventeen*, February 2005, 76

18 Laura Vanderkam, "Hookups starve the soul," *USA Today*, 26 July 2001

19 Tarleton Cowen, "Fling or forever?," *The Daily Princetonian*, 8 October 2001

20 John Palacio, Kevin Newman, "CO-ED DORMS," *ABC GOOD MORNING AMERICA*, 23 October 1998 (7:00 am ET)

21 Interview, 6 March 2005

22 Nora Zamichow, "Anxiety 101," *Los Angeles Times*, 14 October 1994

23 Interview, 6 March 2005

24 "FAQ about SHAs," http://www.sha.ucla.edu/about/shasjob.html

25 Phyllis Schafly, "'Yale Five' Challenge Rule on Co-ed Dorms," *Education Reporter*, September 1998

26 Anna Arkin-Gallagher, "'Yale Five' lose appeal in court," *Yale Daily News*, January 12, 2001

27 Stephanie Cook, "This isn't Ally McBeal. It's the college dorm.," *Christian Science Monitor*, 3 October 2000

28 Interview, 6 March 2005

29 David Limbaugh, "Targeting campus speech codes," Townhall.com, August 16, 2003

30 "Nondiscrimination Policy: University of Colorado at Boulder," http://www.col-orado.edu/FacultyStaff/nondiscrimination.html

31 *Harvard Law School: Catalog 2004-2005*, 240

32 "Berkeley Campus Guidelines Concerning Student Behavior Based on Prejudice," http://www.speechcodes.org/policy.php?id=9962

33 "University Handbook, Section D: Privileges, Benefits, and Responsibilities," http://www.speechcodes.org/pdfs/9426.pdf

34 Robert H. Bork, *Slouching Towards Gomorrah* (New York, New York: ReganBooks, 1997), 48

35 Ibid, 28

36 Ibid, 30

37 Tarleton Cowen, "Fling or forever?," *The Daily Princetonian*, 8 October 2001

38 Kathleen Kelleher, "Birds & Bees," *Los Angeles Times*, 20 August 2001

39 Name changed to protect personal privacy

40 Interview, 6 March 2005

41 Interview, 6 March 2005

42 John Leo, "It's grin-and-bare-it time at U.C. Berkeley," Townhall.com, 4 March 2002

43 Dave Ranney, "Senator plans to watch videos from KU sex class," *Lawrence Journal-World*, May 2, 2003

44 Joe Jablonski, "Porn Studies Latest Academic Fad," Academia.org, October 2001, http://www.academia.org/campus_reports/2001/oct_2001_4.html

45 Eric Rich, "Wesleyan Brings Porn Into The Classroom," *Hartford Courant*, 8 May 1999

46 "Introduction," http://www.yale.edu/wgss/>

47 "About: Concentration in Studies of Women, Gender and Sexuality," http://www.fas.harvard.edu/~wgs/about/about.htm

48 "The ultra-fabulous and not-so glamorous homo class revue!" *TenPercent*, Winter 2002

49 Interview, 6 March 2005

50 Kathleen Kelleher, "Birds & Bees," *Los Angeles Times*, 20 August 2001

51 Interview, 6 March 2005

52 Interview, 6 March 2005

53 Stephanie Cook, "This isn't Ally McBeal. It's the college dorm.," *Christian Science Monitor*, 3 October 2000

CHAPTER 4: POP TARTS

1 "Madge protects Lourdes from kisses," Yahoo! News UK, 12 November 2003

2 Ibid

3 Ben Shapiro, "From virgin to tramp," Townhall.com, September 3, 2003

4 Jamie Marlernee, "S. Florida teen girls discovering 'bisexual chic' trend," *South Florida Sun-Sentinel*, 30 December 2003

5 Richard Luscombe, "US girls embrace gay passion fashion," *The Observer*, 4 January 2004

6 Laura Sessions Stepp, "Partway Gay?," *Washington Post*, 4 January 2004

7 Mim Udovitch, "Madonna" in Ed. Barbara O'Dair, *The Rolling Stone Book of Women in Rock* (United States: Rolling Stone Press, 1997), 341

8 Andrew Morton, *Madonna* (New York: St. Martin's Press, 2001), 202

9 Mim Udovitch, "Madonna" in Ed. Barbara O'Dair, *The Rolling Stone Book of Women in Rock* (United States: Rolling Stone Press, 1997), 344

10 Andrew Morton, *Madonna* (New York: St. Martin's Press, 2001), 123-124

11 "Madonna: A star with staying power," CNN.com http://www.cnn.com/CNN/Programs/people/shows/madonna/profile.html

12 Andrew Morton, *Madonna* (New York: St. Martin's Press, 2001), 127

13 John Skow, "Madonna Rocks the Land," *TIME*, 27 May 1985

14 Andrew Morton, *Madonna* (New York: St. Martin's Press, 2001), 163

15 Boze Hadleigh, *Sing Out: Gays and Lesbians in the Music World* (New York: Barricade Books, 1997), 158

16 Andrew Morton, *Madonna* (New York: St. Martin's Press, 2001), 164

17 Boze Hadleigh, *Sing Out: Gays and Lesbians in the Music World* (New York: Barricade Books, 1997), 156

18 Andrew Morton, *Madonna* (New York: St. Martin's Press, 2001), 104

19 Rashod D. Ollison, "NAUGHTY by NURTURE," *Baltimore Sun*, 17 August 2003

20 Pier Dominguez, *Christina Aguilera: A Star Is Made* (Phoenix, AZ: Colossus Books, 2003), 70

21 Larry Flick, "Aguilera's Expanding Beyond 'Genie'," *Billboard*, 24 July 1999

22 Arlene Vigoda, "Ex-Mousketeer a hit in rat race," *USA Today*, 20 July 1999

23 Amy Reiter, "Aguilera: Touch me!," Salon.com, May 17, 2001

24 Wendy Tokunaga, *Christina Aguilera* (United States of America: KidHaven Press, 2003), 34-35

25 Lisa Lenoir, "HOW COULD SHE?," *Chicago Sun-Times*, 24 October 2002

26 Lisa Lenoir, "HOW COULD SHE?," *Chicago Sun-Times*, 24 October 2002

27 Greg Overzat, "SOME POP STARS GO IN ODD DIRECTIONS AS THEY GROW UP," *Sun-Sentinel*, 21 February 2003

28 Lisa Lenoir, "HOW COULD SHE?," *Chicago Sun-Times*, 24 October 2002

29 Martha Roberts, "CELEBRITY BODIES CHRISTINA AGUILERA," *The Mirror*, 24 June 2004

30 Maggie Marron, *Britney Spears* (New York, Warner Books: 1999), 39

31 Steve Huey, "Britney Spears: Bio," MTV.com, http://www.mtv.com/bands/az/spears_britney/bio.jhtml

32 Nicholas Barber, "MUSIC: HIT ON ME BABY ONE MORE TIME (BUT SEX IS OUT OF THE QUESTION)," *The Independent*, 13 August 2000

33 "Newsmakers," *The Houston Chronicle*, 28 May 1999

34 Brian McCollum, "BRITNEY SPEARS: GOOD GIRL...OR BAD GIRL? TEEN IDOL TAKES DIFFERENT LINES FROM TIME TO TIME," *Detroit Free Press*, 7 July 2000

35 John Harlo, "Pop star will stay a virgin," *Times of London*, 14 May 2000

36 Maree Curtis, "BRITNEY SPEARS—Is the Lolita of pop as innocent as she seems?—The business of being the queen of teen," *The Sunday Telegraph*, 21 May 2000

37 Brian McCollum, "BRITNEY SPEARS: GOOD GIRL...OR BAD GIRL? TEEN IDOL TAKES DIFFERENT LINES FROM TIME TO TIME," *Detroit Free Press*, 7 July 2000

38 Maree Curtis, "BRITNEY SPEARS—Is the Lolita of pop as innocent as she seems?—The business of being the queen of teen," *The Sunday Telegraph*, 21 May 2000

39 Maree Curtis, "BRITNEY SPEARS—Is the Lolita of pop as innocent as she seems?—The business of being the queen of teen," *The Sunday Telegraph*, 21 May 2000

40 Chuck Klosterman, "THE YEAR IN IDEAS: A TO Z; The Consciously Constructed Sexual Paradox," *New York Times*, 9 December 2001

41 Ralph Novak, "Must-See Videos," *People*, 31 May 2004

42 Laura Sessions Stepp, "Britney rage; As she loses her 'innocence,' Spears is moving up on the hate parade," *Windsor Star*, 1 December 2003

43 Richard Harrington, "Keeping Up With Hilary Duff," *Washington Post*, 16 July 2004

44 Richard Harrington, "Keeping Up With Hilary Duff," *Washington Post*, 16 July 2004

45 Mark Binelli, "Confessions of a Teenage Drama Queen," *Rolling Stone*, 19 August 2004

46 Maureen Callahan, "BAD GIRL NEXT DOOR—HOLLYWOOD CHEERS AS LOHAN PUTS WORST FOOT FORWARD," *The New York Post*, 6 June 2004

47 "Celebrity women setting 'bad' examples," *Chicago Sun-Times*, 20 July 2004

48 Mark Binelli, "Confessions of a Teenage Drama Queen," *Rolling Stone*, 19 August 2004

49 Interview, 18 March 2005

50 Name changed to protect personal privacy. Interview, 18 March 2005

51 John Aizlewood, "Kurt's last stand," *The Evening Standard*, 19 November 2004

52 Patrick MacDonald, "1991 interview offered look into mind of a rising rock star," *The Seattle Times*, 5 April 2004

53 Ernest A. Jasmin, Kur Cobain: What was, what might have been," *The News Tribune*, 4 April 2004

54 Jim DeRogatis, "Don't blame ex-Nirvana singer for inciting mail-bomb suspect," *Chicago Sun-Times*, 9 May 2002

55 Ibid

56 David Montgomery, "Great &#38," *The Washington Post*, 6 May 2002

57 Rafer Guzman, "MUSIC REVIEW; Headbangers' debate," *Newsday*, 16 July 2004

58 Jason Ankeny, "MTV.com—Marilyn Manson," http://www.mtv.com/bands/az/marilyn_manson/bio.jhtml

59 "SUNDAY MAIL OPINION: TOO EASY TO BLAME ROCK STAR," *Sunday Mail*, 13 February 2005

60 Hearing of the Senate Commerce, Science and Transportation Committee, "Subject: TV Rating System," Federal News Service, 27 February 1997

61 Mary Eberstadt, "Eminem is right: the primal scream of teenage music," *Hoover Institution Press Policy Review*, 1 December 2004

62 Mary Eberstadt, "Eminem is right: the primal scream of teenage music," *Hoover Institution Press Policy Review*, 1 December 2004

63 Laura Sessions Stepp, "Partway Gay?; For Some Teen Girls, Sexual Preference Is A Shifting Concept," *The Washington Post*, 4 January 2004

64 Paul Bracchi and Will Stewart, "The curse of Tatu," *Sunday Mail*, 11 April 2004

65 Paul Bracchi and Will Stewart, "The curse of Tatu," *Sunday Mail*, 11 April 2004

66 Lisa LaFlamme, "Russian pop duo suffers loss of credibility," CTV News, 2 August 2004

67 Jon Wiederhorn, "T.A.T.U.," MTV.com, http://www.mtv.com/news/yhif/tatu/>

68 Lisa LaFlamme, "Russian pop duo suffers loss of credibility," CTV News, 2 August 2004

69 Paul Bracchi and Will Stewart, "The curse of Tatu," *Sunday Mail*, 11 April 2004

70 Ann Oldenburg, "Britney to little-girl wannabes: 'It's up to parents'," *USA Today*, 24 August 2001

CHAPTER 5: WHERE PIMPS AND HOS RUN FREE

1 Audra D.S. Burch, "thug trend spawns a war for the soul of rap music," *The Miami Herald*, 14 April 2001

2 Renee Graham, "LIMBAUGH'S ATTACK OF KERRY IS A BAD RAP," *The Boston Globe*, 13 April 2004

3 Mark Steyn, "No lie: Kerry's just a wannabe," *Chicago Sun-Times*, 4 April 2004

4 Andrew Miga, "Senator 'fascinated' by hip hop," *The Boston Herald*, 1 April 2004

5 Ibid

6 Tyler Whitley, "SHARPTON BRINGS MESSAGE TO VA.," *Richmond Times-Dispatch*, 7 September 2003

7 Todd Martens, "Norah still tops on Billboard 200," BPI Entertainment News Wire, 24 March 2004

8 "Billboard 2004 The Year in Music," http://www.billboard.com/bb/yearend/2004/rap_2.jsp

9 Ibid

10 http://www.mtv.com/bands/az/pablo_petey/artist.jhtml

11 Lori Price, "Swimming in the Mainstream," *The Dallas Morning News*, 21 October 2004

12 Stephanie K. Taylor, "Pop art propaganda," *The Washington Times*, 1 August 2003

13 Scott Mervis, "BUSTIN' RHYMES," *Pittsburgh Post-Gazette*, 15 February 2004

14 Stephanie K. Taylor, "Pop art propaganda," *The Washington Times*, 1 August 2003

15 Scott Mervis, "BUSTIN' RHYMES," *Pittsburgh Post-Gazette*, 15 February 2004

16 Lori Price, "Swimming in the Mainstream," *The Dallas Morning News*, 21 October 2004

17 "Snoop Dogg: Rap's Slanguistic Sensei," MTV.com,
    http://www.mtv.com/bands/s/snoop_dogg/news_feature_061303/>
18 Michael Z. McIntee, "Tuesday, September 2, 2003—Show #2034," CBS.com Late
    Show with David Letterman,
    http://www.cbs.com/latenight/lateshow/exclusives/wahoo/archive/2003/09/archive02.s
    html
19 "This Week in 1997 Snoop Faces Murder Charges, White Zombie Protested, AC/DC
    Tear It Up," MTV.com, 22 April 2002, http://www.mtv.com/news/arti-
    cles/1453530/20020422/story.jhtml
20 Michelle Malkin, "Jacko and Snoop Dogg's America," Townhall.com, 2 February
    2005
21 "Gangstas," COURT TV'S CRIME LIBRARY, http://www.crimelibrary.com/notori-
    ous_murders/celebrity/shakur_BIG/index.html?sect=26
22 "East Coast VS. West Coast," COURT TV'S CRIME LIBRARY, http://www.crimeli-
    brary.com/notorious_murders/celebrity/shakur_BIG/2.html?sect=26
23 "Gangstas," COURT TV'S CRIME LIBRARY, http://www.crimelibrary.com/notori-
    ous_murders/celebrity/shakur_BIG/index.html?sect=26
24 "East Coast VS. West Coast," COURT TV'S CRIME LIBRARY, http://www.crimeli-
    brary.com/notorious_murders/celebrity/shakur_BIG/2.html?sect=26
25 "CAPE FROLIC FOR BEN AND J.LO," *The New York Post*, 4 September 2002
26 "East Coast VS. West Coast," COURT TV'S CRIME LIBRARY, http://www.crimeli-
    brary.com/notorious_murders/celebrity/shakur_BIG/2.html?sect=26
27 Dennis Harvey, "TUPAC: RESURRECTION," *Variety*, 10 November 2003
28 Sheri Linden, "MOVIE REVIEW; 'Tupac: Resurrection'," BPI Entertainment News
    Wire, 7 November 2003
29 Michael Medved, "Glorification of rapper Shakur degrades African-Americans," *USA
    Today*, 19 November 2002
30 Phil Kloer, "Hip-hop heads weary of today's hard sell on sex, excess," Cox News Ser-
    vice, 26 September 2004
31 Ibid
32 Stanley Crouch, "RAP'S RHYMES DEPLORABLE," *Daily News*, 16 January 2005
33 "the mix: TAKE BACK THE MUSIC: WHAT THEY'RE SAYING," *Essence*, January
    2005
34 "JIM CARREY, AMANDA BYNES, FRANKIE MUNIZ, OUTKAST, ELLEN
    DEGENERES, HILARY DUFF, TONY HAWK, 'HARRY POTTER,' MIA HAMM,
    'SPONGEBOB SQUAREPANTS,' NELLY, LOS ANGELES LAKERS AND MORE
    CAPTURE TOP HONORS AT *NICKELODEON'S 17TH* ANNUAL KIDS' CHOICE
    AWARDS," Nickelodeon Kids Choice Awards Press Area, 3 April 2004,
    http://www.nickkcapress.com/2004KCA/content/winners_release.php
35 The editors, "the mix: TAKE BACK THE MUSIC: WHAT'S REALLY GOING ON,"
    Essence, January 2005
36 "the mix: TAKE BACK THE MUSIC: WHAT THEY'RE SAYING," *Essence*, January
    2005
37 Stanley Crouch, "RAP'S RHYMES DEPLORABLE," *Daily News*, 16 January 2005
38 Tavis Smiely, "Shift in African-American cultural persona," *Tavis Smiley* (9:00 AM
    ET) on NPR, 21 October 2003
39 Chris Cuomo, Catherine Crier, Jon Scott, "I Wanna Be Black," *Fox Files* (21:00 ET)
    on Fox News Network, 10 September 1998
40 Ibid

41 N.R. Kleinfield, "HOW RACE IS LIVED IN AMERICA," *The New York Times*, 6 July 2000

42 Chris Cuomo, Catherine Crier, Jon Scott, "I Wanna Be Black," *Fox Files* (21:00 ET) on Fox News Network, 10 September 1998

43 Jim Walsh, "In the era of Eminem, whites mirror black pop culture," *Milwaukee Journal Sentinel*, 19 November 2000

44 http://dictionary.reference.com/search?q=multiculturalism

45 Dan DeLuca, "What's good for hip-hop is what's good for America," *Philadelphia Inquirer*, 18 January 2004

46 Chris Cuomo, Catherine Crier, Jon Scott, "I Wanna Be Black," *Fox Files* (21:00 ET) on Fox News Network, 10 September 1998

47 Audie N. Cornish, "Harvard Professor Makes Hip-Hop CD," *Washington Post*, 6 November 2001

48 Associated Press, "Bowling Green offers 'Hip-Hop 101' class," *The Enquirer*, 3 June 2001

49 Andrew Guy Jr., "BLING BLING," *The Houston Chronicle*, 4 May 2003

50 Randy Lewis, "The Week Ahead," *Los Angeles Times*, 22 November 2004

51 "Eminem's Grammy glory," *BBC News*, 22 February 2001

52 http://www.imdb.com/title/tt0298203/business

53 Randy Lewis, "The Week Ahead," *Los Angeles Times*, 22 November 2004

54 Carol Midgley, "Young, gifted and . . . black?," *The Times*, 27 March 2003

55 Baz Dreisinger, "BLACK LIKE ME," *LA Weekly*, 7 February 2003

56 Tanya Kersey, "Justin Timberlake: Unjustified Co-Host of Motown Special," *Atlanta Inquirer*, 6 March 2004

57 Eric Boehlart, "GOP 'playa hatas'," Salon.com, 23 April 2004

58 Eric Boehlart, "GOP 'playa hatas'," Salon.com, 23 April 2004

59 Brent Bozell, "MTV-pandering Kerry digs rap music," Townhall.com, 2 April 2004

60 Eric Boehlart, "GOP 'playa hatas'," Salon.com, 23 April 2004

61 Ibid

62 Ibid

63 Ibid

CHAPTER 6: TEENYBOPPERS

1   Karen Bokram, "Karen the editor's PAGE," *GL*, February/March 2005

2   Jana Siegal Banin, "love q&a," *YM*, October 2003, 78

3   Ibid

4   Rebecca Onion, "ask anything," *YM*, February 2004, 17

5   Ed. John W. Wright, *The New York Times Almanac 2004* (New York, New York: Penguin Group, 2003), 388

6   Ibid

7   Kathy Flanigan, "Girl Talk; Do you want your daughter reading this stuff?," *Milwaukee Journal Sentinel*, 29 October 2001

8   Paisley Strellis, "say anything," *YM*, February 2004, 16

9   Ibid

10 Ibid

11 Kathy Flanigan, "Girl Talk; Do you want your daughter reading this stuff?," *Milwaukee Journal Sentinel*, 29 October 2001

12 Rebecca Onion, "ask anything," *YM*, February 2004, 17

13 "EASIER ACCESS?," *YM*, May 2004, 115
14 Kathy Flanigan, "Girl Talk; Do you want your daughter reading this stuff?," *Milwaukee Journal Sentinel*, 29 October 2001
15 "celebrity kissing do's and dont's," *YM*, February 2004, 58
16 "HOW TO HAVE THE PERFECT SUMMER FLING," *YM*, July 2004, 105
17 *Cosmo Girl!*, February 2005
18 Jess Beaton, "Ask College Girl," *Cosmo Girl!*, February 2005, 78
19 "your body questions answered," *Seventeen*, February 2005, 65
20 Kristen Kemp, "YOU OUGHTA KNOW: vulva love," *Cosmo Girl!*, February 2005, 76-77
21 Ibid
22 Ibid
23 Ibid
24 "TOTAL BOY: THE RATING GAME," *Elle Girl*, February 2005, 118
25 "AND THE LAST BOY STANDING IS TREVOR MAHON," *YM*, Dec/Jan 2005
26 "BOY-O-METER," *Cosmo Girl!*, February 2005, 42
27 "EYE CANDY," *Cosmo Girl!*, February 2005, 48
28 *Elle Girl*, 7 February 2005
29 *YM*, Dec/Jan 2005
30 *Seventeen*, February 2005
31 *Teen Vogue*, February 2005
32 *Teen People*, February 2005
33 *Teen*, Winter 2005
34 *Cosmo Girl!*, February 2005
35 "the dating game," *Teen*, Winter 2005, 50
36 Ibid, 51-53
37 *Cosmo Girl!*, February 2005
38 *Teen People*, February 2005
39 *Teen*, Winter 2005
40 *YM*, February 2005
41 *J-14*, February 2005
42 *J-14*, February 2005
43 "celebrity kissing do's and dont's," *YM*, February 2004, 58
44 "stars kiss & tell," *J-14*, February 2005, 28-30
45 Ibid
46 Ibid
47 "HOT, HOTTER, HOTTEST," *YM*, February 2005, 70-72
48 "Pinups: Cuties to cut out and put up," *Teen*, Winter 2005, 62-68
49 "Jesse, oh, yessee!!!," *GL*, February/March 2005, 44-45
50 Christopher Henry, "hit men," *Teen Vogue*, February 2005, 128-129
51 *Teen People*, February 2005, 110-111
52 Ed. Elizabeth Wallace, "total BOY," *Elle Girl*, February 2005, 113
53 Sona Charaipotra, "IS HOLLYWOOD BAD FOR YOUNG STARS?," *Teen People*, February 2005, 75
54 Lori Berger, "LINDSAY SPEAKS," *Cosmo Girl!*, February 2005, 88
55 "how rumors rocked jessica's world," *J-14*, February 2005, 21
56 "STAR TRACKS," *Teen People*, Winter 2005, 16
57 "TALKING FASHION TRENDSPOTTING," *Teen Vogue*, February 2005, 58
58 "does your faith affect your love life?," *Seventeen*, February 2005, 69

59 As told to Zoe C. Courtman, "my religion isn't evil," *Seventeen*, February 2005, 71

60 http://www.witchvox.com/basics/rede.html

61 http://www.witchvox.com/xbasics.html

62 "your body questions answered," *Seventeen*, February 2005, 65

63 Ibid

64 "20 Ways to Love Yourself," *Cosmo Girl!*, February 2005, 110-111

65 Mikki Halpin, "BECOME AN ACTIVIST (and change the world!)," *Cosmo Girl!*, February 2005, 124-125

66 http://worldpeace.org/peacepoles.html

67 Mikki Halpin, "BECOME AN ACTIVIST (and change the world!)," *Cosmo Girl!*, February 2005, 124-125

68 Ibid

69 http://globalstewards.org/petitions.htm

70 Mikki Halpin, "BECOME AN ACTIVIST (and change the world!)," *Cosmo Girl!*, February 2005, 124-125

71 Ibid

72 http://www.freechild.org/issues.htm

73 http://www.freechild.org/hiphop.htm

74 Robert Knight, "Dear Abby Tells Mom to Lose Qualms About Daughter's Porn Sites," Concerned Women for America Analysis/Commentary, 14 November 2002, http://www.cwfa.org/printerfriendly.asp?id=2772&department=cfi&categoryid=cfreport

75 Dear Abby, "Dear Abby: PFLAG's there to help," *Arizona Daily Star*, 12 July 2004

76 Dear Abby, "Dear Abby: After reading th ...," *The Washington Post*, 12 November 2002

77 ANN LANDERS, "ANN LANDERS," *Newsday*, 23 December 1997

78 Ed. John W. Wright, *The New York Times Almanac 2004* (New York, New York: Penguin Group, 2003), 388

79 *Cosmopolitan*, February 2005

80 Lesley Goober, "THE COSMO INTERVIEW: FUN FEARLESS FEMALE OF THE YEAR ASHLEE SIMPSON," *Cosmopolitan*, February 2005, 58

81 "CONFESSIONS," *Cosmopolitan*, February 2005, 46

82 *Cosmopolitan*, February 2005

83 "Emma Taylor and Lorelei Sharkey, "8 PLEASURE MAXING POSITIONS," *Cosmopolitan*, February 2005, 131-133

84 Ted Spiker, "Foreplay Your Guy's Way," *Cosmopolitan*, February 2005, 146-148

85 Peter Hyman, "COSMO'S GUIDE TO CONDOMS," *Cosmopolitan*, February 2005, 138

86 "february cosmo commandments: 10 Ways You Should Never, Ever Test His Love," *Cosmopolitan*, February 2005, 42

87 "cosmopolitan fun fearless men 2004," *Cosmopolitan*, February 2005, 105-124

88 "guy without his shirt," *Cosmopolitan*, February 2005, 76

89 Jennifer Benjamin, "Butt Really," *Cosmopolitan*, February 2005, 68

90 Brooke Le Poer Trench, "guy spy," *Cosmopolitan*, February 2005, 72

91 Ibid

92 "informer," *Cosmopolitan*, February 2005, 64

93 Ed. John W. Wright, *The New York Times Almanac 2004* (New York, New York: Penguin Group, 2003), 388

94 "editor's letter," *Seventeen*, February 2005, 87

95   Karen Bokram, "Karen the editor's PAGE," *GL*, February/March 2005

96   "Girls' Life Magazine Celebrates Its 10th Birthday!," *PR Newswire*, 20 July 2004

97   Ed. John W. Wright, *The New York Times Almanac 2004* (New York, New York: Penguin Group, 2003), 388

98   "Media Insight: Girls' Life Magazine," *PR NEWS*, 6 August 2001

99   Ibid

100   Karen Bokram, "Karen the editor's PAGE," *GL*, February/March 2005

101   Ed. John W. Wright, *The New York Times Almanac 2004* (New York, New York: Penguin Group, 2003), 389

CHAPTER 7: ABERCRAPPY & BITCH

1   Jean Kilbourne, *Can't Buy My Love: How Advertising Changes the Way We Think and Feel* (New York, NY: Touchstone, 2000), 268

2   Tom Reichart, "What is Sex in Advertising? Perspectives From Consumer Behavior and Social Science Research," in Ed. Tom Reichert, Jacqueline Lambiase, *Sex in Advertising: Perspectives on the Erotic Appeal* (New Jersey: Lawrence Erlbaum Associates, 2003), 11

3   Juliann Sivulka, "Historical and Psychological Perspectives of the Erotic Appeal in Advertising," in Ed. Tom Reichert, Jacqueline Lambiase, *Sex in Advertising: Perspectives on the Erotic Appeal* (New Jersey: Lawrence Erlbaum Associates, 2003), 41-46

4   Ibid, 46-47

5   Ibid, 48-50

6   Ibid, 55

7   Barrie Gunter, *Media Sex: What Are the Issues?* (New Jersey: Lawrence Erlbaum Associates, 2002), 197

8   Ibid, 198

9   "TELEVISION ADVERTISING LEADS TO UNHEALTHY HABITS IN CHILDREN; SAYS APA TASK FORCE," American Psychological Association Press Release, 23 February 2004

10   Juliann Sivulka, "Historical and Psychological Perspectives of the Erotic Appeal in Advertising," in Ed. Tom Reichert, Jacqueline Lambiase, *Sex in Advertising: Perspectives on the Erotic Appeal* (New Jersey: Lawrence Erlbaum Associates, 2003), 60

11   "From Diapers to Thongs," BreakPoint Online, 17 June 2002, http://www.pfmonline.net/transcripts.taf?_function=detail&ID=2514&Site=BPT&_UserReference=5481E50B5EBDA49C3FD49BE5

12   Joseph Sabia, "Abercrombie & Filth," *Cornell Review*, 31 August 2001

13   Ibid

14   Joseph Sabia, "Abercrombie & Filth," *Cornell Review*, 31 August 2001

15   Martha Kleder, "Abercrombie & Fitch Sells More Sex Than Clothes," *Family Voice*, September/October 2001

16   William F. Buckley, Jr., "Show your ID before reading," TownHall.com, 20 June 2001

17   Parija Bhatnagar, "Abercrombie: What's the naked truth?," CNNMoney.com, 2 December 2003

18   Chuck Colson, "Abercrombie and Flinch," TownHall.com, 8 December 2003

19   Parija Bhatnagar, "Abercrombie: What's the naked truth?," CNNMoney.com, 2 December 2003

20   Joseph Sabia, "Abercrombie & Filth," *Cornell Review*, 31 August 2001

21 "HOW THE HOMOSEXUALS SAVED CIVILIZATION," *Publishers Weekly Reviews*, 16 August 2004

22 Joseph Sabia, "Abercrombie & Filth," *Cornell Review*, 31 August 2001

23 Roberto Rivera, "Abercrombie & Fitch's Secrets for Success at College," Boundless Webzine, 1999
http://www.boundless.org/1999/departments/campus_culture/a0000133.html

24 Ibid

25 "SPRING 97," http://www.fcuk.com/fcukadvertising/>

26 Julia Finch, "Oh FCUK, where have our customers gone?," *The Guardian*, 17 November 2004

27 "WINTER 98: My place now," http://www.fcuk.com/fcukadvertising/>

28 "SPRING 99: subliminal advertising," http://www.fcuk.com/fcukadvertising/>

29 "WINTER 99: wishful thinking," http://www.fcuk.com/fcukadvertising/>

30 Ibid

31 Ibid

32 Lynda Lee-Potter, "Why I will never buy these clothes again," *Daily Mail*, 22 August 1997

33 "Winter 2001: Guaranteed Fcuk," http://www.fcuk.com/fcukadvertising/>

34 Lynda Lee-Potter, "Why I will never buy these clothes again," *Daily Mail*, 22 August 1997

35 Charles Colson, "Bankrupt at Age Twenty-Five," *BreakPoint with Charles Colson*, 18 November 2003

36 Alissa Quart, *Branded: The Buying and Selling of Teenagers*, (United States of America: Perseus Publishing, 2003), 4

37 "TELEVISION ADVERTISING LEADS TO UNHEALTHY HABITS IN CHILDREN; SAYS APA TASK FORCE," American Psychological Association Press Release, 23 February 2004

38 Juliann Sivulka, "Historical and Psychological Perspectives of the Erotic Appeal in Advertising," in Ed. Tom Reichert, Jacqueline Lambiase, *Sex in Advertising: Perspectives on the Erotic Appeal* (New Jersey: Lawrence Erlbaum Associates, 2003), 61

39 Tom Maurstad, Manuel Mendoza, "THE BUZZ," *The Dallas Morning News*, 20 September 2004

40 http://www.joesjeans.com/>

41 Karyn Monget, "VICTORIA'S SECRET NIXES TV SPECIAL," *WWD*, 13 April 2004

42 Jennifer D'Angelo, "Oh! Oh! Oh...It's Another 'Sally' Ad," FoxNews.com. 13 November 2004

43 "Throw a Streaking Party in 6 Easy Steps," http://www.herbalessences.com/streaking-party/streaking_party.asp

44 Jennifer D'Angelo, "Oh! Oh! Oh...It's Another 'Sally' Ad," FoxNews.com. 13 November 2004

45 Amy C. Sims, "Busty Beer Ads: Sexist or Just Smart Selling?," FoxNews.com, 3 February 2003

46 Shari Waxman, "The twins thing," Salon.com, 30 May 2003

47 Michael McCarthy, "Coors' twins ads a hit with target market," *USA Today*, 2 March 2003

48 Amy C. Sims, "Busty Beer Ads: Sexist or Just Smart Selling?," FoxNews.com, 3 February 2003

49 Michael McCarthy, "Coors' twins ads a hit with target market," *USA Today*, 2 March 2003

50 Barrie Gunter, *Media Sex: What Are the Issues?* (New Jersey: Lawrence Erlbaum Associates, 2002), 204

51 "Children fed diet of skinny images," *The Irish Times*, 27 July 2004

52 Denise Davy, "Body politics: Why do teenage girls so dislike their own bodies?," *Hamilton Spectator*, 27 December 1997

53 Janice Castro, "Calvin Meets the Marlboro Man," *Time Magazine*, 21 October 1985

54 Ibid

55 Tom Shales, "Those Incredible Hunks," *The Washington Post*, 27 November 1983

56 Dan Savage, "SAVAGE LOVE," *OC Weekly*, 7 November 2003

57 Jean Kilbourne, *Can't Buy My Love: How Advertising Changes the Way We Think and Feel* (New York, NY: Touchstone, 2000), 266

58 Greta Van Susteren, "Interview with Rick Solomon, Toure," *Fox On The Record With Greta Van Susteren 10:40 PM EST*, 31 December 2004

59 Sarah Hall, "Paris Hilton Sex Tape Hits the Net," E! Online News, 12 November 2003

60 Anna Cock, "Paris 'in lesbian tape'," *The Daily Telegraph*, 15 November 2003

61 Rush & Malloy, "Photos reveal Paris' lesbian district," *New York Daily News*, 22 November 2004

62 "Late Night with Conan O'Brien: Quotables for the week of November 23-26, 2004," http://www.nbc.com/nbc/Late_Night_with_Conan_O'Brien/quotables/archive/q_11_23_04.shtml

63 Leslie Earnest, "Retail Posts 2.4% Gain," *Los Angeles Times*, 8 October 2004

64 Frank DiGiacomo, "Guess? Paris' Next Move?," *New York Observer*, 2 February 2004

65 Leslie Earnest, "Retail Posts 2.4% Gain," *Los Angeles Times*, 8 October 2004

66 "PARIS OUT OF FLAVOUR," *The News of the World*, 5 September 2004

67 Phil Kloer, "Upscale Vendors Cash In on Pornography," *Atlanta Journal and Constitution*, 17 August 2003

68 Dave Berg, "Porn goes mainstream," *The Washington Times*, 4 November 2003

69 Stuart Elliot, "Porn stars to adorn ads for clothing and footwear company," *New York Times*, 25 February 2003

70 Phil Kloer, "Upscale Vendors Cash In on Pornography," *Atlanta Journal and Constitution*, 17 August 2003

71 Ibid

72 David Lewis, "Brands: the lifestyle you wear," *Wearables Business*, 1 January 2005

73 Claire Schaeffer-Duffy, "Uncle Sam hustle to keep the ranks filled," *National Catholic Reporter*, 21 March 2003

74 Jean Kilbourne, *Can't Buy My Love: How Advertising Changes the Way We Think and Feel* (New York, NY: Touchstone, 2000), 268

75 Janice Castro, "Calvin Meets the Marlboro Man," *Time Magazine*, 21 October 1985

CHAPTER 8: TV VS. VIRGINITY

1 Anne Jarrell, "The Face of Teenage Sex Grows Younger," *The New York Times*, 2 April 2000

2 Brent Bozell, "MTV knows no shame," Townhall.com, 6 February 2005

3 Joanne Jacobs, "IGNORANCE IS BLISS AND, APPARENTLY, COMMON," *Orlando Sentinel*, 13 July 2000

4 Gregory Perez, "Uh huh...uh huh huh uh huh...uh...they're cool," *St. Petersburg Times*, 7 July 1993

5 John Lyttle, "TELEVISION / 'Heh-heh, heh-heh, heh-heh,'" *The Independent*, 28 March 1994

6 Brent Bozell, "MTV knows no shame," Townhall.com, 6 February 2005

7 Ibid

8 Ken Tucker, "New 'World' Order," *Entertainment Weekly*, 17 July 1998

9 "THE REAL WORLD: The True Story of Seven Strangers," MTV.com, http://www.mtv.com/onair/realworld/>

10 Helene Blatter, "True story: 'Real World' holds auditions in S.F.," *Alameda Times-Star*, 6 October 2004

11 "THE REAL WORLD: PHILADELPHIA: Episode 20: Romantic Getaway," MTV.com, http://www.mtv.com/onair/dyn/realworld-season15/episode.jhtml?episodeID=79652

12 "WANNA COME IN?: About The Show," MTV.com, http://www.mtv.com/onair/dyn/wanna_come/about.jhtml

13 "PIMP MY RIDE: About The Show," MTV.com, http://www.mtv.com/onair/dyn/pimp_my_ride/about.jhtml

14 "CRIBS: About The Show," MTV.com, http://www.mtv.com/onair/dyn/cribs/about.jhtml

15 "MY SUPER SWEET 16: About The Show," MTV.com, http://www.mtv.com/onair/dyn/sweet_16/about.jhtml

16 "MY SUPER SWEET 16: Episode 105 Summary," MTV.com, http://www.mtv.com/onair/dyn/sweet_16/episode.jhtml?episodeID=86154

17 Ibid

18 John Motavalli, "Spike TV: Pushing the Limit," *Television Week*, 1 September 2003

19 Phil Kloer, "TV WATCH MTV's 'toon duo gets a shot at prime time," *The Atlanta Journal and Constitution*, 28 December 1991

20 Michael Starr, "THIS YEAR'S SPEARS—BRITNEY'S SIS POPS ON THE SCENE WITH HIT 'ZOEY,'" *The New York Post*, 21 January 2005

21 "Emma Roberts makes her Television Debut in New Nickelodeon Series," PR Newswire, 23 July 2004

22 Senate Committee on the Judiciary, "Children, Violence, and the Media: A Report for Parents and Policy Makers," Congressional Information Service, Inc. Policy Papers, 14 September 1999

23 "Hillary Clinton Tells P. Diddy 'Vote or Die' Slogan Hits Nail On The Head," MTV.com, 5 August 2004

24 Dave McNary, "THE CLASS OF 2000," *The Daily News of Los Angeles*, 11 July 1999

25 Polly Drew, "Parents can slow the swift movement of children becoming young adults," *Milwaukee Journal Sentinel*, 21 November 1999

26 Meena Thiruvengadam, "'Sex and the City' fans take a tour to nirvana," *Chicago Tribune*, 13 February 2005

27 *Sex and the City*, "Belles of the Balls," TBS, 4 January 2005, 9:30 pm EST, http://www.parentstv.org/ptc/campaigns/sexinthecity/main.asp

28 *Sex and the City*, TBS, 3 August 2004, 10:00 pm EST, http://www.parentstv.org/ptc/campaigns/sexinthecity/main.asp

29 *Sex and the City*, "Luck Be An Old Lady," TBS, 15 Feburary 2005, 9:00 PM EST, http://www.parentstv.org/ptc/campaigns/sexinthecity/main.asp

30 Terry Gross, "Michael Patrick King discusses the writing of the HBO series 'Sex and the City'," *Fresh Air* on NPR, 12:00 Noon PM ET, 22 January 2002

31 Ibid

32 Ibid

33 Ibid

34 Teresa Gubbins, "Going out, tuning in," *The Dallas Morning News*, 30 June 2001

35 Sarah Portlock, "NYU students say goodbye to 'Sex'," *Washington Square News*, 23 February 2004

36 Interview, 18 March 2005.

37 Meena Thiruvengadam, "'Sex and the City' fans take a tour to nirvana," *Chicago Tribune*, 13 February 2005

38 Julie Salamon, "The Rating Says PG, But Is That Guidance Enough?," *The New York Times*, 7 January 2005

39 Lyle V. Harris, "Home $ sex, thugs, vulgar roles," *The Atlanta Journal and Constitution*, 2 August 1998

40 Mark Dawidziak, "Showtime sees chance to ditch HBO's shadow," *Cleveland Plain Dealer*, 20 February 2005

41 Gillian Flynn, "Sapphic Designs," *Entertainment Weekly*, 25 February 2005

42 Lily Oei, "EMMY'S NEW BREED: THE L WORD," *Daily Variety*, 17 June 2004

43 Howard Rosenberg, "TELEVISION REVIEW; SEX AND THE STEEL CITY," *Los Angeles Times*, 2 December 2000

44 Rita Zekis, "Size matters, says TV stylist," *The Toronto Star*, 25 February 2005

45 "MADE FOR MAYBELLINE," *Malay Mail*, 21 October 2004

46 Richard Williamson, "Y&R Spotlights Stars for 7-Up Plus," ADWEEK.COM, 22 October 2004

47 Gene Edward Veith, "Friends like these," *World Magazine*, 22 May 2004

48 Tony Scott, "Friends," *Daily Variety*, 22 September 1994

49 Eleska Aubespin, "Issue of unwed mother fails to cause stir," *FLORIDA TODAY*, 16 May 2002

50 Sarah Warn, "Lesbian *Friends*: Legacy of a Sitcom," afterellen.com, May 2004

51 Phil Rosenthal, "No turning back," *Chicago Sun-Times*, 6 May 2004

52 Bonnie Britton, "They're 'Friends' to the end," *The Indianapolis Star*, 6 May 2004

53 Jennifer Frey, "Shelter From Reality in The Company of 'Friends'," *The Washington Post*, 5 May 2004

54 Lyle V. Harris, "Home $ sex, thugs, vulgar roles," *The Atlanta Journal and Constitution*, 2 August 1998

55 Helen Barlow, "And baby makes three," *Sunday Mail*, 8 December 2002

56 Lisa de Moraes, "The Outer Limits," *The Washington Post*, 3 March 1999

57 Michelle Cottle, "The Battle Is Over, but the War Goes On," *Time Magazine*, 6 December 2004

58 Manuel Mendoza, "Family hour steaming up," *The Dallas Morning News*, 12 December 1996

59 Rob Owen, "'CITY OF ANGELS' POSES TIME-SLOT QUANDARY FOR HIT-HAPPY CBS," *Pittsburgh Post-Gazette*, 13 January 2000

60 Erika N. Duckworth, "The ring is the thing," *St. Petersburg Times*, 21 February 1997

61 Manuel Mendoza, "Family hour steaming up," *The Dallas Morning News*, 12 December 1996

62 L. Brent Bozell III, "Shrinking bankroll for TV sleaze," *The Washington Times*, 28 November 1995

63 Andrea Ford, "SWINDLERS USE TV SHOW TO DUPE STUDENTS, REINER SAYS," *Los Angeles Times*, 19 November 1991

64 Melanie McFarland, "FOX'S HANDSOM 'THE O.C.' MAY BE JUST WHAT TEENS CRAVE," *The Seattle Post-Intelligencer*, 5 August 2003

65 Christian Toto, "TUNING IN TO TV," *The Washington Times*, 28 April 2004

66 "The making of Feist," *The Toronto Star*, 15 January 2005

67 Ann Oldenburg, "'The O.C.' stirs latest TV lesbian controversy," *USA Today*, 9 February 2005

68 Ibid

69 Episode #423, "Coda"

70 Hearing of the Senate Commerce, Science and Transportation Committee, "Subject: TV Rating System," Federal News Service, 27 February 1997

71 "Another Powell Departs," *The New York Times*, 24 January 2005

72 Dan Quayle, "THE VICE PRESIDENT SPEAKS," commonwealthclub.org, 19 May 1992, http://www.commonwealthclub.org/archive/20thcentury/92-05quayle-speech.html

73 Andrew Rosenthal, "Quayle's Moment," *The New York Times*, 5 July 1992

74 Ibid

75 Eleanor Clift with Clara Bingham, "The Murphy Brown Policy," *Newsweek*, 1 June 1992

76 Kenneth L. Woodward, "The Elite, and How to Avoid It," *Newsweek*, 20 July 1992

77 Interview with Lisa Schiffer, February 16, 2005

78 Kenneth L. Woodward, "The Elite, and How to Avoid It," *Newsweek*, 20 July 1992

79 Adam Miller, "CANDICE VS. QUAYLE: ROUND TWO," *The New York Post*, 24 July 1998

80 Interview with Lisa Schiffer, February 16, 2005

81 Rebecca L. Collins, PhD, et al, "Watching Sex on Television Predicts Adolescent Initiation of Sexual Behavior," *PEDIATRICS* Vol. 114 No. 3, September 2004

82 Victor Godinez, "TECH BITS," *The Dallas Morning news*, 26 February 2005

CHAPTER 9: PORN AND POPCORN

1 Elliot Paul and Luis Quintanilla, *With a Hays Nonny Nonny* (New York: Random House, 1942), 20-40

2 Noelle Hancock, Blair Golson and Ben Smith, "Runway Rubber-Necking," *New York Observer*, 20 September 2004

3 Lynda Gorov, "STEPPING DOWN FROM THE THRONE," *The Boston Globe*, 4 April 2004

4 Ibid

5 Elliot Paul and Luis Quintanilla, *With a Hays Nonny Nonny* (New York: Random House, 1942), 20-40

6 Marybeth Hamilton, "Goodness Had Nothing to Do with It" in Ed. Francis G. Couvares, *movie Censorship and American Culture* (Washington and London: Smithsonian Institution Press, 1996), 187-189

7 Anthony Slide, *Banned in the USA* (London and New York: IB Tauris Publishers, 1998), 2

8 Leonard J. Leff and Jerold L. Simmons, *The Dame in the Kimono: Hollywood, Censorship, and the Production Code from the 1920s to the 1960s* (New York: Grove Weidenfeld, 1990), 28

9 Ibid, 5-6
10 Steve Sailer, "Film of the Week: 'Femme Fatale'," United Press International, 7 November 2002
11 Nell Minow, "Shocked, Mr. Mogul? Look at the world you tell kids is cool," *Chicago Tribune*, 2 March 2004
12 Jack Valenti, "How It Works," http://mpaa.org/movieratings/about/content.htm
13 Jack Valenti, "How It Works," http://mpaa.org/movieratings/about/content4.htm
14 Jack Valenti, "How It Works," http://mpaa.org/movieratings/about/content5.htm
15 Jack Valenti, "How It Works," http://mpaa.org/movieratings/about/content3.htm
16 Amy Wallace, "SUNDAY REPORT; MPAA'S DOZEN JUDGE MOVIES FOR MILLIONS," *Los Angeles Times*, 18 July 1999
17 Bernard Weinraub, "Fun for the Whole Family," *The New York Times*, 22 July 1997
18 L. Brent Bozell III, "Tinseltown's Abandoned Children?," Creators Syndicate, 29 July 1997
19 "Study Finds 'Ratings Cree': Movie Ratings Categories Contain More Violence, Sex, Profanity than Decade Ago," Harvard School of Public Health Press Release, 13 July 2004
20 Kimberly M. Thompson, ScD, Fumie Yokota, PhD, "Violence, Sex, and Profanity in Films: Correlation of Movie Ratings With Content," *Medscape General Medicine*, 12 July 2004
21 "A Life in Pictures; Jack Valenti," CBS News Transcripts, 27 June 2004, 9:00 AM EST
22 Miki Turner, "Nude or not?," *Chicago Tribune*, 3 December 2004
23 Robert Philpot, "Sizzlers and fizzlers of the summer movie season," *Fort Worth Star-Telegram*, 23 August 2001
24 Bruce Kirkland, "BREAST DEFENCE: BERRY DENIES EXTRA PAY FOR FLASH," *Edmonton Sun*, 5 June 2001
25 Jay Boyar, "BERRY BARES DEEP THOUGHTS: THE ACTRESS TALKS ABOUT NUDITY IN MOVIES AND THE OSCAR BUZZ AROUND HER," *Orlando Sentinel*, 15 February 2002
26 Bruce Kirkland, "BREAST DEFENCE: BERRY DENIES EXTRA PAY FOR FLASH," *Edmonton Sun*, 5 June 2001
27 Ruth Hilton, "SHE PLAYS A FEISTY SPY WHO REVEWALS ALL IN HER NEW HIT FILM SWORDFISH BUT BEHIND THE SCENES, ACTRESS HALLE BERRY HAS HAD TO OVERCOME A SERIES OF REAL-LIFE DRAMAS: I WAS NEVER PAID GBP 375,000 FOR MY NUDE SCENE...IF I WERE SELLING THESE BREASTS I'D ASK A LOT MORE," *The Express*, 27 July 2001
28 Ibid
29 Jay Boyar, "BERRY BARES DEEP THOUGHTS: THE ACTRESS TALKS ABOUT NUDITY IN MOVIES AND THE OSCAR BUZZ AROUND HER," *Orlando Sentinel*, 15 February 2002
30 Ibid
31 Michael Rechtshaffen, "Monster's Ball," *Hollywood Reporter*, 13 November 2001
32 Jeff Simon, "BERRY BOND: OSCAR WINNER SPICES UP 20TH IN BOND FRANCHISE," *Buffalo News*, 22 November 2002
33 Edward Guthmann, "Hot and heavy," *San Francisco Chronicle*, 25 January 2002
34 Mark Rahner, "'Black Hawk Down' relies history; 'Kate & Leopold' messes with it," *Seattle Times*, 19 June 2002
35 "Church in Turmoil; Touring the Neighborhood; Making History," The NewsHour with Jim Lehrer Transcript, 25 March 2002

36 Ann Coulter, "I like black people too, Julia!" Anncoulter.org, 28 March 2002

37 Ibid

38 Miki Turner, "Nude or not?," *Chicago Tribune*, 3 December 2004

39 Jami Bernard, "VIRGIN ON THE RIDICULOUS," *Daily News*, 6 May 2001

40 Andy Seiler, "A-list actresses bare all for their art," *USA Today*, 2 November 2003

41 Gillian Flynn, "The Woolf Woman," *Entertainment Weekly*, 10 January 2003

42 Larry King, "Interviews With Nicole Kidman, Anthony Minghella, Ed Norton, Bill Medley, Kim Cattrall, John Hastings," CNN LARY KING LIVE 21:00), 24 January 2004

43 Mark Kermode, "The power of three," *New Statesman*, 15 December 2003

44 Bryan Burrough, "OVITZ AGONISTES," *Vanity Fair*, August 2002

45 Rick Lyman, "Ovitz Bitterly Bares Soul, And Film Industry Reacts," *The New York Times*, 3 July 2002

46 Linda Stasi, "GAY 'MOB' FLEXES ITS MUSCLE," *The New York Post*, 7 July 2002

47 Jonathan Bing and Dade Hayes, "OVITZ BITES BACK AT H'WD," *Daily Variety*, 2 June 2002

48 Debbie Woodell, "'Gay mafia'? Them's fightin' words," *Philadelphia Daily News*, 16 July 2002

49 "Fallen Giant Sets Hollywood Abuzz," CBSNews.com, 3 July 2002

50 Jonathan Bing and Dade Hayes, "OVITZ BITES BACK AT H'WD," *Daily Variety*, 2 June 2002

51 Lorenza Munoz, "'Dinner' Roasts Ovitz, With 'Godfather's' Help," *Los Angeles Times*, 11 October 2002

52 Rachel Abramowitz, "Meeting the Little People on the Way Back Down," *Los Angeles Times*, 6 July 2002

53 Michelangelo Signorile, "About that Gay Mafia... ," *New York Press*, 9 July 2002

54 Manohla Dargis, "Summer Sneaks; ON FILM; You guys are beautiful," *Los Angeles Times*, 9 May 2004

55 Jon Lockett, "WIFE WON'T LET ME; I WON'T BE YOUR GAY LOVER, SAYS BRAD," *Daily Star*, 13 September 2003

56 Hannah Mcgill, "Playing gay in Hollywood remains a mammoth taboo. Even the most daring actors shirk from it," *The Herald*, 29 February 2004

57 George Rush and Joanna Molloy with Jo Piazza and Chris Rovzar, "MALE STARS ARE DOING A CROSSOVER ACT," *New York Daily News*, 21 June 2004

58 Cristiano Del Riccio, "FILM: GAY HEROES HOT TOPIC IN HOLLYWOOD," ANSA English Media Service, 22 June 2004

59 Rebecca Ascher-Walsh et al, "FALL MOVIE PREVIEW: November," *Entertainment Weekly*, 20 August 2004

60 Bob Crisp, "ANGELINA: MY LOVE FOR FILM GIRL JEN," *Daily Star*, 2 August 2003

61 Paul Tatara, "Review: 'The Full Monty' delivers some belly laughs," CNN.com, 7 September 1997

62 Roger Kaufman, "COUNTERPUNCH; IT'S TIME TO OUT GAY STEREOTYPING IN FILMS," *Los Angeles Times*, 24 January 2000

63 "All-Time USA Boxoffice," IMDB.com, http://www.imdb.com/boxoffice/alltimegross

64 "$100 million movies," WashingtonPost.com, http://www.washingtonpost.com/wp-srv/style/daily/movies/100million/article.htm

65 Jane Ganahl, "The fake-lesbian kiss—sexual revolution or ratings ploy?," *San Francisco Chronicle*, 30 June 2002

66 Religion News Service, "Poll finds youth support for gay rights," *Baptist Standard*, 29 October 2001

67 "Lesbians and Gays Enraged at Hollywood Stereotypes," Gay & Lesbian Alliance Against Defamation Press Release, 21 March 1991

68 Gloria Goodale, "Battles Over Media Violence Move To a New Frontier: the internet," *Christian Science Monitor*, 18 November 1996

CHAPTER 10: THE LOTION PICTURE INDUSTRY

1 Reprinted in Tom Wolfe, *The Purple Decades* (New York: Farrar Straus Giroux, 1982), 287-288

2 Associated Press, " 'Basically, I was normal,' killer says," *The Toronto Star*, 25 January 1989

3 Al Goldstein, "THE PERVERSION OF TRUTH CONTINUES IN ALLEGING A PORN-CRIME LINK," *Los Angeles Times*, 8 February 1989

4 Philip Nobile, "The making of a monster," *Playboy*, July 1989

5 "Sex: the good, the bad and the kinky," *Playboy*, July 1990

6 Ibid

7 Kelly Patricia O'Meara, "Free Speech Trumps 'Virtual' Child Porn," *Insight on the News*, 27 May 2002

8 Janny Scott and John Dart, "BUNDY'S TAPE FUELS DISPUTE ON PORN, ANTISOCIAL BEHAVIOR," *Los Angeles Times*, 30 January 1989

9 Dr. Kerry Hollowell, "America's sexual holocaust," WorldNetDaily.com, 3 April 2004

10 Connie Cass, "Addiction to porn destroying lives, Senate told," Associated Press, 18 November 2004

11 Robert D. Richards and Clay Calvert, "The Politics of Porn," *The Boston Globe*, 27 December 2004

12 Vincent F.A. Golphin, "PORNOGRAPHY: WHEN A PICTURE SAYS MORE THAN MEETS THE EYE," *The Post-Standard*, 4 March 1989

13 Associated Press, "Justices block internet porn law," MSNBC.com, 28 June 2004

14 Reprinted in Tom Wolfe, *The Purple Decades* (New York: Farrar Straus Giroux, 1982), 288

15 http://www.dejavu.com

16 Amanda Castleman, "Beauty for rent," The Online Daily of the University of Washington, 2 October 1996

17 Ibid

18 Associated Press, "Police turn over campus porn movie report," CNN.com, 3 December 2002

19 http://www.barelylegal.com/index.php?page=2&LNK=IBB61&CLICK=461,1,bl, http://www.google.com/search~063q~061barely~043legal~038hl~061en~038lr~061

20 Interview, 10 January 2005

21 Cheryl Wetzstein, "Porn on the web exploding," *The Washington Times*, 9 October 2003

22 "Internet Pornography Statistics," Internet Filter Review, http://www.internetfilterreview.com/internet-pornography-statistics.html

23 Cheryl Wetzstein, "Porn on the web exploding," *The Washington Times*, 9 October 2003

24 "Internet Pornography Statistics," Internet Filter Review, http://www.internetfilterreview.com/internet-pornography-statistics.html

25 Ibid

26 Ibid

27 David Legard, "IM Spam Set to Triple," *PC World*, 29 March 2004

28 Ramona Richards, "Dirty Little Secret," *Today's Christian Woman*, September/October 2003

29 Cheryl Wetzstein, "Porn on the web exploding," *The Washington Times*, 9 October 2003

30 "Internet Pornography Statistics," Internet Filter Review, http://www.internetfilterreview.com/internet-pornography-statistics.html

31 "Internet Pornography Statistics," Internet Filter Review, http://www.internetfilterreview.com/internet-pornography-statistics.html

32 Ramona Richards, "Dirty Little Secret," *Today's Christian Woman*, September/October 2003

33 Editorial, "We've Got Porn," *Christianity Today*, 12 June 2000

34 Paul Strand, "Exposing Faith Through the XXX Church," CBN.com, 7 May 2004

35 "Internet Pornography Statistics," Internet Filter Review, http://www.internetfilterreview.com/internet-pornography-statistics.html

36 David Finkelhor, Kimberly J. Mitchell, and Janis Wolak, "Online Victimization: A Report on the Nation's Youth," National Center for Missing & Exploited Children, June 2000

37 "Internet Pornography Statistics," Internet Filter Review, http://www.internetfilterreview.com/internet-pornography-statistics.html

38 David Finkelhor, Kimberly J. Mitchell, and Janis Wolak, "Online Victimization: A Report on the Nation's Youth," National Center for Missing & Exploited Children, June 2000

39 Ibid

40 Ibid

41 Ibid

42 Dr. Kerry Hollowell, "America's sexual holocaust," WorldNetDaily.com, 3 April 2004

43 David Amsden, "Not Tonight, Honey. I'm Logging On.," NewYorkMetro.com, 20 October 2003

44 Jeffrey P. Moran, *Teaching Sex* (Cambridge, Massachusetts: Harvard University Press, 2000), 156-157

45 Donna Britt, "Man in Crisis Sure to Stand By Her Hand," *Washington Post*, 16 January 2004

46 "ANDERSON COOPER 360 DEGREES 19:00," CNN Transcript, 4 December 2003

47 "DILLER HAS WRIGHT STUFF FOR NBC," *New York Post*, 28 June 2000

48 Stephen Schaefer, "TV; 'Swear' tries to tell truth of Bruce," *Boston Herald*, 6 August 1999

49 James L. Lambert, "Christian Broadcaster Blasts Carl's, Jr. for Ad's Sexual Innuendo," American Family Association Agape Press News, 14 November 2003

50 Associated Press, "Justices block Internet porn law," MSNBC.com, 29 June 2004

51 Ibid

52 Tracy Quan, "Naked ambition," *Los Angeles Times*, 7 November 2004

53 http://www.amazon.com/exec/obidos/tg/detail/-/0060539097/qid=1101072876/sr=8-1/ref=pd_csp_1/103-3783720-8640647?v=glance&s=books&n=507846

54 "Jenna Jameson: World's Most Famous Adult Star and CEO," http://www.jestjennajameson.com/index_bio.html

55 Edward Wyatt, "Sex, Sex, Sex: Up Front In Bookstores Near You," *New York Times*,
     24 August 2004
56 Connie Cass, "Addiction to porn destroying lives, Senate told," Associated Press, 18
     November 2004
57 Interview, 21 March 2005
58 Amber Madison, "Porn and sexuality," *The Tufts Daily*, 16 April 2003

CHAPTER 11: TAKING A STAND

1 TBogg, "Getting all giggly about naked people," 10:02 AM, 22 November 2002,
    http://tbogg.blogspot.com/2002/11/getting-all-giggly-about-naked-people.html
2 The Rittenhouse Review, "AROUND THE HORN," 4 January 2003, http://ritten-
    house.blogspot.com/2003/01/around-horn-blogging-smart-and-simple.html
3 Hot Liberty, "New at Townhall.com!," 6:14 PM, 7 March 2004, http://www.hotlib-
    erty.com/archives/000121.html
4 Radical Cowboys, "Sex Too Young: Ben's Story," 10:33 PM, 16 March 2004,
    http://www.radicalcowboys.com/radical_cowboys/2004/03/sex_too_young_b.html
5 TBogg, "I haven't gotten laid yet, but it's okay because I have a note from God...,"
    9:33 AM, 24 December 2003, http://tbogg.blogspot.com/2003/12/i-havent-gotten-laid-
    yet-but-its-okay.html
6 Ben Shapiro, *Brainwashed: How Universities Indoctrinate America's Youth* (Nashville,
    Tennessee: WND Books, 2004), 180
7 Robert H. Bork, *Slouching Towards Gomorrah* (New York, New York: ReganBooks,
    1997), 142-147
8 Robert H. Bork, *Slouching Towards Gomorrah* (New York, New York: ReganBooks,
    1997), 117
9 Mark Levin, *Men in Black: How The Supreme Court Is Destroying America* (Wash-
    ington, D.C.: Regnery Publishing, Inc., 2005), 201-202
10 Linda Greenhouse, "How Long Is Too Long For Court's Justices?," *The New York
     Times*, 16 January 2005
11 Rhoda Rabkin, "Children, entertainment, and marketing; How to rate the ratings,"
     Consumers' Research Magazine, 1 June 2002

INDEX